Feminist Research Methodology

This book focuses on feminist research methodology, exploring and analysing its constituting methods, theory, ontology, epistemology and ethics and politics, and research issues relating to women, gender and feminism in Sri Lanka. The book examines ways of meaning-making for the political, ideological and ethical purposes of promoting individual and social change, and constructs an example of feminist research praxis.

Using this South Asian country as a case study, the author looks at the means by which researchers in this field inhabit, engage with and represent the multiple realities of women and society in Sri Lanka. In analysing what constitutes feminist research methodology in a transitional country, the book links local research practices with Western feminist approaches, taking into account the commonalities, distinctions and specificities of working in a South Asian context. With an emphasis on general issues and debates in global feminist theory and methodology, the book explores the issues of reflexivity, standpoint, gender, women's agency, empiricism, and feminist politics of Marxism and democracy, positivism, induction, deduction, postmodernism and postcolonialism.

Engaging with and re-conceptualising three traditionally different types of research – women's studies, gender studies and feminist studies – from a methodological perspective, *Feminist Research Methodology* provides a framework for researching feminist issues. Applicable at both a local and global level, this original methodological framework will be of value to researchers working in any context.

Maithree Wickramasinghe is a Senior Lecturer in the Department of English at the University of Kelaniya, Sri Lanka. Her research has explored feminist critical theory and methodology, gender in organizations and workplaces, as well as women and gender in development.

Routledge Research on Gender in Asia Series

1 Women, Identity and India's Call Centre Industry
JK Tina Basi

2. Feminist Research Methodology
Making meanings of meaning-making
Maithree Wickramasinghe

Feminist Research Methodology
Making meanings of meaning-making

Maithree Wickramasinghe

Routledge
Taylor & Francis Group

LONDON AND NEW YORK

First published 2010
by Routledge
2 Park Square, Milton Park, Abingdon, Oxon OX14 4RN

Simultaneously published in the USA and Canada
by Routledge
270 Madison Ave, New York, NY 10016

Routledge is an imprint of the Taylor & Francis Group, an informa business

© 2010 Maithree Wickramasinghe

Typeset in Times New Roman by
Taylor & Francis Books
Printed and bound in Great Britain by
CPI Antony Rowe, Chippenham, Wiltshire

British Library Cataloguing in Publication Data
A catalogue record for this book is available from the British Library

Library of Congress Cataloging in Publication Data
Feminist research methodology : making meanings of meaning-making /
Maithree Wickramasinghe.
    p. cm. – (Routledge research on gender in Asia series; v. 2)
Includes bibliographical references and index.
1. Women's studies – Research – Sri Lanka. 2. Women's studies – Sri
Lanka – Methodology. I. Title.
    HQ1181.S72W53 2010
    305.4095493 – dc22
                        2009016943

ISBN 978-0-415-49416-8 (hbk)
ISBN 978-0-203-86732-7 (ebk)

For Ranil who, despite his wisecracks,
          has unswervingly sustained me.
For Amma, who was the original source of motivation.
For Thatha, who is no longer there to see.
For Englanamma, Papa, Maya and Rashmee,
                    who laid the foundations.
For YPunchiamma, for providing the support services.

Contents

List of illustration   xi
Abbreviations   xii
Acknowledgements   xiii

Introduction: Making meanings   1
  An introduction to the genesis of the book   1
  An introduction to the book's structure and chapters   4
  An introduction to the definitions and parameters of
    making meaning   7

Part I
Methodology matters   11

1   The local context: Archaeology of women's research activism   13

  Archaeology   13
  A glance at women-related issues before 1975   14
  The emergence of WR writing and research   17
    The liberal / democratic agenda   *17*
    Marxist feminism   *19*
  Women's movements and researchers   20
  Feminist research activism   23
    Feminist research activism – more issues of connaissances?   *24*
    Feminist research activism – more issues of savoir?   *27*

2   A paradigm: Women – a paradigm in global knowledge production   31

  Women as a paradigm in global knowledge production   32
  Feminist subjectivities   34
  Feminist ontologies   36
  Feminist epistemologies   39
  Feminist research methods   43
  Feminist theories   45
  Feminist politics / ethics   47

Part II
Aspects of feminist research methodology   **51**

3 Subjectivity: Reflecting on the self as / in making meaning   **55**

Subjectivity and reflexivity   56
Positioning / constructing myself in researching   58
　　Discipline and work roles   58
　　Family   58
　　Ethnicity and religion   59
　　Class   59
　　Politics   60
　　Language   60
Constructing / positioning my frameworks of thought   61
　　Ontological and epistemological bearings   61
　　The research context   64
　　Theoretical and methodological aspects   64
　　Political and ethical concerns   66
Positioning / constructing my approaches and methods   67
　　Texts   67
　　Talk   68
　　Analysis and theorisation   69
　　Reflecting on reflexivity as an expression of subjectivity   71

4 An ontology: Research realities in meaning-making   **73**

Ontology and epistemology   73
The attacks and responses   75
Ontological research politics   76
　　Feminist internationalisms   78
　　Feminist structural reformative intents (gender
　　mainstreaming)   81
　　Feminist localisms   84
　　Feminist personal / political interests   87

5 An epistemology: making meanings of being / doing gender   **93**

The concept of gender   93
Justification for an epistemology of gender   95
Gender as an aspect of being / doing (ontology)   96
An epistemology of gender   99
　　Gender theoretical concepts   99
　　Gender analysis   102
　　Gender political aspirations   105
　　Gender methodologies   107
Gender ontology as epistemology is gender epistemology as
　　ontology   108

6 A method: Literature reviewing as making meaning 110

The method of literature reviewing 111
Constructing a historical trajectory? 113
Classifying types of approaches 114
    The empiricist bent 114
    Action research 116
    Theoretical arguments 118
    Mixed-methods research 122
Other methodological issues 123
    The significance of history 123
    The cultural factor 125

7 Theory: Making and unmaking meaning in theory 128

The pros and cons of applying theorisation 128
Beginning theory 130
The location / situatedness / standpoints and intersections of
    knowledge 132
    A women's standpoint 134
    The perspective of a mother 135
    Disciplinary and ideological affiliations 137
    Intersections of class 139
    Counter-communal stands 141
    South Asian or Asian positionings 143
Making and unmaking theory 145

8 Ethics / politics: Feminist ethics / politics in meaning-making 147

Women's lesser morality versus higher social expectations 147
Feminisms as ethics and politics 148
The ethical problematic of a politics of good 150
    Ethics / politics of altruism 151
    Ethics / politics of liberal democracy 153
    Ethics / politics of Marxism 155
Feminist ethics as political strategy and action 158
    Strategic pragmatism 159
Feminist politics / ethics as methods 161
    Responsibilities and accountability 161
    Sensitivity to respondents 163
    Epistemic community 164

**Conclusions: Towards a feminist research methodological matrix –
making meanings of meaning-making**   **167**

Notes   181
Bibliography   186
Index   208

Tables and diagrams

Diagrams

3.1	Aspects of feminist research methodology	53
4.1	Feminist ontological politics	77
4.2	Ontology / epistemology	92
5.1	Gender ontology / epistemology	97
8.1	Feminist politics / ethics	151
8.2	Levels of feminist politics / ethics	157

Tables

| 4.1 | Feminist ontological / epistemological politics | 91 |
| 9.1 | Feminist Research Methodology Matrix | 170 |

Abbreviations

CBO	Community-based Organisation
CENWOR	Centre for Women's Research
CIDA	Canadian International Development Agency
CP	Communist Party
CSR	Centre for Society and Religion
FTZs	Free Trade Zones
GM	Gender Mainstreaming
IDPs	Internally Displaced Peoples
INGO	International Non-Governmental Organisation
IoE	Institute of Education
JHU	Jathika Hela Urumaya
JVP	Janatha Vimukthi Peramuna
LSSP	Lanka Sama Samaja Pakshaya
LTTE	Liberation Tigers of Tamil Eelam
NGO	Non-Governmental Organisation
SAP	Structural Adjustment Programme
SLFP	Sri Lanka Freedom Party
SSA	Social Scientists' Association
SLWNGOF	Sri Lanka Women's Non-Governmental Organisations Forum
UNCEDAW	United Nations Convention on the Elimination of all forms of Discrimination Against Women
UNIYW	United Nations International Year of Women
UNP	United National Party
WERC	Women's Education and Research Centre
WMC	Women and Media Collective
WR	Women-related

Acknowledgements

When I told people that I was writing a book on feminist research methodology, I provoked a range of responses. They ranged from a slight blankness at the idea of working on feminism to the boredom of working on methodology; from a straightforward grasp of method to the incomprehension of obscurity. Further clarification on my part was required as to what constitutes feminist research methodology.

This is the very reason for my book, since it is my intention to engage with / conceptualise the complexities of the act of research. Many people have inspired, influenced, excited, assisted, supported and promoted me during this project. I would like to express my sincere appreciation for their support and contributions over the last few years. In particular, I would like to place on record the intellectual contributions of my respondents: researchers of women-related (WR) issues in Sri Lanka. Despite their initial diffidence about their capacity to contribute to the topic, it is their acquiescence and generous donation of time, experiences and intellectual capital that forms the foundation of my work. Though political and ethical considerations prevent individual acknowledgement, they know who they are. Many thanks.

It was the capacity-building initiative of the Gender in Commonwealth Higher Education Project (2003 – 2006) by the Institute of Education (University of London) and the Department for International Development (DFID) UK which made research for this book possible. I would like to thank all the project team-members for their confidence in me – Louise Morley, Anne Gold, Elaine Unterhalter and Marianne Coleman, as well as Annik Sorendo. I am obliged to the Women in Public Policy Program of the John F. Kennedy School of Government (Harvard University), for giving me a fellowship to maximise on my time in Boston by accessing some of the Harvard libraries. Special mention must be made of Edith Stockey, Swanee Hunt and Victoria Budson for their warmth during my stay and of Theresa Lundt for her coordinating efforts.

I am grateful to Elsevier for giving me permission to include a revised version of my article originally printed in *Women's Studies International Forum*, Vol. 29(6) Wickramasinghe, M., 'An epistemology of gender - an aspect of being as a way of seeing', 606–611. An updated version of my article,

'Imported or indigenous knowledges? Feminist ontological / epistemological politics' (2007) published in N. de Mel and S. Thiruchandran (eds), *At the Cutting Edge – Essays in Honour of Kumari Jayawardena*, New Delhi: Women Unlimited, has also been included in the book as well as a revised version of my article 'Theorizing the self in writing up research' to be published in the *Journal of the Faculty of Humanities*, University of Kelaniya. An adaptation of my paper 'The possibilities and challenges of postcolonial situatedness, standpoints and intersectionality' (2008) presented at the *Conference on Sri Lankan Creative Writing in English* organised by the Women's Education and Research Centre, Sri Lanka is also included in the book.

I deeply appreciate and acknowledge the informal conversations I had with feminist research activists Kamalini Wijayatilake and Bernadeen de Silva (who are no longer with us), Kumari Jayawardena, Swarna Jayaweera, Eva Ranaweera, Neloufer de Mel, Kumudini Samuel, Sepali Kottegoda, Ramani Muttetuwegama, Sharni Jayawardena, Sunila Abeysekere and Shermal Wijewardena about women's movements in Sri Lanka, which helped to contextualise my work. I am also deeply indebted to Mary E. John for taking time to discuss feminist research methodology in India with me. I am very grateful to Urwashi Batliwala, Anila Bandaranayake, Farida Shaheed, Malasri Lal, Maryam Rab, Samina Quadir, Samina Choonara, Papreen Nahar and Muzmunnesa Mahtab for helping me make research contacts and for generously sharing their work with me.

Aside from the interviews and informal conversations, my work involved extensive literature searching in Sri Lanka. I would particularly like to mention the assistance provided by the Centre for Women's Research and its Information Officer, Savithri Hirimuthugoda, who went out of her way to locate some of my historical references. I would also like to thank the International Centre for Ethnic Studies (ICES), the Women's Educational and Research Centre (WERC), the International Labour Organisation (ILO) Colombo and the Centre for Women's Development Studies (CWDS) New Delhi for facilitating access to their respective collections.

Other friends and colleagues to whom I am exceedingly grateful for finding / transporting some of my source materials are Ralph Bultjens, Mariam Ram, N. Ram, Sharmalee de Silva, Piyumika Ranmuthugala, Priyantha Samaratunge, Luxshman Jayamaha, Sharmini Jayamaha, Thanojie Perera, Druvi Perera, Penny Hood, Nadeen Mahendran, Manique de Zoysa, Nalin Perera, Rangeeta de Silva, Sharmila Daluwatte, Chang Pilwha, Usha Welaratna, Sumudu Welaratna, Neloufer de Mel, Nyokabi Kamau, Jayanthi Kuru Utumpala, Romola Rassool, Minusha Wickremasinghe, Rosita Wickremasinghe, Bradman Weerakoon, Yoshini Gunesekera, Saman Athaudahetti, Sagala Ratnayake, Malik Samarawickrema, Muttaiah Muralitharan, Roshini Athukorala, Ananda Athukorala, Upali Amarasiri and Aruni Deveraja Wijewardena.

I am also grateful to Mary Maynard, Meg Maguire, Diana Leonard, Penny Burke, Marianne Coleman, and Neloufer de Mel for their helpful and supportive suggestions on reading my work.

I thank Shirani Dias and Marie de Silva for painstakingly transcribing all 26 audio-tapes. I also acknowledge the prodigious editing inputs of T. A. D. Chamila Kumari Ratnayake, Penny Hood, Sharni Jayawardena, Rashmee Thiyagalingam, Radha Bandaratilake, Ramani Jayasundera and Leelangi Wanasundera during the various stages of my book; and Jane Chilcott for her keen and penetrating final edit.

I am also much obliged to Vathany Narendran for drawing the initial conceptual diagrams and tables despite her stressful schedule and Radha Bandaratillake for her characteristic enthusiasm and big-heartedness in illustrating the final diagrams.

I mention with gratitude Sandra Perera, who has been exceptionally kind in helping me with computer printouts and other coordinating efforts during the past number of months.

I also record with appreciation the inputs made by Routledge, especially Dorothea Schaefter, Suzanne Richardson, Paola Celli, Heidi Cormode and three anonymous readers in the final redrafting and editing of the manuscript for publication.

I would especially like to acknowledge the consideration and support of Sunil Moonesinghe (who is no longer with us), the warmth and generosity of Faiz and Ameena Mustapha, the friendship, concern and hospitality of Penny Hood, the witty repartee and backing of Rashmee Thiyagalingam, and the logistical assistance and warm affection of Thulasi Sandrasagaram during my stays in London.

My heartfelt thanks go to Ann Gold of IoE for her crucial inputs to my work, generosity in spirit, and friendship, while my deepest gratitude goes to Louise Morley, a bulwark of critical support. I value immensely her suggestions and contributions to my work.

I owe much to Kamalini Wijayatilake who was a caring friend and an always-interested, intellectual sounding board for me. We have tied ourselves in methodological knots on many an occasion; and it is my heartfelt regret that she is not here to celebrate this book.

This book owes a lot to the lifelong ribbing, emotional sustenance and material support provided by the new and old GIs – Thano Fernando, Sharmini Peiris, Amalee Perera, Umanga Thammannagoda, Sharmini Jayamaha, Devika Soysa, Renuka Fernando and Prashanthi (Totsy) Mahinderatne.

I am also exceedingly grateful to my mother Shiranee and my aunt Radha for all their encouragement and support during these months.

Finally, I would like to express my love and gratitude to Ranil, my husband, for tolerating, pressurising, promoting and sustaining me through this project.

Maithree Wickramasinghe
August 2009

Introduction

Making meanings

An introduction to the genesis of the book

This book aims to look at the ways and means by which Sri Lankan feminist activist researchers inhabit, engage with, represent and construct the multiple realities of women and society through research. In particular, it explores ways of meaning-making for the political, ideological and ethical purposes of promoting individual and social change. However, it does so with the understanding that the possibility of representing and constructing complete knowledge of realities is highly problematic and debatable; and that the ultimate aim of social transformation is equally incomplete and relative. Given the play of subjectivity and human capacity, knowledge can only be partial and situated, rather than transcendent (Haraway 1988), and social action conditional and pragmatic. The following sections of the Introduction will acquaint the readers with its topic and structure, give definitions of concepts and terms, and provide rationales for the book. As introductions from a modernist perspective,[1] they will presume to offer a formal beginning to the book and an epistemic construction of my assumptions; while from postmodern[2] perspectives, they will construe fragments of my understandings, subjective positionings and hegemonic authority.

In Sri Lanka, as in many other countries, interest in women's rights and issues came to a head with the institution of the United Nations International Year of Women (1975) and the United Nations Decade of Women (1975–1985). Since then, WR research has boomed in many disciplinary directions, encompassing various interdisciplinary subjects. Yet, on the whole there has been little research that has looked specifically at research methodology in Sri Lanka (for instance, at how Sri Lankan realities are represented / constructed in research; or at the theories or ethics of knowledge and meaning-making). An overview of WR research literature indicated that there were a few, sporadic exceptions (see Goonatilake 1985; Wanasundera 1995). These problematised aspects of research methodology per se, such as using feminist frameworks (de Alwis 1994b; Bandarage 1998; de Alwis 2004a; Emmanuel 2006) or participatory methods (Schrijvers 1996; Jayatilaka 1998); or constructing a women's archive from memories and testimonies (de Mel 2007).

Literature that theorised holistically on research methodology was virtually non-existent. One possible reason for this is that research methodology has usually been understood as research methods, and therefore of secondary importance. Many researchers were inclined to include writing on the theoretical and methodological aspects of their work as an ancillary part of other activist topics. Consequently, there has not been much critical discussion amongst researchers and writers on feminist theories or methods in Sri Lanka. Even definitions or categorisations of what constitutes feminist / gender / women's studies[3] have yet to be discursively debated or theorised.

This may reflect a wider gap in the theoretical and epistemological[4] aspects of research methodology training within Sri Lankan universities. As a lecturer working within academia it was my observation that, where given, methodology training tended to be basic, narrow, discipline-bound, highly technical and dated. At the time I started this book, lectures on the application of scientific methods to Humanities subjects were still being given as 'fresh perspectives' on research methodology. This seems to indicate that research methodology had, in certain instances, not progressed beyond a positivist framework based on empiricism – which sees scientific knowledge as the connection between ideas and realities (Ramazanoglu and Holland 2002).

Furthermore, my personal experience as a graduate student in a Sri Lankan Women's Studies programme (in the mid-1990s) consisted of training in a methodology module which did not reflect extensive awareness of feminist research methodologies. Certainly, at the time, there was insufficient provision for even the most fundamental of methodological debates in the classroom, such as the qualitative / quantitative divide or merger and its implications for feminisms, or the inscription of reflexivity. A colleague and I attending the programme can testify to a degree of anxiety at the time as to whether feminist research methodologies in dissertation writing (such as the inclusion of subjective experiences) would be accepted by the university hierarchy. This reveals the hegemony within academia with regard to what is deemed acceptable and legitimate as serious academic enquiry – since positivism reigns as the institutionally sanctioned methodological approach.

Counter-hegemonic activity within academia, such as utilising feminist research methodologies, took place in an environment of institutional uncertainty. This indicated the vulnerability of the discipline of Women's Studies and its methodologies at the time. While some effort has been made in subsequent years to rectify the situation for the programme concerned, the application of feminist research methodologies in student research is still not considered to be of critical value by the rest of the academic establishment. Yet this state of affairs belies feminist research literature that subscribed to knowledge paradigms and approaches in a discipline like English Studies – given its interdisciplinary epistemological possibilities. English for instance, showed subscriptions to a range of critical approaches including deconstruction (Derrida 1976) which reads a text without prioritising one single meaning.

I too lacked formal training in research methodology until I started my PhD research in the early 2000s. My experiences of researching and writing during the last nineteen years have been governed by personal critical readings on a topic, and guided to some extent by intuition. Intuition, which can be traced to a childhood consciousness of women's oppression, but which I cannot necessarily attribute to shocking experiences of abuse or suppression (except for the control exerted by an overprotective father). However, I could attribute it to micropolitics (Morley 1999), or the little oppressions and injustices of daily life. Instances that come to mind include my extended family respecting male rather than female leadership in domestic emergencies; the much-read children's author Enid Blyton's portrayal of boys as being more exciting than girls; incidences of sexual harassment by a male neighbour and strangers; seclusion and exclusion due to the religious practices of purity and the cultural practices of puberty. To some extent, the resulting experiential and instinctive knowledge of gender differences, inequality and women's oppression translated themselves into part of my research methodology in my work (on Women in Development, feminist literary practice, gender and disaster management, and gender in the workplace). Although I have not theorised on this phenomenon and the general role of intuition in research methodology in my work so far, I believe it is one area of interest that requires future field study.

The more I looked at activist research, the more I became interested in how research processes try to capture, compose or rather make meaning of, the realities within the Sri Lankan context: despite postmodernist implications about the authenticity (if not the possibility) of being able to do so. Furthermore, I believe that in order to make knowledge claims both valid and authoritative (Ramazanoglu and Holland 2002) – despite the inherent instability of such claims – the focus on research methodology is vital. These were the main reasons why I selected this research topic.

For me, research methodology consists of:

- understanding the ways in which the subjectivity of the researcher engages / interacts with the research process;
- awareness of the unstable and often conflated multiple realities of life and researching;
- the influence of assumptions and justifications about knowledge;
- the methods that are applied to collect / construct / analyse data on the topic;
- the theorisations (applied or made) that generalise or deconstruct research interests;
- the ethical and political inferences about the research process (including the methods employed).

I am also aware that any consideration of research methodology is both a theorisation on knowledge and a theory of knowledge production (Letherby

2003: 5). Consequently my book constitutes an epistemological[5] exercise. While this book is by no means the final word on feminist research methodology in Sri Lanka, it may well be a beginning.

An introduction to the book's structure and chapters

The book is structured in two parts. Part I will provide a background to the understandings and practices of feminist research methodology in Sri Lanka and worldwide. The six chapters in Part II will consist of what I will argue to be aspects of feminist research methodology. These are the researcher's subjectivity, ontology, epistemology, methods, theory and ethics / politics. They will be introduced not only as a possible methodological framework for general application / construction in researching, but also as derived from / applied to the Sri Lankan context.

In Chapter 1 I will give an introduction to women's studies and feminist research activism in Sri Lanka with the assistance of Foucault's (1972) discursive conceptual tool of making meaning – archaeology. This is because researching is part of women's activism in the country and needs to be conceptualised against the historical, socio-political and cultural milieu of the island. Therefore, I will construct, trace and frame women's research and writing from 1975 to the present day, profile the women's movement and researchers and consider the on-the-ground politics and economics of research production as well as the epistemological and theoretical issues of feminist research activism.[6]

In Chapter 2 I will change my focus from Sri Lanka's historical and material conditions relating to knowledge production to a consideration of the epistemological significance of women as a shift in knowledge paradigms worldwide. The basis of a paradigmatic swing is usually related to methodology: so I will focus on dominant international feminist research methodologies relating to subjectivity, ontology, epistemology, methods, theory and ethics / politics. These categories will frame ways of meaning-making while accounting for / constructing the commonalities, unities, differences, overlaps and contrarieties in these methodologies. On the whole, this will challenge existing notions of women, gender and feminism as types or approaches to research. Through the frame of women as a paradigm I will highlight the dominant trends and twists in researching so as to give an epistemological background to women's studies and research activism in Sri Lanka.

In each of the next six chapters I will focus on one aspect of research methodology that I deem vital for an integrated framework on feminist research methodology. In Chapter 3 I will argue for the indispensability of the researcher's subjectivity in any conceptualisation of feminist research methodology by considering the possibilities and limitations of doing reflexivity as a method of representing / constructing the researcher's subjectivity in the research process. Therefore this chapter will reflect on the process of researching and writing this book. This will involve reflecting on the multiple frameworks and parameters within which my work is constructed / located, as well as the processes of making meaning (or researching methodology) within the Sri Lankan context. For instance, I will argue the case for an exploratory / theoretical study of women's studies / research activism from a methodological[7] viewpoint using a case study approach because of the general dearth of literature on methodology. It will involve reflexively substantiating the use of particular theoretical frameworks, placing them vis-à-vis my conceptualisations of realities (ontology[8]) and my standpoints on knowledge (epistemology), and the consideration of my subjectivity in terms of ideological, social and disciplinary locations as well as the ethics and politics of researching. It will entail justifying my research methods (a literature review on feminist research methodology,[9] a general overview of women's research activism[10] and the methodological issues originating from textual analysis and interviewing). These include the power dynamics of interviewing colleagues and the use of research literature as examples, illustrations and representations of realities (Mason 2002). Finally, the chapter will look at data analysis and theorisation – for the purpose of developing a methodological matrix that has its origins in local discourses[11] (Foucault 1972), as well as in international debates.

Chapter 4 will concentrate on ontology – but not in terms of grand conceptualisations about the nature of realities such as postmodernism or phenomenology[12] (Harre 2006: 220). Rather, I will envision / focus on the local realities or conditions of existence that impinge on and engage researchers. These are understood as a milieu of competing realities of research or ontological politics. They are: a) the impetus of international influences / legal standards; b) the epistemologies of gender mainstreaming of disciplines and institutions; c) contemporaneous socio-political developments that provide local imperatives; and d) the internal personal political drive of researchers. I will argue that these ontological politics of researching are symbiotic with the epistemologies of research.

Chapter 5 will focus on a dominant epistemology in research – gender. I will argue for the concept of gender as an epistemology or theory of knowledge that is based on an aspect of existence – gender. To make this point, I will identify the following ontological characteristics of gender: a) gender as comparison and contrast – that is the sense of being either male or female; b) gender as a process of identification and differentiation involved in the making of a woman's identity and in 'transgendering'; c) gender as an abstract (or the translation of gender into a universal) that constitutes 'being' / 'doing' women; d) gender as personification – when inanimate objects are seen as male or female; e) gender as ideal or prototype for future realities. It will be my central argument that these aspects of reality, or ways of doing / being gender, are also simultaneously aspects of epistemology or ways of knowing gender. These ontological aspects direct the theoretical constructions, principles of analysis, ideological / political objectives and specific methodologies that constitute gender epistemology.

In Chapter 6 I will look at another aspect of feminist research methodology – research methods. I will identify literature review as a research method, paying attention to an aspect of research methodology that is often neglected or taken for granted. It is my argument that reviewing research literature is not only a separate research activity to collect data or to contextualise the topic; but rather, that it also represents / constructs the epistemic evolution of the research subject. I will take the example of my own literature review of feminist research methodology in Sri Lanka to make this argument. It will reflect on the formal possibilities of literature review, such as constructing a historical trajectory, and classifying types of methodological approaches based on empiricism, action research, theorisations and mixed methods. It will also take into account other methodological issues such as the significance of history and culture. I will argue that a literature review is crucial for local feminisms as it not only legitimises previous research but also establishes a foundation on which further knowledge is generated, and should thus form a distinct epistemological project despite the conceptual problems of the instability, subjectivity and arbitrariness of such a modernist project. The literature review will be undertaken not necessarily as a critique, but as another way of making meaning.

Theorisation will be the crux of Chapter 7. I will construct theory on methodology mainly from interviews with researchers, but also through 'nuancing' Western theorisation to suit the local situation. In a context where researchers do not articulate their standpoints in the textual discourse, I apply the theoretical concepts of feminist standpoints (Harding 2004b), intersectionality (Grillo 2006) and situatedness of knowledge (Haraway 1988) to Sri Lankan researching. Discussions with feminists and my own understanding lead to the making of theorisations which are grounded as well as nuanced. At the same time they are unmade by, to some degree, the nuanced application of postmodernist perspectives. This chapter illustrates my underlying argument in the book that making meaning in research involves adopting / adapting a fusion of modernist / postmodernist approaches to realise the process fully.

The final Chapter, 8, will concentrate on researchers' concerns with the political and ethical implications of the research process in Sri Lanka. As a feminist, I believe that politics and ethics need to be intertwined within the research process. I will argue that research constitutes a feminist ethical politics of 'good' and consider the problematic of its very location in 'goodness' – whether it be in altruism, democracy or Marxism. I will also look at feminist ethics as political strategy / activism, and the politics / ethics involved in the usage of research methods. On the whole, the practical, on-the-ground problems and the political gains accrued from research activism are problematised as they need to be engaged with at strategic levels (including that of strategic pragmatism).

The chapters of Part II will thus form individual case studies of the different aspects of the umbrella case study on feminist research methodology. The amalgamation of these six aspects of methodology in researching delineates a matrix for methodological practice within the Sri Lankan context in particular, and the global context in general. Yet, it must be noted that these methodological guidelines are offered, not as a concrete framework, but as methodological possibilities that would help women's research activism to become intellectually robust and politically solid, and to withstand the criticisms that are levied against such research – especially in Sri Lanka.

An introduction to the definitions and parameters of making meaning

In this book, 'women's research activism' is defined as writing by women, on women / gender / feminisms for purposes of activism (from creating consciousness to agitating for policy changes to initiating parallel action projects). This writing emanates mainly from the non-governmental sector rather than the universities. My focus of interest will be limited to work on Sri Lanka that is published in the English language, because the bulk of women's research activism and writing since 1975 has been in English – despite growing bodies of knowledge in the Tamil and Sinhala languages.

WR research and writing refer to literature identified as written by women that centres on women as a topic or standpoint of interest. This includes women's issues (such as puberty or violence against women) from feminist as well as non-feminist perspectives; and work on general issues (such as poverty / the media) from feminist and gender perspectives. Research refers to formal published research studies and writing refers to less formal books and articles. I will consider, as exceptions, a couple of works by men, and collaborations by women / men, where they specifically express feminist views.

I rely on international feminist writing / theory to clarify, enlarge, expand and rationalise my work. These are from 'the West' (the UK, USA and Europe), and 'the globe' (including Western and other countries – especially India). I also depend on dictionaries and glossaries to define and elaborate some of my points.

Respondents are women researchers who were interviewed for their viewpoints and discourses on women's research activism and research methodology. They include researchers from academia, independent research institutions, freelance researchers and consultant researchers.[13] Several informal discussions with Sri Lankan, Indian and Pakistani feminists were also taken into consideration for the book.

'Discourse' (Foucault 1972: 107–108) for the purpose of the book, refers to the ideas, standpoints, theorisations and debates that are represented / constructed in research and writing, as well as those articulated by participant researchers during interviews.

'Feminism' is conceptualised as the consciousness, analysis, critique of, or any form of activism against the psychological, ideological, political, structural and micro forces of power and its transmissions that particularly affect women. It also implies the continuing promotion of alternative choices and commitment to changes for women (and men) via personal identities, divergent ideologies / discourses, socio-political and cultural structures / practices – locally and internationally. 'Feminisms' in the plural is used to convey the pluralism and contestations within feminism (Warhol and Herndl 1997) as well as its locatedness and changing nature given that there is usually no singular strand of feminism adhered to in research.

Research 'methodology' I take to be distinct from 'methods' (Ramazanoglu and Holland 2002), although there is a common tendency to conflate / confuse the term 'methodology' with 'methods'. A simple definition is 'a study of or the theory of the way that methods are used' (Dunne et al. 2005: 163). Unlike Harding (1987) and Letherby (2003) who see methodology as divorced from methods and epistemologies, I conceptualise methodology as constituting methods, theorisations, epistemology, ontology and subjectivity as well as the ethical and political considerations of researching, in a way similar to that theorised by Dunne et al. (2005).

The term 'research praxis' refers to the fusion of theory (to some degree) with the practice of feminist research activism. It assumes that at least some of the stated intentions of feminist research methodology are realised in research practice and that the methodologies utilised at ground level are theorised, despite the epistemological and practical problems of transformative and emancipatory research (Lather 1986, 1991; Stanley 1990a; Letherby 2006). In fact, this book is an attempt at research praxis.

I understand and construct the phrases 'making meanings' and 'meaning-making' as compounded metaphors. This is a play on words, to indicate how researching research methodology also involves researching research. Making meanings refers mainly to my own act of researching from several theoretical perspectives. Meaning-making denotes research and writing by others. Both making meanings and meaning-making are conceptualised as having multiple connotations. They refer to the general practice of researching, or the discovery / construction / representation / interpretation of realities through methodology. They imply the discursive possibility not only of discovering knowledge, but also of constructing it. The phrases will also be used to indicate the making of collective sense, through a formal, accepted academic process via the use of research methodology, for an epistemic community. Finally, they will be conceptualised as making personal sense – through the processes of personal experiences (Collins 1990) and of assimilation at an individual psychological level.

I will use the singular pronoun 'I' to refer to myself reflexively: primarily as a feminist researcher and subliminally in terms of my other identities – notwithstanding the instability of the self. Despite the antipathy of some feminists towards the collective pronoun 'we', because of its assumptions of male, or white feminist, as norms (Kramarae and Treichler 1985), I use it for two purposes. First, I want to convey the implied ethos of the sisterhood (however tenuous) of feminists in Sri Lanka, since they do unite from time to time for political purposes. Second, I use it to indicate the work of myself and co-authors.

It is an accepted scholarly practice that writing on specificities other than the Anglo-American is constantly expected to qualify itself by name and location. In fact, 'Western' is taken to be the norm, while the local is expected to be clarified / defined. Whilst fully aware that I am writing for a global readership, I will attempt to challenge this hegemony in my book. I therefore take the Sri Lankan context as the norm. Any references to global literature will be qualified as such.

Part I
Methodology matters

1   The local context

Archaeology of women's research activism

What are the historical sites of the realities with which this book engages and of which it forms part? This chapter aims to introduce and situate the development of women's consciousness and research activism in the country due to its importance for an understanding of Sri Lankan feminist research methodology. To do so I will subscribe to the discursive methodology[1] of archaeology (as conceptualised by Foucault 1972). This will include a brief, descriptive and subjective historical trajectory of the country's socio-political developments, a profiling of researchers and an engagement with the ground politics and economics of women's studies research and writing. It will also include a discursive sketch / construction of women's knowledge from before and after 1975, and some of the macro- and micro-politics relating to knowledge production.

Archaeology

In searching for a framework to encompass / compose women-related (WR) research in Sri Lanka, I find that Krishnaraj's (2006) understanding of a discipline as having specific conceptual tools, a distinct theoretical vocabulary and defined analytical frameworks to be problematic. This is in view of certain informalities and interfaces of research with activism, as well as the predominantly non-academic locations of women's studies in Sri Lanka. There is a difficulty in sometimes divorcing feminist ideas from feminist action (Chaudhuri 2004). Therefore a broader understanding of a disciplinary domain such as Foucault's (1972) concept of 'archaeology' is much more pertinent to this situation. Thus, for instance, I will selectively apply Foucault's (1998) concepts of savoir and connaissances to WR knowledge, women's movements and action. By archaeology, Foucault specifies:

> not exactly a discipline but the domain of research, which would be the following: in a society, different bodies of learning, philosophical ideas, everyday opinions, but also institutions, commercial practices and police activities, mores – all refer to a certain implicit knowledge (savoir) special to this society. This knowledge is profoundly different from the (formal)

bodies of learning (des connaissances) that one can find in scientific books, philosophical theories, and religious justifications, but it (savoir) is what makes possible at a given moment the appearance of a theory, an opinion, a practice.

(Foucault 1998: 261)

While I differ from Foucault's (1998) theorisation when conceptualising of the interactions between savoir and connaissances, archaeology is important to how I conceive of the background, birth and evolution of Women's Studies. Foucault's savoir refers to implicit knowledge; within the overall environment and discursive conditions that make the production of formal knowledge (connaissances) possible. Connaissances is conceptualised as the discourses of Women's Studies as found in the canon or oeuvre of WR research and writing stemming from a new global paradigm in knowledge (Chapter 2). While I am suspicious of the idea of a disciplinary canon, in terms of an originating point of a particular discipline, the singularity, stability and evenness of its evolution, and the rationality and reason of such a trajectory, the essentialism of such a monolithic vision is also another vital way of making meaning and conceiving of epistemology. The chapter encompasses savoir by constructing / focusing on the implications of the country's political and economic imperatives, knowledge-generating institutions and practices, ideas and assumptions, women's movements and activism. These relations (savoir) make connaissances possible. For instance, the sporadic bursts of Sri Lankan women's demands for education and universal franchise in the late nineteenth and early twentieth centuries make possible the domain of women's studies in today's context. Consequently, connaissances needs to be studied not on its own terms but in conjunction with 'institutions, laws, processes and procedures, common opinions, norms, rules, morality, commercial practices and so on' (Scheurich and McKenzie 2005: 848).

In my application of archaeology, I would like to emphasise the relationship between connaissances and savoir as interdependent. Not only does savoir make connaissances possible, but connaissances also results in savoir – the two concepts counter-producing one another. What can be seen as formal knowledge (such as research on gender) leads to commonplace practice (of gender as a consciousness).[2] Furthermore, what is savoir in one context may be connaissances in another. Yet, my application of archaeology is selective in this book – solely to produce a more discerning perception of the state and evolution of different forms of knowledge production and meaning-making in research activism.

A glance at women-related issues before 1975

In Sri Lanka, consciousness of discrimination against women and women's struggles for equal rights and social justice have been traced intermittently from the nineteenth century onwards in various sections of the populace

(Jayawardena 1985, 1986, 1995a; Cat's Eye 2000b; de Alwis and Jayawardena 2001; Jayawardena and de Alwis 2002). I view women's writing on WR issues (connaissances) as an extension of this consciousness and struggle (Jayawardena and de Alwis 2002) or savoir. It is with the problematic objective of establishing trajectories of women's writing that I glance at what was written about women before the United Nations International Year of Women (1975). I then provide a more in-depth look at the subsequent growth of research in the country. However, the tracing of such trajectories of explicit knowledge (connaissances) can only be subjective and artificial projects that are illustrative of the power dynamics of knowledge production and meaning-making (savoir).

The earliest allusions to Sri Lankan women in the English language was in the seventeenth century by Robert Knox (1966) when he makes incidental references to women in describing aspects of Ceylon[3] and its inhabitants during this period. In one of the first travel biographies ever written, Knox represents Cingalese[4] women purely in terms of their sexuality – as being primitive, polyandrous, unclean 'whores' (Knox 1966: 173). As pointed out by Goonatilake (1985), a number of descriptive articles in journals and newspapers (predominantly by male writers) in the nineteenth century alluded to women in relation to socio-cultural practices (marriage and divorce customs, puberty rites, social welfare efforts, healthcare and education). These dominant public portrayals of women situate them essentially in the private sphere of life where they are perceived as alien subjects who possess a different biology and culture to that of men. Certain 'dark' areas of women's lives such as puberty, childbirth, and marital customs are taken to need investigation and public perusal from the standpoint of male knowledge and authority.

de Mel and Samarakkody (2002) trace the earliest writing by women in English to travel narratives about Ceylon, and commentary on the Empire by British and American visitors to the island during the nineteenth century. Other literature, by local women writers, from the 1860s onwards, took creative forms and genres: such as folklore, ghost stories, adventure narratives, historical fiction and social satire (ibid). These found a space in public discourse (i.e. newspapers and supplements, journals and magazines). Of note in the content of these writings in the early nineteenth century is the notion of 'the new woman' (de Mel and Samarakkody 2002: 43), which was perhaps a result of the political and social undercurrents of the modernist movement in the West which conceptualised a 'modern role' for women. It is worth observing here that 'modernity' and 'westernisation' are recurrent themes (aspirational in this instance, but often derogative or alien) when looking at feminism and women's activism in Sri Lanka.[5]

Early research activism can be seen as writing (by men and women) that advocated social change for women in magazines and newspapers during the latter part of the nineteenth century. As in the other British colonies in Asia such as India and Thailand, this related to the continuing debate on women's education. In Sri Lanka, it was linked to the setting up, firstly of Christian, and later of Buddhist schools for women (de Mel and Samarakkody 2002). Jayawardena (1986) traces one reason for this to the missionary objective of educating girls to pass the Cambridge examination so as to improve their marriage prospects. Other motives entailed becoming proficient in domestic / social skills required to be exemplary wives of men from the upper classes, and to 'reach the highest ladder of fame, to regenerate their sex, and to distinguish themselves ... ' (Buddhist Schools Magazine of 1895 quoted in Jayawardena 1986: 124).

This led to a new class of educated and professional women who became politically active, who travelled, and who formed a number of women's organisations[6] (Cat's Eye 2000c). Jayawardena (1993) records how, through their lectures and public-speaking, these middle and upper class women were active in political and social life during this period. Though their activism did not last, and though they were not as militant as the suffragette groups in Britain, this first generation of women activists and women's organisations can be seen as the historical predecessor to the contemporary women's movements in the country. This can be seen particularly in their role vis-à-vis the burning political, social and welfare needs / rights of women. The Women's Franchise Union of Ceylon (1928), for example, headed the demand for women's voting rights and political participation: leading to the attainment of universal franchise in 1931. In the process it had to fend off attacks on women: charges that franchise rights were 'Western' and therefore not part of the indigenous culture or traditional feminine virtues, and that they were symbols of modernity and elitism (de Alwis and Jayawardena 2001). Most of the debate on the issue took place in the Sinhala / Tamil press of the period, though some writing on the issue is also evident in the English press (ibid.). These developments can be seen as the antecedents of the continuing public discourse on women, which sees feminism as a Western import still linked to modernity – despite the inroads of postmodernism (Chapter 4).

In the late 1920s and 1930s, women were also active in left wing political organisations such as the Ceylon Labour Union and Labour Party, the Surya Mal Movement, the Lanka Sama Samaja Pakshaya (LSSP) and the Communist Party. Not only were these women advocates of radical social changes in society, but they also 'broke with tradition making cross-caste and cross-ethnic marriages, thereby defying both patriarchs and British rulers' (Cat's Eye 2000b: 24).

By the 1940s, the women of the Eksath Kantha Peramuna (EKP or United Women's Front), a coalition of women political activists from the parties of the Left, wrote newspaper and magazine articles on the plight of working women. They focused on working and living conditions, and low wages, and put forward a radical feminist agenda (Jayawardena and de Alwis 2002). Although they attempted to integrate women's concerns into the larger socialist agenda (de Mel and Muttetuwegama 1997), their position on women's liberation was, however, subordinate to class concerns, given the central political interests of these women.

The emergence of WR writing and research

So far I have illustrated the different origins and discontinuities of WR writing in the country and linked the phenomenon to some of the historical developments of the period – despite the questionability of the exercise (Foucault 1972). In the 1970s, local women's activism (first as individuals and then as groups) and the influence of Western / global feminist consciousness (savoir) resulted in the burgeoning of WR research in Sri Lanka (connaissances). This can also be related to the international agenda espoused by the United Nations (UN) with regard to women's rights,[7] issues[8] and gender needs / interests.[9] Research can be conceptualised as savoir in terms of creating consciousness and connaissances when it comes to the theoretical and other tools that are espoused.

The liberal / democratic agenda

The institution of the United Nations International Year of Women in 1975, the first UN Conference on Women (Mexico, 1975), and the subsequent United Nations Decade for Women (1975–1985) were publicly significant events on women's issues in Sri Lanka. Other international initiatives supported by Sri Lanka included the United Nations Declaration on Human Rights (1948), as well as the United Nations Convention on the Elimination of all forms of Discrimination Against Women (UNCEDAW) in 1979. These initiatives were designed to address problems that affected women, to provide equal opportunities, and to integrate women as co-partners in national development (University of Colombo 1979).

The National Committee appointed by the government to coordinate activities to celebrate the First UN Conference included radical left wing politicians such as Vivienne Goonewardene (LSSP) and others from the Sri Lanka Freedom Party (SLFP) and Communist Party (CP). They, together with Manel Abeysekera from the Foreign Ministry of Sri Lanka and Swarna Jayaweera from the University of Colombo, accompanied Sri Lanka's woman Prime Minister Sirimavo Banadaranaike to Mexico City.

At the time, the fact that Prime Minister Sirimavo Bandaranaike (the first woman Prime Minister in the world) addressed the conference created further interest locally. However, in her speech, Bandaranaike (1975) reduced the goals of the United Nations International Year of Women (UNIYW) to one overarching concept of equality. She made a distinction between what she saw as the negative aspects of equality such as 'militancy', 'protest' and 'revolt', and the positive aspects such as 'benefits' and 'integration'. Unfortunately, she did not address the urgent need for multiple strategies to achieve equality. However, she argued that the status of women could not be looked at in isolation from other aspects of development – and that development had to be a unified process. A valid point, which was later reflected in global feminist perspectives, especially as advocated by the Gender and Development (GAD) movement (Overholt et al. 1984; Moser 1993) with its emphasis on gender relations.

Bandaranaike then made a case for an 'Asian' viewpoint – in what can perhaps be seen as one of the earliest attempts at a women's standpoint[10] (Chapter 7) – when she promoted what she called a Buddhist concept of equality. This was primarily culture-based and conceptualised as being in harmonious partnership with men. However, the exact nature of this model or its exact location in Buddhism is not clear. This polarisation between the East and West is characteristic of Bandaranaike's stand on international politics during her tenure (1970–1976). It attributes a homogeneity and immobility to all Asian women as well as to Western women that is detrimental to the diverse identities of women. Furthermore, her faith in the equality of women on the basis of Asian culture needs to be analysed as being centred more on women's (so-called) choice pertaining to motherhood, and a valorisation of its responsibilities as far as women are concerned. Although Bandaranaike's speech grapples critically with the implications of women's equality, development and choice, it does not visualise women as individuals in their own right with specific needs, or conceptualise progressive social change for women.

As a result of the Sri Lankan State's commitments to the UN and of local activism by women, the Women's Bureau of Sri Lanka (1979) was established by the Ministry of Plan Implementation. Later, in 1983, the Ministry of Women's Affairs was instituted, initially in affiliation with other ministries. The Ministry was also bound to report each year to the UNCEDAW Committee on the status of women in Sri Lanka, while women's non-governmental organisations (NGOs) prepared their own shadow report (see SLWNGOF 1999; CENWOR 2001), which provided an alternative perspective from the state's.

At the individual level, the early 1970s saw a small group of women in Sri Lanka reading Western feminist writers de Beauvoir (1972)[11] and others such as Friedan (1963), Boserup (1970), Greer (1971), Millett (1971), Rowbotham (1973) and Rosaldo and Lamphere (1974)[12] of the second wave of feminism in America and England. Like the first generation of women activists in Sri Lanka, some of this group had studied and travelled abroad and were involved in an informal study group. These included researchers and activists like Kumari Jayawardena, Eva Ranweera, Bernadeen de Silva, Swarna Jayaweera, Manori Muttetuwegama and Hema Goonatilake. They had led the preparations for the UNIYW from 1974 (and onto the Decade for Women), through activism via newspapers, pamphlets, public lectures, networking, and organised visits from foreign feminists.[13]

Early research (in English) which prioritised change for women was carried out by women academics.[14] A forerunner in the area is a compendium of short articles in the Economic Review of September 1976 which situated women in the development initiatives of the period (Economic Review 1976b). A more formal and comprehensive research study that was undertaken by the women scholars of the University of Colombo was the Status of

Women Survey in 1979. This was influenced by the Indian study on the topic that Muzundar (2008) projects as a foundational text in India. It considered women as a specific category, and implicitly or explicitly highlighted the inequalities and inequities of their situation (Chapter 6). These women, as well as others researching at the time, can be considered the second generation of feminist writers / researchers.

The critical point here is that with UN sponsorship, women's research and activism became concretised. They acquired tangible aspirations and resulted in state and other structures and mechanisms for women, as well as a specific discourse based on women, development and equality within the particular framework of the UN standards for the UN Decade (1975–85). At the same time, the evolving consciousness about women's issues triggered feminists and researchers to move beyond the continuing UN mandates to other compelling areas of local, personal and institutional research interests such as development, historical and gender issues (Chapter 4). What can be identified as liberal democratic feminist activism[15] (Chapter 8) in Sri Lanka, though not unified or universalised, has over the years aspired towards a multiplicity of goals.

Marxist feminism

Samuel (2006a) comments on parallel developments in the Sinhala-speaking context that supported women's activism based on Marxist principles:

> In 1976, the Marga Institute published Kanthava Samajaya Vimukthiya (Women, Society, Liberation) in two volumes which contained a series of articles translated by Sunila Abeysekera ... Volume 2 however was truly a handbook for the Marxist. It made a case for socialism and feminism by including appropriate writings from across the spectrum of revolutionary founding fathers ... that theorized on women and socialism. Included were Vladimir Lenin, Leon Trotsky, August Bebel, Mao Tse-tung and Fidel Castro. Also included were radical selections from Alexandra Kolontai, Sheila Rowbotham, Maria Mies and Della Costa which introduced a revolutionary perspective into a range of everyday women's concerns from labour to violence, abortion and housework. The Volume employed the inspired strategy of presenting a range of experiences that spanned the world from China to India, and Iran to Vietnam.
>
> (Samuel 2006a: 26)

Other Marxist writing that emanated from this era came in the form of pamphlets and booklets – for instance, a booklet in Sinhala entitled Kantha Vimukthiya[16] published by the Centre for Society and Religion (CSR) in 1975. Edited by the Catholic priest and social justice advocate, Tissa Balasuriya, it promoted women's liberation and was notable for its analysis of the situation of women in Sri Lanka. Samuel points out that:

it opened with a discussion on Women's Liberation by Balasuriya and included three other substantive articles on the 'Semi Slavery of Sri Lankan Women' (Tissa Balasuriya, CSR); 'Discrimination against Women' (Bernadeen de Silva, CSR) and 'The Participation of Women in the Social Reform, Political and Labour Movement of Ceylon' (Kumari Jayawardena). Another contribution ... a collection of misogynist 'sayings on women' was further developed into a popular pamphlet with excerpts of oft-quoted verse from religious texts and folklore interspersed with critical comment, and distributed under the title 'Kantha Handa' (Voice of Women) at May Day rallies in 1975 by Kumari Jayawardena, Sunila Abeysekera and Mala Dassanayake (LSSP).

(Samuel 2006a: 30)

In English, the journal Logos published by the CSR brought out an issue entitled 'Women in Asia' edited by Bernadeen de Silva to mark UNIYW. It contained a pioneering article by Jayawardena on women's participation in socio-political reform and the Labour Movement in Sri Lanka (1975). Consequently, these parallel movements of women's research activism in English and in Sinhala or in liberal democrat and Marxist politics cannot be seen as completely separate or homogenous entities (Chapter 8). There were often women from all communities Sinhala, Tamil, and Muslim involved in these initiatives, which were often on common issues. In this section, I have illustrated that savoir not only led to conditions conducive of / for connaissances, but connaissances often became savoir as far as some developments in feminist research activism were concerned.

Women's movements and researchers

From an understanding of the interfaces and overlaps between connaissances and savoir, I move on to the consideration of savoir – or the historical conditions and developments that make the domain of feminist research activism and Women's Studies possible. Stagnation in economic growth during the 1970s (due to import and foreign exchange restrictions, high unemployment levels and food shortages) led a new United National Party (UNP) government to initiate radical changes in economic policy from 1977. These involved the introduction of a Structural Adjustment Programme (SAP) sponsored by the World Bank and the International Monetary Fund (IMF), according to the prevalent economic matrix. Successive programmes of structural adjustment after that resulted in extensive transformations of the Sri Lankan state and economy. The State became lethargic and relinquished its involvement in public / welfare services as economic restructuring and privatisations took place. This resulted in private sector intervention in the service sectors, especially in urban locales, and in NGO initiatives (especially in microdevelopment) in rural areas. The environment created by the availability of funding from international and bilateral agencies resulted in an increased international non-governmental organisation (INGO) presence, and a boom in NGOs and community-based organisations (CBOs).[17] Women also began to feature in the focus of these NGOs, amongst the development issues of the time such as infrastructure development, welfare assistance, healthcare, education and skills training, community development, income generation schemes and the environment (Fernando and de Mel 1991; Wickramasinghe 2000).

Women's groups and NGOs that were development-oriented, activist-oriented and research-oriented emerged (Jayaweera 1995), as did federations of women's groups at grassroots and other levels. As consciousness strengthened amongst local women and the internationalisation of gender and women's issues grew, the mandates of these organisations addressed the diversity of women's needs.[18] These ranged from welfare assistance to rural women's skills training; from credit schemes to Women's Day activities; from peace initiatives to support for the elimination of violence against women; from legal literacy to policy interventions; from gender training and research to media-monitoring. The diversity of these activities and programmes shows the multi-faceted dynamism of women's activism in Sri Lanka. It has been argued that this constitutes women's movements rather than a single movement (Jayawardena 1985; Wickramasinghe 2000; Jayawardena and de Alwis 2002). This is because groups that are diverse and fragmented come together periodically to establish coalitions, protest, advocate and lobby on contingent issues.

Given that this book relies both on the written and articulated opinions of WR researchers, I refer to one of my interview respondents, Farida, in discussing the issue further. Farida argued that this fragmentation was because 'the movement is quite scattered at the moment; it is scattered because the movement has become "projectified" over a period of time'. She attributed this fragmentation to INGO funding practices which support short-term projects rather than sustained interventions. This viewpoint is partially valid since the interests of some organisations are limited to the project. Yet, my own experiences as a feminist activist have been that, despite their defined and focused interests, many women's organisations and individual feminists coalesce frequently on anti-war protests, issues of violence against women, human rights, the tsunami and political participation (Chapter 8). Rather than interpreting these configurations of women's movements as a limitation they need to be perceived as a feminist politics of unity and difference. Why should we, as feminists, expect or impose on one another a commonality of political interest? I argue that what is strategically necessary is for women's movements to both differ and converge on the basis of pragmatism and contingence. This is conceptualised in terms of feminists and women of many hues working strategically and pragmatically through mutual compromise towards common junctures, while at the same time working independently and consistently towards individual goals and objectives based on differences in their agendas.

Here it is important to account for feminists / women within the epistemic community of Women's Studies who are not part of a formal organisation:

especially since the individual conscious and unconscious subjectivities of researchers in knowledge and meaning-making are irrefutable (Chapter 3). Of the women researchers that I interviewed for this book, Sadia, a women's activist / researcher has this to say:

> Some of the older women come from the Left movement to feminism but with a very strong socialist frame ... Then ... in the 70s, you get women ... influenced by 1968, by Vietnam, revolutions in Nicaragua ... Then ... by the1980s ... yet another generation ... for whom there is globalized influence, globalized knowledge, IT, exposure to international academia, Women's Studies abroad, postmodernism though one may not be necessarily grounded within progressive politics – of movement-oriented politics ... And then the next generation like ... who all have the luxury of being in academia to some extent as they grew up fairly cushioned. Some women are not in engaged politics ... especially the militarized politics of today – as it alienates a lot of English-speaking young academics.

> (Sadia)

This quotation reflected Sadia's take on the numerous facets in the collective identities / subjectivities of researchers. It traces the battery of issues regarding the political grounding, ideological standing, language, disciplinary positionings, external influences and events, and personal interests of researchers. Both global politics and local politics have figured in feminist consciousness / knowledge. However, Sadia's visual pertains to a particular group of researchers who have openly identified themselves as feminist researchers (a number of whom have been educated abroad[19] and have international academic experiences in Women's Studies since the 1980s and 1990s (Chapters 4 and 8). Sadia (ibid.) also talked of an alienating split away from the militarised politics in the country by some of the English-speaking academics. While such an understanding is essentialist and biased towards a view of feminist politics as overt resistance, it does not acknowledge interlinks between researchers and the divergent forms of feminist activisms. As in other Asian countries,[20] Sri Lankan researchers have multiple roles in life: from professional roles to activist roles to gender roles. Often they are academics or professionals; members of women's NGOs and CBOs; they sit on local, governmental, national, regional and international bodies; they are involved in advocacy and lobbying in the government, the private sector and rural and urban communities; they are also involved in protests and demonstrations. Given the unstable economic and political fortunes of the country, many researchers are aware of the opportunities available to them outside Sri Lanka. My interviewees spoke of a conscious decision to stay / work in the country, resisting decades of white and blue-collar labour migration.

Nevertheless, it is worth noting the privileges associated with the English language as discussed by Wanasundera:

The ability to access financial resources required for research, especially external assistance, peer group interactions, participation in professional activities within and outside the country, their high visibility locally, and resources at their disposal were some of the factors that kept research activity confined to few and within urban areas.

(Wanasundera 1995: 348)

The international community is, in terms of agenda-setting, interaction, and funding opportunities, weighted towards those who are skilled in the English language. However, within the last few years INGOs such as CIDA[21] have started funding WR research in Sinhala / Tamil, and have sponsored translations. The last decade has seen an increase in the presentation of WR research in Sinhala by individual researchers.[22]

Feminist research activism

A related development in the institutionalisation of women's movements has been the prominence of research activism. By this, I mean the role and significance of researching and writing as a form of feminist activism, especially as the idea of the activity itself can be conceptualised as intersections / overlaps between savoir and connaissances. Research activism[23] encompasses the following:

- Research / writing for general purposes of consciousness-raising and education.
- Research / writing designed to formulate, lobby, or influence policy and legislation.
- Research / writing in preparation for or in conjunction with a specific developmental or welfare intervention.
- Research / writing that prepares institutions for gender mainstreaming and reformation.
- Research / writing that evaluates gender mainstreaming / reformation.
- Research/ writing that is utilised for feminist protest.

This then is a dynamic understanding of research – as a form of activism not only confined to consciousness-raising and education. It is seen as connected to a gamut of other activisms in addition, as my work in the following chapters will illustrate. Yet defining feminist research activism as above should not camouflage the complexities of the process. As Sadia an interviewee whose origins are in NGO work, she made a very pertinent point for instance, about the subtleties of researching the feminist movement:

Most activists are too busy to write down about their work. Also, they are not trained. Academic research may not be accessible to the activists. They may not have the tools to understand it ... It can be alien, have academic authority. Activists do a lot – it may not get written down, it may not be considered important. They'll only be oral histories. So, we have to think of what constitutes research – as other forms of research are not valued as official research.

(Sadia)

Speaking of her involvement in subaltern[24] historical research, recording the lost voices of working-class women activists, Sadia (ibid.) argued that, for her, there was always a political intent in researching. In this instance, it involved making visible the invisible and thereby giving recognition and value to the activities of working-class women. However, the ethical problem of the authoritative standing of the research as research (as well as in the English language) and the continuing disadvantages of some activists are areas that need further consideration. The above quotation also exemplifies a polarity between action and writing – where writing (connaissances) is perceived as an activity that is given more value by academia, while activism (savoir) is neglected. The following questions posed by Sadia further exemplifies a revisioning of the strict division between connaissances and savoir. What constitutes research and is it only possible in written form? What about different (non-research) knowledge possibilities in particular social / cultural contexts? How should such knowledge be indicated / evaluated? While a conceptualisation of connaissances and savoir as two divergent entities is problematic, nonetheless such a distinction necessarily needs to be made first – before considering the exceedingly blurred and unstable interfaces / overlaps between the two.

As far as the content of WR research / writing is concerned, early development-oriented research has today evolved in many directions and covers a variety of topics. Yet, despite this expansion of research interests by the 2000s, there are still some areas such as sexuality, religion and the woman's body which have not received adequate attention. Writing on sexuality, when attempted, is couched in the discourse of workers' and health rights – as in the case of two studies on sex workers (see Miller 2000; Abeysekera 2005a). Wijewardene's (2007) work on transgendering makes an interesting exception (Chapter 5). Abeysekere, S. (2005) touches on lesbian relations, but only in the context of sex workers. Tambiah (2004) looks at women's sexuality and the female body in relation to the Penal Code Amendment of 1995 which tried to liberalise abortion, amongst other initiatives (Chapter 6). The gap in research contradicts the existence of lesbian researchers in the WR domain, and gay / lesbian / transgender activism in the country. Yet this needs to be understood in the context of the backlash against such interest groups in recent times, and the influence of market ideology (Maguire and Ball 1994) in the neglect of the funding of certain WR topics due to economic interests.

Feminist research activism – more issues of connaissances?

There is a common perception (savoir) that research literature can be categorised into women's, gender and feminist research. Three of my respondents tried to define what they did as research practitioners (connaissance). Kiyana, a researcher in her sixties, described her interest in women's research as follows:

> I have got catapulted to do women's research over the years. By women's research, I mean, I look at women … in art and history … I focus on women – pre-modern representations, ancient women, how they have been represented, things like that – so I don't do gender research or feminist research.
>
> (Kiyana)

For Kiyana, women's research was distinct from gender and feminist research because it focused on women. This meant discussing the ways in which women were represented in the historical data that she used. She particularly did not want to be identified as a gender or feminist researcher. Often, the rejection of gender in researching emanates from those who identify themselves as feminists – especially as they fear that expanding the focus to men depoliticises women's oppression (Chapter 5). Yet Kiyana did not identify herself as a feminist researcher either. Researchers who disown the feminist label usually do so because they find the stereotypical notions that have been associated with feminisms to be radical (Chapter 7). While it can be argued that women's research is a discipline, a standpoint and a category of research, for me women's research is a paradigm in knowledge – where the epistemological focus is on women, as argued in Chapter 2.

For researcher Aruni, who has been working in grassroots development projects and research for an INGO, gender research involved the following:

> My work is in gender – gender relations. The conceptual standpoint I have been taking is that in any area men and women perform distinctly different roles in society, and because of that, their life experiences, expectations, needs, capabilities, their difficulties are different … within that framework I try to find out what are the differences, what are the capabilities, what are the difficulties, what are the strengths.
>
> (Aruni)

Aruni saw gender as a conceptual framework (or frameworks) that relates to gender roles and relations as conceptualised by Moser (1993). For her, gender involved considering the differences between men and women, and incorporating them in her work. Due to her affiliation with development work, gender had practical implications for Aruni. However, as will be discussed in Chapter 5, gender can be conceptualised as more than a theoretical / practical framework: it is my argument that gender is an epistemology.

On the other hand, Zulfica proudly announced that she was a feminist:

> I am a feminist; I am self-taught in feminist theory. One thing is, you have to look at the power dynamics in society – this involves looking at

class, poverty, conflicts, race and so on. How this affects women. And the end result of research should be empowerment – of the individual and structures. Consciousness-raising and change in structures. Of course, I can't directly link this to our research but we seem to have conscientised the judges of the Quasi Appeal Courts. Now their judgments are more pro-gressive – we have a woman lawyer from our organisation to represent clients. She argues the case so well that judgments are more favourable towards women. But these dynamic efforts need to be kept going constantly.

(Zulfica)

Her idea of feminism entailed a holistic view of various power-plays or intersection of oppressions within society – in terms of how they affected women. She also advocated the use of multiple methods to empower indivi-duals and social structures, and told an anecdote about structural change due to research activism by her organisation. Here the understanding of what is termed as feminist research has an indisputable link to the politics of power and a desire / action for social change. In this context, Zulfica echoed my own standpoint and reading of feminism as a form of ethical politics (Chapter 8). The above example also shows that formal knowledge of connaissances invariably impacts on savoir and vice versa, in what can be seen as a cyclical relationship. The theoretical aspirations of formal knowledge led to informal institutional knowledge and activism in this instance.

However, there are more tempered readings of feminist research activism. Another interviewee, Wasanthi, articulated the following sentiments regarding women:

And it becomes more comfortable to talk within that framework, and see that their conditions are improved – what I mean is that they have not been confrontational. But sort of a 'softly softly' approach, you know what I mean? Say ... without challenging the status quo. Actually, we have not challenged the patriarchal structure forcefully enough. That is my feeling. Whether we can achieve what we want to achieve through the way we are doing without being confrontational, I don't know whether that is possible.

(Wasanthi)

Wasanthi (ibid.) conveyed her ambivalence about the liberal / democratic feminist approach of working within the existing status quo. Yet this is based on a stereotypical perception that feminism – particularly Western feminism – is symbolic of confrontation. I realised during the course of my research that I myself have in fact been guilty of such unconscious bias. Two other inter-viewees in my study also saw confrontation as 'radicalism'. Such views belie and negate Sri Lankan women's periodic protests and agitations – against the war, for instance. Having argued thus, it must be conceded that the bulk of activism has been attempted through strategic means: negotiation, lobbying and action research. It is, however, highly debatable whether this reflects the dominant Buddhist ethic of tolerance in Sri Lanka as has been generally presumed. It is also worth mentioning here aspects of feminism which are more instinctive: what my respondent, Sakunthala, a quantitative researcher, identified as 'a gut feeling' with regard to her own commitment to women's research. This 'gut feeling' is a subjective, unconscious, instinctive factor propelling WR research activism, and it requires further investigation.

Conforming to modernist reasoning centred on dualisms, I now juxtapose this unconscious, even emotional partiality of feminisms (Jagger 1989) with the contention that Sri Lankan WR research lacks theorisation by feminist researchers (Goonatilake 1985; Wanasundera 1995). This seems dated in the face of new research studies: work in anthropology, cultural studies, and social science for example, explore the theoretical boundaries of contemporary Sri Lankan women in armed combat (Rajasingham-Senanayake 2001), nationalism (de Mel 2001) and militarism (de Mel 2007). It is possible that this criticism of Sri Lankan research as lacking theory is based on a perception of the research not formulating local or indigenous theorisations. Of course, postcolonial understandings of travelling theory (Said 1983) discussed in Chapter 7, hybridity (Bhaba 1994) and multibridity (Chapter 3), as well as postmodernist critiques of binary oppositions, deconstruct the idea of theory being divided into local and Western[25] or even into inductive and deductive. This is because research studies that employ a women's perspective or operate on arguments of women's rights or gender equity / equality or local conceptualisations of patriarchy[26] also have an element of induction. While empirical work based on inductive methods of surveying and interviewing (take the examples of Jayaweera 2005 or Wijayatilake 2002) also have deductive assumptions and frameworks. These studies do not always 'theorise' through systematic and well-developed arguments of synthesis or deconstruction. Nonetheless, they 'begin' theory (Chapter 7) through middle-order theorisations (de Groot and Maynard 1993a) combining both deductive and inductive analysis (Chapter 3). It is possible that the focus on beginning theory as opposed to full-blown, comprehensive theorisations results from the location of a great number of WR studies in the NGO sector and not in academia, where the objectives of research may centre on 'a needs-base' and a pragmatic approach. While the next section deals with the savoir of feminist research activism, it needs to be reiterated that the boundaries between savoir and connaissances are not always clear.

Feminist research activism – more issues of savoir?

WR research in English from academia, though pursued sometimes within university fora, is not always published,[27] unlike research from the NGOs.[29] The non-existence of a formal discipline of Women's Studies at undergraduate level, and the relative lack of emphasis on research (as opposed to teaching within higher educational institutions), may have impacted on this. Often the production of and forum for WR research has been situated in NGO environs rather than in the academy (Reuben 1978), as is the case in Sri Lanka. This 'new academia' is seen to be flexible and unstructured, with surges of activity and the potential for continuing growth as long as funding sources are available, again prompting a re-evaluation of savoir and connaissances. In contrast, due to the free education system in the country and a staunch resistance to the privatisation of universities, the impact of market ideology within higher education is limited – unlike in the UK, for instance (Maguire and Ball 1994). However, higher education is in the process of sporadic reconstruction through World Bank-related and internal initiatives. Conversely, Women's Studies teaching[30] has, since 1988, been located primarily in the universities with the exception of a few initiatives by NGOs.[31] Today, several state universities have also integrated gender / women's perspectives into undergraduate, diploma and graduate courses[32] in various disciplines, often promoting gender / WR topics and perspectives in dissertation writing. Here, the local debate has been centred on whether there should be a separate Women's Studies discipline or whether gender should be integrated into all subjects (Jayawardena 1995a). Currently both strategies are in operation, giving the dual advantages of compartmentalisation and mainstreaming.

However, this picture of dynamic WR research and activism is perhaps compromised by the influence of globalisation and what is generally seen as the commercialisation of research. There are allegations that certain researchers take advantage of their mastery of WR discourse (in terms of familiarity with theoretical frameworks and technical jargon) and their academic qualifications to cultivate contacts within the INGO sector, to exploit the funding sources available. These researchers' commitment to feminist politics has been questioned within the feminist research domain. Research motives are seen to be tainted by interactions based on exploitation and self-aggrandisement, and the politics of the research process as being eroded by commercialism and the interests of market ideology (Maguire and Ball 1994) or global capitalism. While these allegations are disturbing, they also reflect early feminist assumptions that feminism is based on superior, higher ideals of sisterhood and unity. Furthermore, they assume that feminist politics should strive to be pure and uncoloured by negative characteristics of exploitation, competition, self-interest and personal dislikes (Mohanty 2003). Post-modern feminism has exposed the misleading fallacies of such moral polarisations (that naturally assign 'goodness' to women and 'badness' to men) as being based on essentialism and biological determinism[33] / reductionism (de Lauretis 1989; Martin 1994).

What is required in today's context is not misplaced idealism, or rejection, but an approach to feminism that is inclusive, strategic and pragmatic. This should take into consideration the multiple facets and realities of the research context (such as funding concerns and other motivations), and build on what has been achieved. This is important in the context of complex and far-reaching global and other forces that are part of, intersect or impinge on the local scenario. Universities, for example, which should be the bedrock of research, are increasingly under financial pressure to adjust structurally to the demands of economic reforms and changing employment requirements through needs-based teaching and researching.

When it comes to NGO research, the question always arises as to who decides the research agenda, topics and questions. As far back as 1985, Goonatilake (1985: 36) saw the researcher as 'having to attune herself to criteria laid down externally'. While the shifting nature of funders' research mandates (according to globally identified interests) cannot be denied, there is nonetheless space for negotiation by researchers – as evidenced by the multiplicity of issues and directions in research literature.

Respondent Kamini, a feminist academic working in an activist organisation, articulated the following about the donor / NGO relationship:

> As an organisation ... if you look at our annual plan there are studies that we want to do. You will find that some of them have never been done. They are pushed out. Because you just can't get funding for those things. Nowadays – you put in violence issues, some economic issues, peace or rehabilitation. Donors all have their own priorities ...
>
> (Kamini)

Dhamani, an ardent proponent of anti-positivism, related her experience of how this divide manifested itself in research praxis:

> I wanted to trace a study of women from different ethnic groups in the north and east of the country, multiethnic groups, and look at how the war has shaped their responses to the tsunami. But this INGO was not interested in funding that. What they wanted was a nine-month turnaround ... give some kind of a preliminary report. They were more interested in things like the distribution of aid. Now, some part of my study would have looked at the distribution of aid because it is absolutely important. But I would have looked at it from its gendered aspect ... we know how aid can get politicised, how women may not see any ... and how women have been shaped by the war as well as the Tsunami. They just downgraded the whole proposal.
>
> (Dhamani)

In this instance, what could have been a more insightful, comprehensive research study was redirected into one primary objective – that of evaluating impact. This highlights the current mantra of institutional productivity and efficiency that is an influencing factor in the direction and content of research.

However, despite these constraints, researchers have managed to obtain funds for research proposals designed solely by them, according to their own interests and priorities. This reveals the complex tensions between the autonomy of the research focus and global funding sources. Another trend seems to be the regional research projects undertaken by transnational women's NGO networks and initiated by research centres.[34] Here too, there has been room for negotiation: to make way for country issues or to design the research project according to the local environment. However, this may not always be the case with research consultancies, where researchers are commissioned by organisations, and given specific Terms of Reference (TOR) for the research project. Yet, personal experience proves that I have – as a consultant researcher – been able to formulate and even change the TOR. I reiterate here that the multiplicity of issues and directions of WR research literature negates the argument that the research focus is solely dependent on funding priorities. Certain research interests – such as the current focus on women's political participation – can be attributed to global prioritisation especially at the UN level, but research is equally situated in local imperatives, institutional impulses and personal politics (Chapter 4).

In this chapter, my depiction and construction of trajectories of WR research since the nineteenth century have resulted in an understanding of the links between research and the multiple historical, political and socio-cultural realities in the country. It is a relationship that is contingent not only on women's activism over the years, but also on Sri Lanka's development processes, the conflict situation and other external factors. The close alignment of research with women's movements is what makes it useful to think in terms of research activism as archaeology. However, the boundaries between women's research (connaissances) and the ontological conditions (savoir) producing research were seen to be / constructed as blurred. Furthermore, the assumed binaries of WR research (theory versus empiricism, academia versus NGO, scholar versus activists, and funding directives versus independent research) require revisioning so as to reflect / compose the complex interactions of archaeology. Yet as argued earlier, savoir and connaissances were also conceptualised as separate, oppositional concepts. Archaeology was also understood as a meta-concept or a theorisation evoked to encompass / construct / represent women's studies and feminist research activism in the country.

2 A paradigm

Women – a paradigm in global knowledge production

If Sri Lankan theory on research methodology is under-theorised, there is a distinct possibility that international theory on research methodology is over-theorised. I pose the following questions from research literature on methodologies reviewed within the international fora. What are the common histories and experiences, feminist understandings and objectives assumed by Women's Studies worldwide? What are the differences? How can these dominant methodological issues of feminisms be understood / conceptualised?

Admittedly these are broad, generalised questions and answering them is understandably an undertaking of challenging proportions, given the assumptions implicit in the separation of local from global methodologies; transitional from developed nations; and the possibilities of differences, commonalities and unities within regions. Consequently, it is with some degree of apprehension that I undertook this chapter. The objective of this chapter, nonetheless, is to explore and construct methodological issues within global contexts as a means of contextualising Sri Lankan work and of giving relevance to this book beyond the Sri Lankan realm. Consequently the responses to these questions conform to my overall methodology of concurrently looking for and composing unities and dissensions, commonalities and disparities, oppositions and conflations.

This chapter originates from my problem with the tendency (particularly in Sri Lanka) to envisage feminist research as genuine political research; gender research as commercial research; and research on women as neutral research (Chapter 1). Such assumptions are misleading in view of the shared aims and assimilations of feminisms, gender and women in both local and global research. The common factor in the three types of research is, quite simply, their focus on women / woman. In fact, the illusory category of women / woman is the nexus of all women / feminist / gender-related research and methodology, and represents a global paradigm that breaks away from the generally established norms and principles of research, irrespective of whether it is a compensatory model based on women's disadvantage (Raj 1988) or an aspirational model of gender equity / equality. In this chapter, I will define or compose the ways in which researchers relate to and engage with this paradigm – methodologically. Consequently, it is a chapter that focuses on connaissances or formal bodies of learning (as understood from Chapter 1).

Women as a paradigm in global knowledge production

The concept of a paradigm in knowledge is commonly held to originate with Thomas Kuhn and his idea of how scientifically unexplainable anomalies in scientific traditions and practices lead to the conceptualisation of new foundations for scientific practice (Kuhn 1970). These new methodological foundations are put forward to explain and resolve the existing anomalies. Althusser is cited by Foucault (1998: 281–282) as calling this phenomenon 'an epistemological break' with regard to the advent of Marxist economic analysis. Though Foucault (1998) himself disagrees, arguing that Marx modifies the economic analyses of Ricardo, he concedes a break only when it comes to the Marxist theory of society.

My understanding straddles both positions. A paradigm is not a distinctive action undertaken by a specific knowledge maker, but rather, an extended break – comprising new (multiple) knowledges and cross-fertilisations in epistemology (understood as connaissances in Chapter 1) that for a time ignites the collective intellect of a particular epistemic community. When such a process is conceptualised as taking place from a postmodernist viewpoint, its origins may not always be clear and its history and progress may be discontinuous and non-linear. Furthermore, as in Foucault's (1972) episteme (a similar concept to a paradigm), it may be necessary to make allowances for contradictory and opposing theorisations to co-exist within a paradigm. Yet, from a modernist position, it is possible to identify and construct the beginnings, continuities and linearity of a paradigm. I see this overarching concept as symbolic moments in knowledge production which can be understood to have led to the phenomenon of worldwide Women's Studies from the 1970s onwards.

The term 'paradigm' is 'not so much a theory, more a theoretically derived worldview which provides the categories and concepts through and by which we construct and understand the world' Stanley and Wise (1993: 153). When applied to social science research 'paradigms are not only produced from the doing of scientific work, they also play a key role in providing covert reference points; paradigms bind people together in a shared commitment to their discipline' (Oakley 2000: 27). In other words, a paradigm not only provides a knowledge base, a framework and method for researching, but also a sense of an epistemic community as conceptualised by Stanley and Wise (1993) and Ramazanoglu and Holland (2002). This is in the form of a socially produced community that takes upon itself the authority to speak for and from a specialised knowledge base. Yet while Women's Studies worldwide constitutes a critical swing of the knowledge paradigm, it can only be conceptualised as a transitional moment of emerging, competing knowledges – given Lather's (1991) discussion of the various critiques of paradigms.

To reiterate, the 'birth' of a new discipline needs to be conceptualised as involving Foucault's archaeology of both savoir and connaissances (Foucault 1972). It is connaissances in the way that it spans and straddles multiple disciplines, and appropriates / incorporates many knowledge-making models, and diverse theoretical standpoints. It is savoir in how it revolutionises knowledge production and meaning-making through appeals to experience, emotions, activism and networking.

As conceptualised by Kuhn (1970), I contend that this paradigm shift arose from a series of anomalies in existing knowledges. It began with a consciousness of women's subjectivities – of individual and collective women becoming conscious of themselves as women; and with an understanding of ontology – of the various forces, institutions, and micropolitics that led to oppression and inequalities. It occurred for epistemological reasons – from identified gaps and misrepresentations in existing knowledges with regard to women in virtually all disciplines; and from the realisation that conventional research methods could not investigate or construct women's realities and that there was thus a need to formulate new methods. It came about from a lack of theoretical concepts and frameworks to define / encapsulate women's lives and oppression and finally, from a political / ethical understanding of how knowledges about women were generally considered informal and illegitimate.

Christine Delphy has critiqued existing knowledges for their ignorance of social oppressions:

> All knowledge which does not recognize, which does not take social oppression as its premise, denies it, and as a consequence objectively serves it ... Knowledge that would take as its point of departure the oppression of women would constitute an epistemological revolution.
>
> (Delphy 1981: 73)

Delphy (1981) makes explicit the connections between knowledge and power. The power to critique / deconstruct old knowledge claims, and the power to make new knowledge claims from a women's standpoint, were the original means by which a paradigm based on women was created and established.

Usually, discussions relating to a paradigm are held at the expense of a contrasting paradigm – examples being that of the qualitative versus quantitative paradigms or the interpretive versus normative paradigms (Burrell and Morgan 1979; Cohen and Manion 1997; Oakley 2000). This reflects the oppositional or binary thinking of modernism. I am temporarily conceptualising a women's paradigm as forming a binary opposition to established codes of knowledge, solely in order to convey the departure or deviation from existing knowledge. I am not arguing that the two paradigms represent universally dissimilar ideals that are mutually exclusive and eternally in conflict. Furthermore, despite the attempts of such a paradigm to produce counter-knowledge and methodology that is true to those who are subjugated, these too can only be partial and situated (Haraway 1988). Consequently, my conceptualisation of a women's paradigm in research is based on assumptions of an ordered, coherent worldview as well as an awareness of the non-linear, unstable, fragmented disunity in such an overarching concept.

In the next section I will review how feminist researchers internationally have engaged with and contributed to a women's paradigm through various research methodologies. Given the impracticable breadth of such an exercise, the section is not based on an exhaustive literature review, but on a selective highlighting of trends, issues and dilemmas. Research methodologies or ways of meaning-making have been identified or composed by me as they relate to the researcher's subjectivity, ontology, epistemology, methods, theory and ethics / politics, because they continue to be thematic areas of interests for researchers.

Feminist subjectivities

As far as methodology is concerned, subjectivity refers to a consciousness of the internal self (in terms of thoughts, emotions, experiences, beliefs, assumptions, intentions, imagination, and consciousness of the self and others) – as well as the external identities imposed by society. Subjectivity can also be understood as a dimension of ontology: in that it is a consciousness of the self as a reality. Yet there are many accounts of subjectivities: from Modernist accounts that portray the subject as stable, conscious, individualistic, in control and possessing agency, to French feminists who discuss how the self is constructed as a coherent autonomous self through the exclusion of others. Psychoanalysis emphasises the significance of the unconscious in subject positionings, while Irigaray (1974) asserts that Western philosophical discourses are phallocentric and that as a result women can only define themselves through male terms. Furthermore, postmodernists deconstruct the subject's consciousness as fluid, vacillating, arbitrary and paradoxical, and its positionings as multiple and fractured (Irigaray 1974; Foucault 1980a; Braidotti 1994; Debold et al. 1996; Butler 1999; Althusser 2000).

On the whole, feminist interest in subjectivity was initially located in the political consciousness of the self as a woman (MacKinnon 1982), especially as a victimised woman (Bartky 1978; Harding 1987) or as an agent of resistance or self-determination (Mani 1992; de Mel 1996). These subjectivities are conceptualised in two ways: first, as the consciousness of the self as a constituent member of women (a collective); and second, as the awareness of the self as a biological / gendered woman (an individual). This was often because the concept of 'women', in the plural, was a politicised category used for the aspirational objectives of feminisms. But Oyewumi (1997: ix) points out that there was 'no pre-existing group (*of women*) characterised by shared interests, desires or social position' in Yorubaland before its encounter with the West. Furthermore, not all societies make the division between men and women their primary form of social ordering. For instance, Oyewumi (1997) discusses social ordering according to age hierarchies in Yoruban societies. Although critiqued as simplistic and essentialist, this homogenous overarching perception of women (as women) served to institute them as a category of analysis and an oppressed group in the global imagination. As a consequence, women as ontology were transformed into an epistemological category by the act of researching, despite the questionability and instability of discursive representations of illusory masses of women (Haraway 1990; Butler 1999).

Similarly, the concept of 'the woman', in the singular, also enters women's studies discourses – because of the hitherto ontological gaps and misrepresentation of the woman. First, it does so as a biological entity essentially based on sight (Oyewumi 1997); and second, as a social construction (de Beauvoir 1972; Oakley 1972). The consciousness of subjectivity as a woman in terms of the physical body has been theorised as follows. 'Corporeal' feminists have identified the biological differences between the man and the woman as a central cause for male control – through physical strength as well as socio-cultural discourses. Reproduction, in particular, was recognised as a bodily site of inequality in the woman along with sexuality and sexual orientation (Firestone 1979). 'Difference' feminists on the other hand, affirmed, valorised and celebrated bodily differences as sources of power. Cixous (1976) talks of an 'ecriture feminine' which is symbolic of the woman's body; and Gilligan (1977) argues for the woman's unique moral development as opposed to the man's. These understandings of subjectivity (and ontology) were founded on sexual differences as natural, and therefore resulted in oppositional, static, stereotyped representations of the woman. Another highly influential view of subjectivity as a woman was founded on gender as a social / cultural division and therefore artificial and changeable (Oakley 1972). 'Sex roles' feminists underrated the biological, and theorised that socialisation processes were the sources of inequalities; and that transformations in social structures and processes could therefore lead to gender equity / equality. Yet, paradoxically, the burden of the social constructionist[1] (Hepburn 2006) argument of gender may have served to render the woman and man passive objects. This is because very rigid conceptualisations of social, structural and ideological forces of conditioning could compromise personal agency (Jacobs 2003). Butler (1999) engaged with feminist assumptions of a woman's subjectivity as static and 'accomplished' by theorising gender as performativity, thereby focusing on the identity politics of subjectivity. She saw sex and gender as a continuous process that was being constantly constructed and sustained by individuals through repetitions, rituals and performances.

A significant volume of feminist ontological representations and constructions relies on both social constructionism and biological determinism to understand and construct women's subjectivities (Chodorow 1978; Hubbard 1990). These unify centuries-old ontological assumptions, made from Plato to Descartes in Western philosophy, of a mind / body bifurcation. Fuelling these debates further are completely different ontological perspectives which argue that the concept of biology itself is arbitrary and socially constructed (Wittig 1981; Oyewumi 1997; Butler 1999; Moi 1999). As a result, things seen as natural and predetermined (such as biological differences) are merely conceptual classifications. In this understanding, both sex and gender differences are seen as social constructs and therefore partial to change according to developments in knowledge and technology despite some physiological and genetic aspects of a woman (or a man, for that matter) that have resisted scientific innovations / challenges – such as ageing.

Underlying these conceptualisations of the woman is the supposition, often based on notions of heterosexuality, of the woman's relationship to the man – as the opposite (Rich 1980; Wittig 1981). This has led to extensive parallel thinking on masculinities (especially by the men's movements and gender theorists) that have influenced feminist understandings of gender and femininities. Once again, the assumption reinforces heterosexuality as the norm as opposed to other sexual orientations – despite the historical, social, cultural and discursive production of the ensuing variations in sexualities (Foucault 1980a; Rubin 2006). In response, lesbian feminists have advocated the abandonment of compulsory heterosexuality. Instead, they have conceptualised a 'lesbian continuum' (Rich 1980) by including all the woman-centred experiences of women, devoid of a sexual focus. While conceptualisations of lesbian subjectivities have been monolithic at times (for instance, the discussion of the concept of lesbian as superseding categories of men and women by Wittig in 1992), these have been destabilised by Queer theory which highlights personal identities and questions notions of deviancy and transgression.

While the politics of sexuality was seen as key to gendered and politicised subject positions (Rubin 2006), so were other conscious and theorised intersections in subjectivity such as experiences located in class, race / ethnicity, indigenous groups, caste, language, geography, age, transgender, disability, non-Western, postcolonialism and nationalism (Collins 1991; Harstock 2004; Sandoval 2004; Harding 2004c; Narayan 2004). Weedon (2003) traces the subjectivities or subjects assumed by various epistemological and theoretical approaches. Here, understandings of hybridity (Bhaba 1994) as well as 'multibridity'[2] (Chapter 3) are helpful in engaging not only the pluralism of subjectivities but also the crosscuts, intersections, overlaps, simultaneity, fragments, arbitrariness and continuing evolution of subjectivities. By and large, these possibilities also convey the extent to which subjectivity is situated in multiple and often contradictory fields of power. For the main part, despite their abstractness, the discursive concepts of women / woman have been partially successful in promoting concrete, historically located, social, psychological and cultural understandings of the experience of being woman / women.

Feminist ontologies

Ontology refers to consciousness of realties of the self (or being) and understandings / conceptualisations of the forms, nature or aspects of reality which impinge on, are part of, or motivate research processes.[3] Ontology can therefore be conceptualised as experienced at several levels. There might be grand all-encompassing perceptions of metaphysical realities centred on life, absence, presence, time, space, geography, history, etc.; overarching epistemological or theoretical ontologies involving postmodernisms, constructivism, modernism, realism, etc.; discursive, creative and imaginary realities of literature, art, culture, cyberspace, and history, etc.; internal subjective realities of the self related to the psyche, linguistics, the body, being or becoming, sexuality and dying, etc.; experiential realties that are located in relations of gender, socio-politics, class, economics, development and culture, etc.[4] Individuals can be seen as experiencing and negotiating with these intersecting multiple realities simultaneously and critically: depending on their heightened consciousness of the moment.

Feminist engagements with ontology began with an awareness of the following: the relative absence of women in most versions of realities; rampant androcentrism even when or where women were present; unconscious assumptions of the male as the norm; the dominance of male perspectives and bias; pervasive sexism in numerous knowledge domains and accounts. This understanding led to filling gaps vis-à-vis women: a highly compensatory political act of correcting epistemological absences or silences, and deficiencies or misrepresentations in the sciences, social sciences, history, development, the arts, literature, culture and family (see de Beauvoir 1972; Boserup 1970; Friedan 1963; Greer 1971; Millett 1971; Oakley 1972; Rowbotham 1973; Rosaldo and Lamphere 1974; Smith 1974; Jayawardena 1986). While history does provide evidence of feminist observations and constructions of realities from time to time, the present ontological shift in the West is traced to the second wave of women's movements in the UK, USA and Europe. In African, Asian and South American countries such a focus on women gained momentum with the global assimilation of United Nations (UN) and local initiatives in the 1970s, which led to reports on the status of women as well as other seminal studies, especially in development (Zinsser 1990). They spanned women's education, economic contributions, political participation, health, legislation, agriculture and households as well as country-specific issues (see Wanasundera 1995 for Sri Lanka and Shaheed 1997 for Pakistan). Though less keen to attribute blame for the condition and oppression of women than their Western counterparts, they nevertheless presented panoramic views of women's situation in various fields of activity (Chapters 1 and 4). From a methodological perspective these were political attempts to promote the women's side of the coin and thereby reverse male-as-the-norm, androcentric perceptions of life.

Alongside these ontologies of the situations of women were ontologies of causality. Usually these were conceptualised as mono-causes of women's oppression: such as patriarchy, reproduction, male violence, the male psyche, unpaid labour, or compulsory heterosexuality. Historical research mapped women's oppression as spanning centuries of civilisation and assumed common overarching narratives of women's oppression. Postmodern, cultural and postcolonial approaches established experiential ontologies that argued for the specificities of women's experiences due to specificities of national contexts, cultural contexts and subjective contexts. Take the examples of the historical dual subjugation of black women in the USA and UK or the imperialist / postcolonial realities of denial, marginalisation and oppression of indigenous women in countries like the USA, Canada, New Zealand, Australia, etc. (see Smith 2008). Take feminist engagements with the nation state as a result of state-sponsored nationalisms, communalisms and religious fundamentalisms – generally at the expense of women (Shaheed 1997; Chhachhi 2005; Chakravarti 2008), especially in the Middle East and South Asia. Take the periodic militarisations and war situations of the latter half of the twentieth century in countries like Bosnia, Pakistan, India, Ireland, Israel, South Africa and Sri Lanka that have had long-drawn repercussions on women as victims and agents (Manchanda 2001; Meintjes et al. 2001; Skjelsbaek and Smith 2001; de Mel 2007). Take feminist concerns of neoliberalisation, globalisations, development and displacements; as well as migrations and diaspora, especially in the cities of the West (Jackson and Pearson 1998; Brah 2003; Cornwall et al. 2007). Take the dominant subjectivity-based realities of the West that revolve around the politics relating to the body or being, such as lesbianism, transgendering, abortion, weight issues, pornography, disability and illness (Rich 1980, 2003; Dworkin 1981; Wittig 1992; Rubin 2006).

Feminists also focused on ontologies of change, especially in transitional countries. Understandings of development hold a key position – especially in relation to the epistemologies of Women in Development (WID) perspectives as well as Gender and Development (GAD) methodologies. But by the 1980s WID's assumptions about 'adding women in' were exposed, as women became compartmentalised, marginalised and manipulated by patriarchal exigencies and development stereotypes (Overholt et al. 1984; Jackson and Pearson 1998; Wickramasinghe 2000; Nzegwu 2002). The aspirational myths of gender equity / equality pertaining to the economic empowerment and political participation of women from the 1970s onwards, that drove research activism, came under judicious critique in the 2000s: especially in the face of religious fundamentalisms and when co-opted by neoliberal forces in India (John 2004b; Batliwala and Dhanraj 2007). The instrumentalisation of gender through the development of methodological tools for mainstreaming, measurement and evaluation has had mixed results (Miller and Razavi 1998a; Kabeer 2003; Cornwall et al. 2007). It has highlighted the processes of implementation at the expense of outcomes, while granting limited consciousness within institutional spheres (Chapter 4).

Re-visualisations of realities according to alternative ontologies are also a part of feminist projects for change. Early work, which included women-centred domestic formations and lifestyles in imaginary women's communities envisaged by Auerbach (1978) or Gilman (1979) for example, was important for lesbian and separatist feminism. Ontologies such as those of gender mainstreaming have alternative visions and practical frames of institutional societies supporting gender equity / equality inscribed in them (Moser 1993; Kabeer 2003). Other imaginaries were diverse and spanned from Sara

Ruddick's (1980, 1992) visualisation of the possibilities of maternal peace politics, to Vandana Shiva's (2008) re-evaluation of the discipline of biology from three intersecting standpoints: feminism, ecology and the Third World. These transformative elements in ontologies are based largely on faith in the human capacity for change, assumptions about feminist agency and under-standings of cause / effect.

In contrast, postmodern conceptualisations of realities focused on anti-foundations, fragmentations, pragmatisms, instabilities, localisations and insecurities. These thwarted the certainty, consistency, stability and founda-tionality of master-narratives of oppression. A foundational concept such as gender relations, for instance, was no longer a universal or homogeneous cate-gory, rather it was relational and context-bound (Flax 1987). The 'woman' was no longer a unitary category in conceptualising change, but a unifying one for purposes of 'strategic essentialism'; while women's alliances and soli-darity were re-theorised in terms of a politics of identification, instead of a politics of identity (de Lauretis 1989; Brah 1993; Maynard 1995). Given the diversity composed and surfaced by feminisms globally, and despite the poli-tical threats posed to feminisms through the undermining of 'a fundamental cause' or 'a grand narrative of women's subordination worldwide' by post-modernisms, feminists have found it expedient to incorporate postmodern visualisations in their understandings of ontologies. This is because post-modern perspectives can provide alternative understandings of feminist con-troversies and prevent tendencies towards oversimplification, essentialism, reductionism and stereotyping.

Irrespective of whether these are modernist or post-modernist con-ceptualisations, feminist ontology in all its layers and intersections is at the core of a women's paradigm in knowledge production – even though such a paradigm is conceptualised at an epistemological / discursive level. These apprehensions of realities are what become transformed into theorisations, analytical frameworks, justification and validation in the production of knowledge and meaning-making: in a word – epistemology.

Feminist epistemologies

Epistemology can be conceptualised as the reflexive focus on ways of know-ing the ontological realms of the research process: through all-encompassing epistemologies of realities centred on time, space, geography, history, pre-sence, absence; epistemological narratives of poststructuralisms, empiricism, constructivism, rationalism, critical realism; subjectivity-related epistemolo-gies of the psyche, the body, being or becoming, sexuality, dying; epistemo-logical theorisations pertaining to experiences of gender, socio-politics, class, economics, culture and other differences. Epistemology is also related to constructions and representations within the cultural spheres of literature, artefacts and other creative works. Epistemology is concerned not only with what constitutes knowledge but also knowing, and how we consciously and unconsciously understand / analyse / construct / apply / justify / theorise / critique / validate these knowledges. Given the difficulties the human consciousness experiences in separating realities from knowledges of those realities, there has been a symbiotic link made between consciousness of ontology and the conceptualisations of epistemology in Western knowledge traditions since the time of Aristotle.

Feminisms, as a totality, can be considered to be an oppositional epistemology to the existing voids, androcentrisms, male standards, prejudices and sexisms in existing knowledges. Feminists have critiqued dominant and varied modernist epistemologies such as empiricism, biological determinism, rationalism and culturalism.[5] In order to do so they of course had to use other epistemologies such as feminist Marxisms, postcolonialisms, poststructuralisms and psychoanalysis. It is therefore possible to observe and compose a dynamic interplay of critiques and counter-critiques within feminist epistemologies. For instance, John (2004a) has argued that a number of Indian feminists, in particular, have taken oppositional standpoints to the normative of 'Western' or dominant global feminist debates on the basis of divergent cultural differences. The worldviews of positivism that valorise empirical epistemologies related to neutrality, objectivity, scientific observations, testing and experimentation have been exposed by feminists as being ultimately reliant on the subjectivity of the knowledge producer (Haraway 1988). Smith (2008), in particular, exposes the inherent imperialist values that colour positivist research among New Zealand indigenous groups from an indigenous perspective. The authority and validity of positivist accounts, vis-à-vis the knowledge they produce about women, have been severely damaged (Harding 2004b).

On the other hand, feminists have used empiricism to combat the bigoted and repressive ideas about women that emanate from cultural traditions. Narayan (2004), for example, has argued that the European Enlightenment's traditions of liberalism, rationalism and positivism are needed to oppose the negative values, prevalent in Indian culture, that degrade and stereotype women. Epistemological arguments of gender equality, justice and neutrality have been readily accepted in the legal domains of many countries. At the same time, culturalist rationales from ethnic, religious and historical traditions that have proved seemingly positive to women, such as the valorisation of motherhood, have been utilised to maintain the status quo (Narayan 2004). Similarly, epistemologies of postcolonialism, Marxisms and psychoanalysis have served to demonstrate the assumptions, omissions and justifications in prevailing knowledges pertaining to subjectivity in terms of class, race and other intersections. Moreover, poststructuralist insights into language (Weedon 1987) have further undermined the fixity, homogeneity and totality of knowledges and discourses, and exhibited them as partial, fragmented, contingent and politically informed. It is apparent that these diverse epistemologies have been exploited for the political objectives of feminisms: they should not necessarily therefore be constructed as irreconcilable binaries or as contrarieties. Rather, they should be allowed to coexist, as argued by Foucault (1972), vis-à-vis an episteme and understood as pragmatic and strategic methodologies in meaning-making.

Feminists have also proposed alternative epistemologies relating to the filling of knowledge gaps and the 'feminising' processes of knowledge production. Filling knowledge gaps includes identifying, naming, constructing and giving value to issues with particular significance for women's bodies and sexuality that have hitherto been ignored in knowledge and meaning-making (such as gender, female foeticide, sexual harassment, dowry, lesbian and transgender identities, abortion, sati, pornography, marital rape, cliterodectomy, menopause, anorexia, sexual and gender-based violence including domestic violence). In the Social Sciences existing knowledge has been critiqued / feminised as advocated by Smith (1974) while in the Humanities knowledge has been critiqued based on such epistemologies as Gynocriticism (Showalter 1979). Gynocriticism originally sought to theorise on women as producers of textual meaning, based on postulations about female creativity, women's history, themes, structures and genres in writing, as well as about a specific women's language. It strives to bring women from the margins of knowledge-making to the centre, as points of analysis and reference in the Humanities. Furthermore, it tries to invent new and women-specific standards / values / perspectives / methods that are different to men's (Jagger 2008). Sexual differences and the hitherto unknown facets of women's experiences were central to Gynocriticism, but from a universalist perspective that does not account for the differences amongst women across the board – especially in the public domain.

The assumptions of homogeneity and universality in Western feminist theorisations have been seriously undermined by epistemologies of differences that have greatly developed understandings of the diversity and multiplicity of the subjectivity, identity politics and personal experiences of women. The politics related to the representation of research 'participants' by researchers is one area that has caused epistemological predicaments. For instance, Alcoff (2008) discusses the possibility, the ethical problem and the impact of speaking for others; Lyons (1999) considers the power the Western researcher has over whether and how to include the perspective of the researched vis-à-vis women ex-combatants in Zimbabwe. Standpoint theories are proposed as an epistemology of overcoming some of these issues by linking the subjectivity of the knowledge-producers to the knowledge produced. Subjectivity is not only ontology (being a component of it), but also epistemology (Chapter 5). Standpoint epistemologies can account for the different categories of women's subjectivities and identities that lead to theorisations about different realities relating to classes, races / ethnicities and indigenous groups, castes, languages, geographies, ages, lesbianism, sexual orientations, transgenders, disabilities and non-Western (Collins 1991; Harding 2004c; Harstock 2004; Sandoval 2004; Narayan 2004; Ghai 2008; Rege 2008). Standpoint is seen as containing the perspectives of the oppressed, and is valorised for possessing the capacity to reflect the vantage point of the oppressed, and 'subjugated knowledges', with authority and authenticity. However, the epistemic privilege of 'sub-jugated knowledges' is discredited, given the multiple locations and position-alities that can provide only limited knowledge (Collins 1991; Narayan 2004). So knowledge is not only partial, it is also not innocent, given its assumptions and intentions (Haraway 1988). Standpoint theory has also been critiqued for using such knowledges as a normative standard and for presuming the fixity of experience (Hughes 2002). On the other hand, the implied relativism / pluralism and homogeneity, and its emphasis on the conscious subjectivity of the researcher (Harding 2004a), have also come under attack. 'Relativism is a way of being nowhere while claiming to be everywhere equally' (Haraway 1988: 581). Nonetheless, Stanley and Wise's (1993) counter-argument about not evaluating standpoints in terms of authenticity or relativism, but rather as situated, specific and local to the researcher, is of value. The standpoint debates have evolved from collective politics and researchers' ethics to expand on epistemological issues concerning the situatedness of knowledge (Haraway 1988; Skeggs 1994; Engelstad and Gerrard 2005) and intersectionality (see Fonow and Cook 1991b, 2005; Mauthner et al. 2002; Hesse-Biber and Yaiser 2004a) which can account for layers of multiple differences, shifting stand-points and porous boundaries.

Key critiques of overarching epistemologies are based on allegations of essentialism. For example, Oluwelwe (2000: 104) has asserted that many gen-erations of Western writers have stereotyped African women as 'timid, passive and family-oriented' thereby homogenising them into victims: in contrast to the dynamism of Western women who fight against male chauvinism in their societies. False, separatist dichotomies indicative of Western philosophical thinking are frequently constructed between the qualitative and quantitative, women and men, emotion and reason, nature and culture (Narayan 2004). Furthermore, these bipolarities are given gender-stereotyped characteristics and values. Essentialism can be defined as the attribution and highlighting of certain properties and elements to define something, even if it does not necessarily possess these properties and elements (Shorter OED cited in Andermahr et al. 1997: 67). Essentialism also takes place, not only through reductionism and stereotyping, but also through compartmentalisation and universalisation as well as through constructions of fixity, homogeneity and dualisms (Plumwood cited in Hughes 2002; 17–18). I myself argue in Chapter 8 that essentialism also involves prioritisations and attributions of difference, without taking into account certain commonalities. For many feminists, these postmodernist insights relating to essentialism pose a critical problem, since essentialisms tend to dilute the political intent of feminisms. This is because critiques based on essentialisms are self-reflexive and end up critiquing the assumptions of feminist goals. In turn there are many critical positions on essentialism (Weedon 1987; Alcoff 1988; Franklin and Stacey 1988; de Laur-etis 1989): my epistemological position sees essentialism as another way of meaning-making. As Spivak asserts:

it is not possible, within discourse, to escape essentialising somewhere. The moment of essentialism or essentialisation is irreducible. In deconstructive critical practice, you have to be aware that you are going to essentialize anyway. So then strategically you look at essentialisms, not as descriptions of the way things are, but as something that one must adopt to produce a critique of anything.

(Spivak 1990: 51)

Another option is to resort to 'strategic essentialism' (Franklin and Stacey 1988), given that essentialism is inevitable, if not essential (!), in meaning-making.

Feminist research methods

Research methods relate to the ways and means of collecting and constructing data; the analysis, structuring and writing up of data; and are reliant on the researchers' subjectivity, ontology, epistemology, theory and ethics / politics. Methods and approaches include surveys, interviews, case studies, discourse analysis, genealogy, observation, focus groups, participatory methods, action research, content analysis, deconstruction, ethnography, oral history, needs assessment, close readings, etc. Feminist methodologists have been particularly preoccupied with the question as to whether there is a particular feminist method; for instance, based on women's experiences, or locating the researcher in the same plane as the subject, or in doing research for women (Harding 1987). However, methodological attempts at unification or a prescribed feminist method were abandoned in the face of the differences in feminist thinking on research approaches. Furthermore, in discussing methods, feminists tend to get caught up with issues of epistemology (especially relating to subjectivity), due to the interdisciplinary nature of feminist inquiry, as well as issues of postmodernism, postcoloniality and psychoanalysis that have influenced this trend.

Critical appraisals of existing research methods by feminist researchers led to an initial valorisation and appropriation of qualitative methods as being more appropriate for reflecting or composing women's experiences than the presumed objectivity of quantitative methods. This polarisation led to what was perceived as a clash in knowledge paradigms (Burrell and Morgan 1979; Oakley 2000). But later work acknowledged that quantitative methods, despite (or as a result of) representing and composing experiences through generalisations and predefined categories, had an impact on policy and political action. While qualitative methods were seen to embody the divergent experiences of individual women, they were also problematised (Ribbens and Edwards 1998) for their dependence on constructivism, interpretivism and inductivism, in particular. Consequently, the clash in paradigms has given way to an appreciation of the specific uses of both quantitative and qualitative methods (Jayaratne 1983; Jayaratne and Stewart 1991; Reinharz 1992;

Oakley 2000). Furthermore, triangulation arising from the mixing of data, methods, theories and investigators is used not only as a method of validation (Flick 2006), but also as a method of portraying and constructing a greater scope, span, shade, depth, dimension and finer distinction in the knowledges produced.

Feminist methodologists have consistently provided additional insights into qualitative and quantitative methods from feminist perspectives (see Reinharz 1992). Delphy (1981) has argued that stratifying women according to social positions or class becomes highly problematic due to factors such as employment, occupation, marriage and parental background. Both Oakley (1981) and Ribbens (1989) have talked of the implications of interviewing women for feminist research in view of the political commitments of feminism. On the other hand, the dynamics of focus group interactions are examined by Wilkinson (2004) for their meaning-making potential through consciousness-raising and action, as well as the inclusion of under-represented groups. Given the relative neglect of literature reviewing in Sri Lankan research, I will propose literature reviewing as an important epistemic method, particularly for feminist researching, in Chapter 6. The assumptions about data collection have also been critically exposed, resulting in experimentation in quantitative methods. Nearly four decades after Boserup (1970) highlighted the roles of women in developing countries, Waring (2008) has critiqued a number of global counting systems for discounting the contributions of women to household economies. She has discussed alternative models that are elastic and indeterminate and can account for the shifting contributions of women and the varying priorities and impacts of change, as well as alternative measurements.

For feminists, research sources have not been confined to one particular discipline. Consequently, not only is feminist research multidisciplinary in terms of disciplinary sources and perspectives, but it is also interdisciplinary in that it uses cross-disciplinary theories and methods so that new, dynamic fields of study are created over time (such as violence against women or the girl child or women in conflict studies). These fields of study sometimes transcend disciplines in terms of the data and information taken into account (resulting in transdisciplinary work). The problems of doing interdisciplinary / multidisciplinary / transdisciplinary studies include the need for varying expertise on the part of the researcher, and the lack of a specific disciplinary focus that can lead to unmanageable research (Andermahr et al. 1997). However, the rationalisation of knowledge as partial (Haraway 1988) as well as the usage of reflexivity are useful in overcoming some of these drawbacks. Reflexivity can also be seen as a method of analysis and writing up[6] as it involves articulating the positioning of the researcher and internal workings of research methodology.

When it comes to data analysis, inductive methods have been useful for empirical work – especially as a means of eliciting theory from women research participants. This is seen as an alternative to overarching, foundational theorisations that often guide data generation. In particular, grounded theory has been heralded as an analytical method that can avoid theoretical over-determinism and researcher-enforced definitions (Lather 1986), given that research can be undertaken without any theoretical assumptions (Strauss and Corbin 1998) or extensive background reading (Reinharz 1983). However, it has also been argued that, given the political objectives of feminisms, feminist research can never be completely inductive or theory-free (de Groot and Maynard 1993a; Morley 1996). 'Feminist' research is situated in feminist theoretical perspectives, objectives, assumptions, ethics and politics. This is why scholars de Groot and Maynard (1993a) talk of a middle-order approach that is derived from refining concepts in existing theoretical frameworks, and the generation of new ideas from the analysis of new empirical situations. This approach combines inductivism with deductivism in data analysis as a means of engaging with the political and theoretical assumptions as well as the field data of feminist empirical research.

On the whole, data analysis from deductive perspectives of feminism and gender has been at the core of research (the theoretical concepts relating to these analytical frameworks will be discussed in the next section). Gender analysis frameworks and gender equity indexes / indicators are methods (see Moser 1993; March et al. 1999; Kabeer 2003; Leach 2003; International Labour Organisation and Employers' Federation of Ceylon 2005) frequently used in gender mainstreaming research. These methods add an element of formality and structure to data: predominantly according to pre-ordained guidelines, categories, frames and matrixes that are considered to be necessary for practical interventions and action. The challenge in using these tools is to ensure that they are flexible enough to encompass totalisations, specificities, commonalities and differences simultaneously.

Feminist theories

Theory is understood and constructed here as an identified system of conceptual rules, structures, assumptions, reasonings and rationales as to how the subject of research is understood. Andermahr et al. (1997) summarise theory as follows: for positivists, theory needs to be objective and verifiable and provide frameworks for the production of scientific knowledge; for non-positivists, theory can be subjective and falsifiable: it can 'interpret' data and help to 'construct' knowledge or meaning. Theory can have formal frameworks, axioms, propositions and configurations and be an essential guide to practice and politics for Structuralists. Yet, with post-Structuralism, the prestige and authority associated with theorising has been dispersed amongst other discourses; grand theories have become highly suspect: indeed, theories are seen to be contingent and unstable.

Feminists have adopted, adapted, expanded and experimented with many theories from politics to development; from literary criticism to anthropology; and from sociology to law. From the 'problem that has no name' (Friedan 1963), theorisations on feminisms per se have centred on different theoretical interests, at different times, in different places. Understandings of women as victims of oppression and requiring equality with men were influential in the West, especially in the 1960s and 1970s (Beasley 1999). Gross (1987) has discussed not only theories of equality, but also theories of difference as addressing women's oppression. Equality has come under fire for its assumptions about measurements (of identicalness and antithesis) in making women 'the same as men', without accounting for sexual differences between men and women or the differences identified by identity politics, postmodernism and poststructuralism, and postcoloniality (Hughes 2002; Scott 2003). Difference has also become problematic due to essentialism (Felski 1997), and theorists have been grappling with notions of fixity (Braidotti 1994), intra-group hierarchies and intersections and overlaps within difference (Hughes 2002; Grillo 2006).

Patriarchy, in particular, has been a crucial feminist conceptualisation worldwide – though of less import in the West in recent times. Patriarchy has had the capacity to represent the oppressive and exploitative system of men's dominance in societies in totalist terms. It has been seen as an ideology, a socio-cultural and material structure and the cause as well as the effect of women's oppression. Some of the key causal conceptualisations of patriarchy have been in relation to the family (Millett 1971), reproduction (Firestone 1979), male violence (Rich 1980), class and economic relations (Barrett (1988), and social structures (Walby 1990). Patriarchy has been criticised for its ahistorical and static features as well as its reliance on structure and monocausality. Contemporary research in countries like India and Sri Lanka conceptualise patriarchy as varying according to different contexts (such as matrilineal Muslim communities in India (Dube 2002). Agarwal (1988) gives an introduction to the interplays of the modernising institutions of the state, community and household in patriarchy, based on the experiences of South Asian and South East Asian countries. Kandiyoti (1988) has portrayed patriarchy as an interactive relationship between women and men in sub-Saharan Africa, the Middle East and East Asia, where women adopt strategies of negotiation and bargaining, as well as active and passive forms of resistance against power-holders. Sangari (2008: 523) has talked of crosscutting multiple patriarchies that 'are part and parcel of wider social formations', and 'are related to, embedded in, structured or enabled by' these.

In transitional countries, a dominant concept and theoretical framework relating to individual and social change is that of women's empowerment – especially in relation to development. It was originally promoted to counter the dissatisfaction felt with some WID[7] initiatives. However, the term 'empowerment' remains a highly contested one (Wickramasinghe 2000). While early UN appropriation of empowerment was primarily related to capacity building (Mohanty 2008), it has also been associated with welfare efforts, grassroots mobilisation, access to resources, participation in development, and conscientisation (Karl 1995; Wickramasinghe 2000; Mohanty 2008). Batliwala (1993) envisions the concept as an individual / collective process whereby the powerless are able to gain access and control over material and knowledge resources, and challenge ideologies of subordination. However, when empowerment has been translated into action it has often stopped at grassroots economic empowerment. Furthermore, empowerment was not conceptualised from the perspectives of grassroots women, often ignoring the domestic and public power dynamics and spaces (Banerjee 2008). In response to some of these criticisms, Wee and Shaheed (2008) have proposed a grounded research framework for women to empower themselves in Muslim contexts, which is inclusive of different levels of micro, macro and meso-power plays, disempowerment and possibilities for empowerment.

Gender is another feminist concept that has multiple meanings globally: as an analytical category, as well as a thought category; it is also an ideology, a social process, and a social product as argued by Krishnaraj (2006). While I have already looked at gender as subjectivity, I will be arguing in Chapter 5 that it is also an epistemology arising from ontology. Therefore, I limit my discussion here by referring to gender as theoretical concepts of identities, roles and responsibilities, relations, needs and interests, as well as gendered characteristics, behaviours, performances, etc. (Young 1988; Moser 1993; Butler 1999; Wickramasinghe 2000). On the whole, dominant theorisations of feminisms highlighted above have been explored from multiple and competing epistemological perspectives. They not only signify their relationships with ontology and subjectivity but also methods, ethics and politics.

Feminist politics / ethics

Politics refer to the overall motivations, objectives, impact and outcomes of research. In fact, research, by the very nature of its stated objectives, has a political interest (Hammersley 2006) as it is aimed towards the production of knowledge, creating individual consciousness and empowerment and overall improvements in micro / macro structures and practices. Ethics refer to a concern for the ways of conducting research: to ensure that the goals, processes and outcomes of research are not compromised or impeded – even by default. While it may be optimistic to conceptualise politics and ethics together (Chapter 8), they are inseparable and should be understood as permeating all methodologies and aspects of research.

Early feminist action politics in the West were aligned to the political movements of liberalism, Marxism, socialism and radicalism. At the same time, feminists have seen / composed foundational concepts of feminisms (such as equality, equity / difference, identity, empowerment, gender and women) as political issues. On the other hand, feminists have had mixed feelings towards ethics in general, often seeing ethical principles as patriarchally constituted and religiously aligned, and as yet another way of controlling women and men (Gilman cited in Kramarae and Treichler 1985: 143). Today, ethics increasingly encompass a concern for the researchers' engagement and negotiation with humans (respondents / research funders / colleagues, etc.). Research ethics and politics initiating social change in individuals,

structures and practices (see Fonow and Cook 1991) have become epistemologically intertwined with the representation and construction of knowledge
(Ramazanoglu and Holland 2002; Maynard 2004). Consequently, Birch et al.
(2002a) have talked of amalgamating the empirical and the theoretical when
considering ethics.

When it comes to field work, feminists have concentrated firstly on the ethics /
politics relating to research sources and methods and to the researcher, such
as access and informed consent (Reay 1995; Miller and Bell 2002; Thorne
2008), and the power dynamics in interviewing (Oakley 1981; Finch 1984;
Ribbens 1989). A compelling epistemological issue that surfaced as a result
was that of the intrinsic power of the researcher in the research process. This
has led to discussions on privilege, truth, location and the possibility of full
representation of respondents and their realities (Collins 1991; Reinharz 1992;
Mauthner and Doucet 1998; Birch and Miller 2002; Mockler 2007; Alcoff
2008). While an insider / outsider perspective (Collins 1991; Griffiths 1998) can
engage with some of these issues, it raises additional questions of betrayal
(Reay 1996; Islam 2008). As a result, reflexivity (Griffiths 1998; Mauthner
2000) has been employed as a method of problematising research dilemmas
even if it cannot resolve some of the epistemological issues concerned. One
attempt to resolve the powerlessness of the research participants has been via
participatory research: though the extent to which this is possible or desirable
depends on the participants and the researcher having a mutual agenda (Birch
and Miller 2002). Another effort at responsible researching that attempts to
address the assumed chasm between discourse and action has been through
action research (Mies 1991; Schrijvers 1996). Khanduja (2005: 276) defines
action research as focusing 'on the immediate consequences and applications
of a problem, and not upon general and universal applications; nor upon the
development of a theory or model'. However, the possibilities of action
research fulfilling the miscellaneous expectations of research participants may
not always be realistic (Chapter 8).

There have been ethical / political questions regarding the de-politicisation
of feminisms due to postmodernist and poststructuralist deconstructions of
foundations, master narratives, causal theories, certainty, stability and totalism
(Gross 1987; Fraser and Nicholson 1990; Maynard 1993, 1995). The concept
of difference has been a key issue with Gilligan (1977) when discussing the
significance of accounting for differences in moral reasoning by girls and boys.

Yet assumptions and constructions of bipolarities within differences such
as universalism and cultural relativism (Ahmed 1998) have led to 'othering'
and the category of 'third world women' (Spivak 1993; Mohanty 2003). Thus
the uncritical appropriation of this key conceptualisation / deconstruction in
postmodernism (difference) has raised doubts over the very possibility of
postmodern ethics. This is because postmodern critiques have deconstructed
political objectives, values, standards and processes of legitimisation and
replaced them with possibilities of differences, dissentions (Ahmed 1998) and
delegitimisations.

I have argued that the turn to women constituted a new paradigm in knowledge worldwide: conceptualised as an extended methodological twist in existing knowledge that is stable as well as unstable; continuous as well as discontinuous; traceable as well as untraceable. A paradigm of women is not then offered uncritically as being able unanimously to resolve the methodological problems and contradictions provoked within – such as the inherent friction between a collective women's reality and an individual woman's. Nor does it offer an epistemological resolution for essentialism, or the means to overcome the structural limitations of social constructivist frameworks such as patriarchy and gender relations.

A paradigm of women is seen to be composed through experimental changes, and inventive additions and deletions to methodologies of knowledge production – the key international strands and debates of which I have underscored up to now. Sri Lankan feminist research methodology forms part of and is enabled by this global paradigm of knowledge as well as by the particularities of the country situation. Though these global methodologies were dealt with under the separate frames of subjectivity, ontology, epistemology, methods, theory and ethics / politics, they can also be understood as inter-related through differences, assimilations, divisions and overlaps. While this argument was not explicitly stressed, it will serve me in conceptualising, in Part II of this book an integrated feminist methodological matrix based on these porous frames. There, I will apply this methodological framework to Sri Lankan research and also argue for its application in other global contexts.

Part II

Aspects of feminist research methodology

When I started researching feminist research methodology in Sri Lanka, I originally meant to engage with the methodological implications of the three research typologies in the local context: women, gender and feminism (Chapter 1). However, the more embroiled I became in the research process, the more my interviews, research texts and theoretical reading persuaded me to re-envision feminist research methodology in line with the categorisations of methodologies that I had conceived of and identified in Chapter 2. From there it was a modernist leap in perception (of logic and rationalism) to conceptualise a matrix of feminist research methodology consisting of different dimensions of subjectivity, ontology, epistemology, method, theory and ethics / politics.

As a result, in Part II of the book, I will explore and construct feminist research methodology in Sri Lanka as an umbrella case study arising from the archaeology of Women's Studies and research activism in Sri Lanka (Chapter 1) and the global paradigm of women (Chapter 2). Each of the next six chapters will deal with six constituent case studies of (what I argue are) aspects of feminist research methodology. Yet with postmodernist insights (relating to meta-theory, homogeneity and difference) I will represent, apply and construct the conceptualisations of subjectivity, ontology, epistemology, method, theory and ethics / politics as crosscutting, intersecting or overlapping dimensions within this overarching framework.

While the above methodological aspects are understood to be indispensable concerns for any research project, the precise ways in which they were seen to operate would be reliant on the subjectivity of the researcher in each research context. Consequently, this methodological matrix could be operated in any situation, on the assumption of similarities in general experiences and specificities in local. Of course, the Sri Lankan particularities would resonate powerfully with transitional countries, given some of the commonalities and differences in their geographies, histories, cultures and experiences of globalisation.

This particular conceptualisation of research methodology originated in a model by Dunne et al. (2005). It was nuanced and refined by my theoretical readings of feminisms, and determined by the particularities, gaps and possibilities within the Sri Lankan context. The rationales for focusing on these specific aspects of feminist research methodology are as follows. I will focus on the exposition and construction of researchers' subjectivity (through reflexivity) in Chapter 3, since it has become an important feature for epistemology and validity in feminist research globally. While the subjectivity of the researcher is understood as permeating all aspects of research methodology, I have composed it as a crosscut given the need to concentrate on it discursively in writing up research. Chapter 4 will focus on case studying ontology as local and international ontological currents (also conceptualised as a matrix) that direct research epistemologies because of their significance in the local context. The chapter on epistemology (Chapter 5) will focus on gender because of the way that gender is conceptualised as going beyond mere theoretical interests into the epistemological: as an epistemology that originates in one's sense of being / doing (ontology) and knowing (epistemology). Chapter 6 on method will concentrate on literature reviewing as an important epistemic project for researching and constructing formal knowledges in light of a distinctive gap in this activity locally. Chapter 7 will case study theory – specifically theory-making – from or about spoken knowledges, and it will focus on the standpoints, intersections and situatedness of knowledge. Finally, in Chapter 8, I will case study feminist ethics and politics, given the synergy between these two motivations, and argue that they constitute feminisms in Sri Lanka.

The above understandings do not foreclose the possibility of simultaneously conceptualising key methodological concepts in other ways: such as women as a critical approach rather than a discipline in India (John, 2008); or gender as a form of critical analysis by Nordic researchers Jarviluoma et al. (2003); or feminisms having open-ended possibilities in Western feminist theory (Beasley 1999). Rather, they allow the potential for simultaneously divergent, conflating and conflicting approaches to meaning-making.

Diagram 3.1 (Aspects of Feminist Research Methodology) serves to illustrate the overarching framework of feminist research methodology as well as the inter-relationships between and amongst subjectivity, ontology, epistemology, method, theory and ethics / politics.

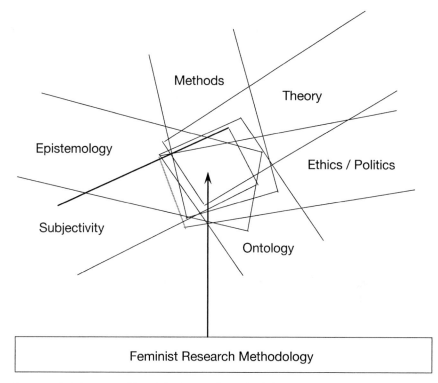

Diagram 3.1 Aspects of Feminist Research Methodology

3 Subjectivity

Reflecting on the self as / in making meaning

In this chapter I will consider / construct the significance of the researcher's subjectivity as an all-encompassing aspect of feminist research methodology. Hitherto, Sri Lankan researchers in Women's Studies have been conditioned to a great extent by the positivist[1] paradigm / tradition of knowledge-making that values the criteria of objectivity, impartiality and reliance on 'neutral' scientific methods. Consequently, they do not always account for the researcher's subjectivity in research. On the contrary, they actively strive to erase the presence of the researcher from the research process and from the writing up.

New developments in epistemology / theory and research methodology, influenced by sociological and cultural studies (including psychoanalysis, constructionism, interpretivism, postmodernisms and postcolonialisms), have exploded the myth of objectivity and theorised on the significance of the researcher's role in the research process (Haraway 1988; Morley 1996; Ramazanoglu and Holland 2002; Jarviluoma et al. 2003; Adkins 2004; Harding 2004). I subscribe to the view of attributing the researcher's subjectivity, an integral crosscutting role in feminist research methodology (along with ontology, epistemology, theories, research methods, ideological politics and ethics). Reflecting on the subjectivity of the researcher in researching can give validity, methodological rigour and credibility to a research study. So, how should research activists conceptualise the subjectivity of the researcher? What should be the roles and responsibilities of the feminist researcher in these post-eras,[2] given some of the penetrating and divisive debates about postmodernisms, postcolonialisms, post-Marxisms and perhaps even postfeminisms?[3]

One objective of this chapter is to consider what roles the beliefs, thoughts, emotions, experiences, assumptions, intentions, imaginations and consciousness of the self play in researching. How can the researcher engage with her / his subjectivity? Here I argue that the subjectivity of the researcher can be engaged through the practice of reflexivity – the method of consciously including and constructing the role of the researcher in the research and writing up process. Another objective of this chapter is to discuss the ways in which reflexive research can be done: I will take the research conducted for this book as an example.

Subjectivity and reflexivity

The subjectivity of the researcher (Chapter 2) is conceptualised by me as a constant interplay and contestation of ontological, social, psychic, corporeal and discursive forces – leading to conscious agency and passive subjection, as argued by Althusser (1977). The split subject, as posed by poststructuralists, is always in a state of fluidity: being continuously constituted and resisted (Foucault 1980a); articulated and reversed; positioned and erased. It is consequently understood only in terms of paradox and contradiction (Braidotti 1994). In modernist understandings the subject is taken to be rational, agential, autonomons, and self-reflexive. In any event, subjectivity may never completely correspond to social identity.

Consciously reflecting on the self in and as making meaning is a method that is often used to express subjectivity in research. In fact, reflexivity has become almost a habit of gender in late-modern Western societies (Adkins 2004), given the focus on, and the authority of, the individual's experience in popular culture. Adkins bases her argument on Bourdieu's thesis of critical reflexivity as 'constituted in circumstances where there is a lack of "fit" between the habitus (the feel for the game) and the field (game itself), that is when synchronicity between subjective and objective structures are broken' (Adkins 2004: 191).

I conceptualise reflexivity as an epistemological / theoretical standpoint and a method / practice in researching that accents and includes the individual's experiences, opinions, insecurities, and emotional perspectives as opposed to a view that strives to be abstract, generalised, objective or definitive. In complete opposition to positivist values, it is argued that another researcher working on the same research material is unlikely to come up with the same interpretations and research results. Reflexivity requires the researcher to talk and write in terms of the subjective 'I, me and myself' that are generally discouraged, rejected and 'illegitimised' or invalidated in positivist research. This need not imply, however, that the researcher is in absolute control of her / his consciousness and subjectivity.

Let me begin by defining the act of reflexivity in research as 'the process of monitoring and reflecting on all aspects of the research process from the formulation of research ideas to the publication of findings, and when this occurs, their utilization' (Jupp 2006: 258). Thus, reflexivity is an overarching action of consciousness that straddles the entire research process from the germination of the research hypothesis to the final outcomes. But how far is this possible, given the role of the writer's unconsciousness in this process? Ramazanoglu and Holland (2002) identify and differentiate reflexivity as an act of critical consciousness located in the subjectivity of the researcher, since it involves 'reflecting critically on the consequences of your presence in the research process' (Ramazanoglu and Holland 2002: 158).

This does not mean that the researcher does not leave traces of his / her unconscious in the research output. It means that the researcher needs to engage critically with the conceptual, cerebral and emotional aspects of the research process as far as it is consciously possible. Morley argues that this involves 'emotional and theoretical literacy on the part of the researcher, who can engage sensitively with the research study while / because s/he is aware of her/his own responses, values, beliefs' (Morley 1999: 19).

While this will still not allow the researcher access to his / her unconscious it will explore 'the hesitancy, uncertainty and caution arising from researchers' understanding of the theoretical complexities of a particular topic' (Morley 1996: 139). It may call for the researcher to highlight the personal feelings involved in the research project, and the time and emotional energy devoted to writing up – to the extent that the researcher was conscious of these. The ideological, political and moral concerns fuelling research that are generally ignored, or deliberately expunged from the research process, are brought to the forefront. This is done on the basis that the doctrine of 'objectivity' is a fiction that needs to be unmasked, as all knowledges are partial and situated (Haraway 1988; Harding 2004b). It is also an admission of the fact that the unconscious of the researcher cannot be consciously accessed or articulated. As there cannot be value-free, impartial or objective research, I subscribe to the view that strong objectivity can only be achieved through strong reflexivity (Bourdieu and Wacquant 1992; Harding 2004a).

While the debate on reflexivity has covered a number of issues, it is important to establish the difference between a confession and a reflexive account. In some ethnographic genres, confessional narratives may centre on fieldwork experiences and strategies – especially relating to investigative techniques (Seale 1999). Reflexivity, on the other hand, as defined earlier, involves a number of other possibilities as well. There could be the individual reflexivity of the researcher writing herself / himself into the text. Equally, there could be collective reflexivity practised by the researcher and the research participants in the research process. What I call collective reflexivity can be seen as a reaction to the influence of postmodernist realisations that the authorial self is unstable, and therefore meta-narratives need to be de-centred in favour of the multiple and often contradictory voices (polyvocality) of the researched (Seale 1999). Collective reflexivity can centre on the research subjects' or participants' reflections on the meaning of the experience under investigation and on feedback on research methods, as exhibited by Mies (1991). This would necessarily involve giving attention to the participant women's lived experiences and the representation of their voices in constructing knowledge. Constructing and representing such voices can be achieved through such means as the inclusion of poetry or drama, and other creative ways of recording or reflecting on the different experiences of the respondents (Richardson 2000). Reflexivity can also be expanded further to encompass audience / readership reactions and reflections on the meaning of research once it has been published (ibid.).

Throughout the book I will critically contemplate and demonstrate my subjectivity – by writing reflexively. The theoretical understanding of subjectivity will be put into methodological practice through reflexivity. In the introductory sections, I have already framed and situated my work by examining not only the context of justification (methods) but also the context of discovery (the origins of research, the impetus for the researcher and the research process) as argued by Harding (1990). In the following sections, I will turn inwards and contemplate my subjectivity, the research context, my understandings of realities and knowledge-making processes, my theoretical and methodological influences, and finally the political, moral and ethical concerns that underpinned my research and writing up.

Positioning / constructing myself in researching

Reflexivity involves exposing the subjective locations of the researcher. In the next sections I will focus on my discipline and work roles and facets of my identity (such as family, ethnicity, class, language and politics). I will reflect critically on how I was positioned in writing up research as well as the extent to which my identity constructed and positioned my work.

Discipline and work roles

I feel that the fact that my entry into the field of research methodology was not through philosophy was important in rationalising the directions of my work. Discipline-wise, my original training was in English Literature under the aegis of Humanities, though I was subsequently nursed in the interdisciplinary domains of Women's Studies. My study of feminist research methodology was driven by the theoretical tools of English, Education and Sociology, and by my reading on the subject. My training in English Literature made me familiar with feminist literary theories and with criticisms of varying theoretical hues (Wickramasinghe 2002) spanning the Anglo-American tradition to post-colonialism and poststructuralism. Later, while researching for my Masters on the topic of women / gender and development practices, I trained myself in conducting sociological research according to positivist paradigms. My PhD provided me with formal training on research methodology in general and feminist research methodology in particular. This training and subconscious conditioning in the above theoretical traditions and the disciplines of English Literature and Women's Studies were central to my methodological decisions, including those to do with sampling research texts, theories utilised and so on.

Family

Despite my good intentions of being disciplined about the research process, there were facets in my life that impacted on my work. These were beyond my control because of the woman that I was, am, have to be, and want to be. Some of these attained particular significance during the period under question, to the extent of shaping my research decisions. I am the only descendant of an ailing mother and my father is dead; I am the wife of a leading legislator holding public office; and I am a feminist activist and writer. As a result, the decision as to where I worked on my research was dependent on my mother's state of health – important in the context of access to libraries. There were compulsions to abandon my work sporadically as a result of the vagaries of my husband's political career – elections and electoral victories or defeats, renovating and moving houses. There were feelings of grief and unrest following the untimely death from cancer of a close friend and colleague, which sharpened my sensitivity to certain social issues instead of others. Throughout the research process I was handicapped with bouts of rheumatoid arthritis and resultant backaches, neck and arm pain which influenced the type of data analysis I undertook.[4]

Ethnicity and religion

Another significant feature of my identity is my ethnicity – especially as there are always tensions between how one conceptualises oneself and how one is perceived within the different social strata of the Sri Lankan context. Despite being brought up as a Sinhala Buddhist, I have extremely strong personal convictions towards religious pluralisms, ethnic diversity and multiculturalisms as important personal, ideological and political commitments. The language of naming (as pointed out by Watson and Maguire 1997) places me in a privileged position within the Sri Lankan milieu as a member of the dominant Sinhalese community. For me, such social attributions of racial and religious 'purity' and 'legitimacy' are compromised in the current context by divisions within and across races, by centuries of regional invasions and minor migrations to the island (North Indian / South Indian / Arabian / Malay / Chinese to name a few), as well as by the country's colonial traditions of Portuguese, Dutch and British rule. These have resulted in the construction of ambivalent and hybrid identities, as conceptualised by Bhaba (1994). Moreover, many Sri Lankans, irrespective of class, are affected by the fragmented realities of globalisation. These include opportunities for global travel, global information technology and communication, as well as education, entertainment and employment (as racial, economic and language factors allow). It may therefore be more relevant to think in terms of 'multibridity', rather than hybridism. I use this term to imply the multiple influences defining a person's life – of being simultaneously, thought not uniformly informed of the indigenous, as well as the numerous global knowledge traditions (Western, Middle Eastern, South Asian, Eastern and other cultures). Such positionings were crucial in conditioning my various ontological and epistemological standpoints as well as my selection of and access to the theories adopted in my work.

Class

My position as a middle-class academic who married into the political class of the country posed further complications. There is no doubt that I occupy a position of class privilege, although I believe that my training in multiple knowledge traditions has sensitised me to this and to related issues of language, education and power. Because I have access to a certain degree of symbolic power and privilege associated with politics, I am also in danger of being stereotyped due to these same factors. This is not a denial (Giddens cited in Maguire 2005: 4) or a distraction in class awareness. My reluctant positioning within the public view as a politician's wife (despite a deliberately low media profile and firm emphasis on an independent identity) makes me vulnerable to certain assumptions in a context where women are still primarily seen as male appendages. These same assumptions have also been a factor in discrimination against me – given the politically charged atmosphere arising from divisive party politics – because of the insistent attribution of my husband's politics to me, confusing and erasing my own identity, subjectivity and individuality. While this could be a case of the personal being the political – where one's choice of partner is taken to reflect personal beliefs, values and politics – an unqualified understanding can negate the differences and commonalities within personal relations. Such perceptions may have had the potential to determine research interactions with my respondents even though I was not aware of it in an overt sense.

Politics

My positioning within the women's movements and feminisms in Sri Lanka was sometimes compromised, because I occupy the simultaneous positioning of an insider and outsider, as conceptualised by Collins (1991). On the one hand, my academic and other feminist work as a writer legitimises my ideological, political and ethical standpoints – within professional and academic contexts. I also network with different women's organisations within the country and have close friendships with other feminists. On the other hand, what is perceived as my privileged socio-political positioning provides me with access to, and the capacity to utilise information and mainstream political contacts for feminist activism. However, these apparent advantages disadvantage me as well, and sometimes have the potential to dispossess me of my identity when it comes to articulating views that can be politically exploited, given the extreme polarities of race, religion, and mainstream politics within the country. Feminist protest action, for instance, could be linked to my husband's political party as a result of my presence – in a context where many women's groups in the country choose to be apolitical and have no party affiliation. There was a possibility, as far as both class and political issues were concerned, that my respondents may have been influenced by my identity (although, as noted earlier, I was not consciously aware of such a possibility given that I was acquainted with most of my respondents).

Language

It was also important to consider the contradictions of working in the English language in a context where the national languages are Sinhala and Tamil.

Within the country, there is an assumption that English can function as a link language, bridging the ethnic and cultural bipolarity of the indigenous languages and contemporary politics. Of course, there are also reactionary forces that see English as an undesirable remnant of colonialism.

The multibridity of many Colombo-based non-governmental organisations (NGOs) / international non-governmental organisations (INGOs) gives rise to English being one of the working languages. A considerable amount of women's research is done in English for this reason and because global developments on women, gender and feminism that influence local discourses and disciplines are accessed through the English language. However, consciousness-raising work, as well as gender training amongst local communities at the grassroots, is executed in either Sinhala or Tamil, depending on the locality. It is thus possible to see three interconnected linguistic dimensions to the discourses on women, gender and feminism. But this also results in a degree of compartmentalisation, and the marginalisation and exclusion of some issues between the discourses in English and the endemic languages. Given that I worked in the English language, my research was directed by and positioned within this dimension.

Constructing / positioning my frameworks of thought

In the following section I will discuss another aspect of subjectivity – how I constructed / positioned my frameworks of thought in researching.

Ontological and epistemological bearings

To begin with, I will consider my diverse assumptions, both explicit and implicit, about the nature of the world and reality, as well as about the way in which it should be investigated. My ontological standpoint does not necessarily fall under the stereotypical classifications of the nominalist (subjectivist) or realist (objectivist) paradigmatic divide as debated within the social sciences (Burrell and Morgan 1979; Cohen and Manion 1997; Oakley 2000). On the one hand I assumed that there is an external material reality. There exists a corpus of women's research in published and unpublished forms; stacked in libraries and sold in bookshops; tangibly consulted by students, researchers, educationists and policy-makers. This is a positivist conceptualisation of an a priori reality and history (Foucault 1972). On the other hand, there is also lodged in my mind a perception of such research which is entirely reliant on the way that I conceptualised or cognised (unconsciously as well as through observation and reference) this corpus of research. This is more in line with postmodernist and social constructivist / constructionist[5] (Hepburn 2006) perspectives which hold that 'meaning is socially constructed; all knowledge is created from the action taken to obtain it' (Holstein and Gubrium 1995: 3).

This obviously signifies that there are as many multiple conceptualisations of realities as there are people. The realities that are conceptualised at individual and collective levels could be seen as tangible, reliable and uniform; or conversely, as conflicting, fluctuating and elusive, depending on one's ontological standpoint.

Accordingly my research 'field' constituted a conceptual and material one – that of the discipline and discourses of women's research in Sri Lanka since the United Nations International Year of Women in 1975. Its domain (Foucault 1998) is constituted by opinions given by local researchers, and by feminist writings and research, in conjunction with my reading of global feminist theories and methodologies, and my own experiences as a feminist researcher.

The resultant / related epistemological field involved the consideration of textual conceptualisations and verbal opinions, defined methodologies and indeterminate practices. Often these contradicted one another. I was also aware that this field is temporal and constantly changing; that the research context and content are continually developing; and that research ontologies themselves are continually evolving and in a constant state of flux.

In reflexively considering ontological and epistemological assumptions it is vital that I discuss the influences of modernism and postmodernism. Modernism has been a diverse and contested project dominating the twentieth century – spanning everything from realism, positivism, structuralism and rationalism to postcolonialism, Marxism and feminism. For feminists, it has involved traditional ways of rediscovering, re-visioning, and re-interpreting, as well as experimenting with, material reality (Andermahr et al. 1997). Then again, from the latter part of the twentieth century, postmodernisms, poststructuralisms and deconstruction have revolutionised feminist engagements with realities (especially language), often in ways that obscure and nullify feminist knowledge and politics. Foucault posits that:

> the human sciences that have appeared since the end of the nineteenth century are caught, as it were, in a double obligation, a double and simultaneous postulation: that of hermeneutics, interpretation, or exegesis – one must understand a hidden meaning. And the other: one must formalize, discover the system, the structural invariant, the network of simultaneities.
>
> (Foucault 1998: 263)

But as Naples (2003) points out, constructing bipolar positionings reduces the complexities of both epistemologies (in this instance, modernism and postmodernisms) in a way that constructs oppositions for each side. Butler (1999) argues that, in fact, theorisations in terms of strict modernist or postmodernist formulations have changed drastically because of cultural appropriations and translations.

I myself do not see modernism and postmodernism as forming a strict dichotomy when researching.[6] I therefore investigated the topic of feminist research methodology by amalgamating a number of knowledge theories that can be viewed as both complementary and contradictory. This involved incorporating not only modernist/ positivist approaches, such as structuralism[7] (Caws 1995), but also an understanding of the conditions of postmodernism and possibilities of poststructuralism.

To illustrate this argument, I can refer to my conceptualisation of feminist research methodology. This subscribes to a conscious, structuralist, theoretical positioning that not only attributes relations amongst six components, but also unifies them under the overarching conceptualisation of research methodology. It is my understanding that whether we like it or not, our unconscious ascribes structures to our apprehensions of realities. Yet, it is equally possible to be aware of the instability and arbitrariness of these same aspects of research methodology. Thus, these same aspects of feminist research methodology can be simultaneously understood as crosscutting, overlapping, contradictory and heterogeneous.

In this context, developing conceptual literacy (Hughes 2002) in terms of being simultaneously sensitive to pluralisms and contestations in meanings as an ongoing process (without closure) was useful. This is because 'arguments over meanings should be appraised as political acts that are designed to shape how we should know our social worlds. They are enacted from implicit or explicit theoretical positions based on implicit or explicit beliefs' (Hughes 2002: 178).

I use this type of deconstruction to convey how the attribution of relations or structures is subjective, unstable and arbitrary. I also use it to dismantle strict definitions and demarcations of meanings. I take the prerogative of considering deconstruction as part of my methodology – more precisely and simply as a form of ontological analysis – despite Derrida's aversion to conceptualisations of deconstruction as analysis or critique (Derrida 1999). I apply the term 'deconstruct' in the book to conceptual unravelling rather than to the discursive. I do not rely on discourse deconstruction in the conventional sense: rather, I deconstruct concepts (Hughes 2002).

I envisioned my approaches to making knowledge and meaning as having elements of structuralism (Caws 1995), social constructionism (Hepburn 2006), conceptual analysis (Hughes 2002) and deconstruction (Gillies and Alldred 2002). Here, the complementarities, complexities, constraints and contradictions of these processes need to be conceptualised. I reject both the view that neither texts nor transcripts (interviews) can comprehensively mirror reality, and the converse view that they are merely textual (Holland and Ramazanoglu 1994). I argue that this may not necessarily invalidate my viewpoint that research possesses the capacity to reveal and expose. I hold the middle ground therefore, since I am able to understand that 'there is some level of reality which can be accessed through people's accounts, but also to accept that there is no precise solution as to how exactly this can be done' (Holland and Ramazanoglu 1994: 145).

In this context, rather than engaging further with the traditional dichotomy of what is considered true or false in knowledge within the social sciences

(Burrell and Morgan 1979), I wish to advance my viewpoint that research knowledge constitutes elements of both truth and falsity: to the extent that what is experienced as a particular reality by the researched is framed by the research topic, and is interpreted, recontextualised (Bernstein 1990) and constructed into research by researchers. With the above understandings, I move to an inclusivist positioning that incorporates variations of positivism, empiricism, structuralism, as well as interpretivism, constructivism, relativism and deconstruction.

The research context

As far as the research context is concerned, there were many tumultuous events in the country during the period of researching and writing this book. There were instances of periodic violence and sporadic warfare due to the raging ethnic conflict in the north and east of Sri Lanka; there were successive elections, acts of violence, abductions and extrajudicial activity which reflected the unstable political situation in the country; and then there was the unforeseen natural disaster of the Asian tsunami in 2004. These events, I believe, evoked certain emotions in me and made me better disposed towards certain ways of making meanings than others. For example, given the local realities that directly impinge on the research process and engage researchers my conceptualisation of ontology was as a matrix of competing realities of research (Wickramasinghe 2007). Conceptualised as feminist ontological / epistemological politics they were a) the impetus of international influences and legal standards; b) the epistemologies of gender mainstreaming of disciplines and institutions; c) contemporaneous socio-political developments that provide local imperatives; and d) the internal personal political drive of researchers (Chapter 4). My own research arose from, and was related to, all these factors: it originated in the gaps relating to research practice in Sri Lanka; it was funded by the Gender Project 'Gender in Commonwealth Higher Education' conducted by the Institute of Education, University of London; which was informed to an arguable degree by international feminisms as well as by the methodologies of gender mainstreaming.

Theoretical and methodological aspects

This book is constructed on the implicit assumption that research is generated and utilised for a number of purposes: its political, ethical and educative capacity to reveal and expose; to include and mainstream; to influence decisions and give rise to policy; to catalyse change for women (and men) in various sites and levels of society (Chapter 1). This somewhat essentialist idea of education leading to social transformations has been articulated in many ancient cultures from the Chinese and Indian to the Greek and Roman civilisations, as well as by the European Renaissance and the Enlightenment movement. This faith in the capacity of research interventions to engender change (in individual consciousness and actions, in economic standards, in politico-social structures, and in cultural practices) can be associated with feminist internationalisms[8] and gender mainstreaming. These are based on liberal feminist engagements with individual rights, equality, justice and equal opportunities (Maynard 1995; Bandarage 1998). They are also linked to the emancipatory narratives of Marxism and the leftist movements in Sri Lanka. Of course, the concept of change needs to be defined and evaluated, both contextually and subjectively, as to the situation before and after research / related interventions, and as to in what ways change kept occurring.

Admittedly, the extent to which this is possible is highly debatable, as has been problematised by feminist postmodernists. They urge the reconsideration of what are considered to be the disciplinary-bent, meta-theoretical implications, the synthesis, unifications, foundational beliefs, essentialist arguments, overarching conceptualisations and conclusions (Flax 1987; Gross 1987; Alcoff 1988; Lather 1991; Brah 1993; Maynard 1995; Oakley 2000) of research. Consequently, I am aware that we can no longer take concepts such as 'women' or 'education' or 'change' or 'empowerment' or 'ethics' for granted. The philosophical tendencies of the Enlightenment towards meta-theory and universalisations must be tempered with generalisations – what might be seen as patterns or middle-level theory – that can sustain certain common meanings (Flax 1987; Maynard 1995).

My interest in the location of knowledge production arose due to certain pedestrian allegations that have been levelled against feminisms in Sri Lanka. Consequently, another theoretical objective on my part as a researcher was that of investigating charges of how Sri Lankan feminist activism was imbued with Western concept(s), and therefore alien to the local cultures (Chapter 4).

Mohanty (2003: 461) argues that there cannot be a unified global perspective of women because 'a place on the map is also a place in history'. The particularities of the Sri Lankan historical and cultural context mean that global theorisations on methodology were not always appropriate to the local context. In this instance, it is useful to consider Narayan's (2004) argument on how positivism has its uses in India, despite being condemned in Western feminist debates for not being able to portray the experience-based politics that are central to feminisms (Chapter 2). Similarly, Sri Lankan researchers Jayawardena and de Alwis (2002) try to situate their work, not within the contours of epistemology, but within local politics:

> Our central concern here will be to highlight different kinds of political struggles in which Sri Lankan women have participated both collectively and publicly. It is the specificity of the struggle, we wish to argue, which informs activism and rather than reading a particular response as either reactionary or progressive, essentialising or empowering, we wish to focus on its political efficacy and contingency.
>
> (Jayawardena and de Alwis 2002: 247)

I too feel that posing the above issues as oppositions (as globalism versus localisms or Western versus Sri Lankan) cloud the intricacies and layers of meanings that are possible within this debate. My theoretical position is one that takes into consideration the country's colonial inheritance and contemporary currents of globalisation. This includes a consciousness of postcoloniality (Said 1978; Bhaba 1994) and the related concepts of neo-imperialism, globalisations, hybridity (and multibridity), race and nation.

Political and ethical concerns

It was my understanding that for research to be feminist it should have explicit or implicit political / ethical objectives to engender change, and should be sensitive to the different levels and dimensions of the research process. First, in terms of politics, this book attempts to raise consciousness about, and problematise for fellow feminists / scholars the methodological aspects of meaning-making. Second, in terms of ethics, it tries to provide a methodological model that allows for research which is more holistic and sensitive while taking into account specificities and uncertainties. Consequently, there are implicit and explicit pedagogic intentions directing my work.

My political and ethical stance is one of fusion rather than a singular positioning. It entails pluralism, as well as political and ethical pragmatism. Politically, vis-à-vis feminism, I do not necessarily associate myself with the customary political categorisations of Marxist, liberal or radical feminisms (Gross 1987; Maynard 1995) associated with the West. At times, I subscribe to certain foundational conceptualisations of Marxism by focusing on class. I also advocate gender mainstreaming or changes to existing institutional structures that are envisioned by liberal feminism. Furthermore, I support lesbian feminism – part of the radical feminist agenda. I do not distinguish between equity and difference approaches to gender – but adopt both – sometimes simultaneously when it suits the occasion (Wickramasinghe and Jayatilaka 2006).

As far as ethics were concerned, a prominent issue while researching was that of confidentiality versus representation with regard to my interviewees. I had previously given my respondents a pledge of confidentiality, assuring them of anonymity. However, this imposed anonymity prevented me from acknowledging these respondents' individual contributions to my research. My only consolation was the fact that these respondents have the power in their own right to represent themselves: they have opportunities and access to Women's Studies discourse and fora if they so desire or require.

Assurances of confidentiality also resulted in a dilemma for me when it came to representing my interviewees. Given the familiarity amongst researchers within the circuit, and their specialisations / locations in specific disciplines, detailed references would have resulted in the identification of respondents. As a result, I was compelled to focus more on the voices of the interviewees rather than on their identities. I allude to facets of the research-ers' identities, intersects, contexts and affiliations only when absolutely neces-sary. Consequently, there is only partial representation of researchers in the study – not only in terms of subjectivity and bias, but also in terms of com-pleteness or totality (Haraway 1988).

Positioning / constructing my approaches and methods

> A case study is both a process of inquiry about the case and the product of that inquiry.

> (Stake 2005: 444)

In considering my research approach and methods, I need to justify designing a case study of feminist research methodology as opposed to other approaches. I chose the approach of a case study because I was venturing into the hitherto unexplored terrain of women-related (WR) research and writing, and because I was interested in investigating and constructing the intangible concepts, as well as the material practice of feminist research methodology in Sri Lanka. The case study was constituted through a series of literature sur-veys on women's studies and research methodology, textual analysis of selected research texts, and interviews with feminist researchers in different disciplines. This was based on the assumption that texts and speech would be reliable and valid methods of capturing and constructing the topic under discussion.

Texts

There were constraints in literature reviewing and textual analysis that require reflexive consideration. The decision to focus on WR research / writing in English was made because the bulk of WR research and writing since 1975 has been in English. However, some of the seminal activism and writing on women's oppression in the 1970s are found in Sinhala / Tamil grey literature (such as pamphlets and booklets[9]), while during the last decade writing in Sinhala has grown considerably. These were not taken into account, due to time and language limitations.

In this book, I understand and use the term 'textual analysis' as follows. On the one hand, it is rooted in the Hermeneutic[10] tradition of being from the viewpoint of the reader though originating in the frame of reference of the researcher (Scott 2006). This assumes a certain degree of stability and coher-ence on the part of the researcher and reader. On the other hand, other poststructuralist writers, such as Derrida (1976) and de Man (1999), stress the instability and fragmentation of both the reader and the researcher. Their method of analysis incorporates the interpretive task of exposing / decon-structing the inconsistencies and incoherencies of the text. My method of textual analysis combines both these methods.

Talk

The concept and materiality of feminist research methodology are not confined to what was expressed / practised in texts, but also encompass the opinions of participant researchers (my respondents) as well as my subjective interventions into the research process. Interviews with 27 researchers afforded me the possibility of gaining insights into these researchers' ontologies, epistemologies, theories, methods, politics and ethics. They provided key information and viewpoints that supplemented the literature surveys and textual analysis. The sample of researchers who were interviewed for the book constituted the three main ethnic groups, Sinhalese, Tamil, and Muslim, as well as those of mixed ethnicity. They came from several generations[11] within the time scale spent in the field of women's research and writing. Many of the researchers are from middle-class backgrounds and they work in academia, NGOs, INGOs and independently.

One issue that needs highlighting is the vulnerability of the interviewee in the face of what was perceived as an intimidating interview topic – despite being familiar with the feminist theorisations disclosed. Consequently, it is possible that my respondents may have felt some degree of insecurity and anxiety about performing in the interview as women researchers (Butler 1999). The interviews may have been perceived as assessments of performance and thus may have led to a degree of insecurity, given the view that theorisation required substantiation through reading up on Western feminist theory (Chapter 7).

I originally approached the participant researchers (peer respondents, as discussed by Platt in 1981), because of their professional status and experiences, with the idea of inviting them to be involved in participatory processes of knowledge production and making meaning. However, while these interviews were sites of new collaborative knowledge production (Riddell 1989; Lather, 1991; Holstein and Gubrium 1995), they were not necessarily participatory processes. This was because the respondents did not necessarily share my research interests (as discussed by Letherby 2006); nor were the interviews reflexive interactions between myself and the respondents, with rare exceptions. Furthermore, it was debatable whether the respondents possessed the required information in the required format, and to what extent they were prepared to engage with the methodological significance of the questions.

There was, nonetheless, an easy establishment of rapport (Oakley 1981) between my respondents and myself, since we were 'members of a shared community' (Platt 1981: 77) of women's studies as well as friends and colleagues. This was indicative of my position as an insider within the women's movements of the country, despite my simultaneous outsider status due to socio-political positioning. Though I had expected my public identity to impinge negatively on interviews with some of the respondents whom I knew less well, this was not overtly the case. I was consistently treated with cordiality, respect and friendship as a colleague, rather than an 'outsider'. For my part, it made me conscious of Stacey's (1991) argument that research inevitably involves elements of inequality, exploitation and betrayal; though the objective should be to minimise this.

While most researchers seemed genuinely at ease with me, I suspected a few interviewees of trying to establish their command over the interview by challenging its boundaries. This was done by discussing unrelated anecdotes during the interviewing sessions. It led to a certain degree of submerged tension for me, as I began to lose control over the interviews' semi-structured schedule. The power dynamics of the research process became evident in these instances (Ribbens 1989). Even though these respondents were researchers themselves, and technically my equals, the reasons for this can be attributed to the particularities of the Sri Lankan context. For instance, ageism is rampant in Sri Lankan culture and a couple of older researchers may perhaps have felt compelled to assert themselves. One researcher, who considered herself foremost as an activist, was self-conscious and insecure due to her lack of 'academic credentials'. Another researcher was somewhat condescending in her attitude – possibly due to the fact that she had already worked on feminist research methodology and was perhaps threatened by my entry into the field.

I found the work of early feminist researchers (Oakley 1981; Finch 1984; Scott 1984; Riddell 1989), who discussed issues related to feminists interviewing women, useful in thinking about my own work. In fact, Morley (1999) had experienced some of the issues that I faced during the course of my interviews: one such issue being the implicit power (although challenged) I had as the interviewer – inevitably, due to my status and my control over the parameters of the interview (Giddens cited in Letherby 2006: 89). Moreover, the overall power over the entire process also rested with me as the researcher (Ribbens 1989) in terms of physical control, data selection and inclusion, and data interpretation and representation (Fontana 2002; Reinharz and Chase 2002).

> Patterns of thought are and have always been crucial objects of sociological analysis. What we deny is that the subjects of these thoughts and behaviours can provide in themselves validation of the sociological correctness or of the absolute correctness of their thoughts. The thoughts and accounts of those investigated have no ontological primacy. Patterns of thought, in order to be objects of sociological inquiry, must be converted into data.
>
> (Cain and Finch 2004: 520)

Analysis and theorisation

One of the main challenges in data analysis was the immensity and diversity of the data available, identified and generated for the book. Obviously I had some idea of the theoretical approaches that I was going to be using, but how was I to sort the data? What would I include or reject? What would I represent and construct? What would I prioritise or ignore? On the one hand, in terms of my modernist objectives, what themes and conceptual frameworks was I going to use? On the other hand, according to postmodernist perspectives, how was I going to deconstruct the data that I had constructed?

During the initial processes of data analysis I sought to do the following: to identify and isolate specific methodological frameworks and to consider how they have been conceptualised and practised in multidisciplinary and diverse ways. I also sought background reading on the ways in which research methodology was theorised as methods and epistemologies / theories / politics / ethics / standpoint (Martin 1994; Morley 1996, 1999; Olesen 2000; Ramazanoglu and Holland 2002; Letherby 2003). Furthermore, I wanted to consider the wider implications of such conceptual usage (Hughes 2002), and to interpret how research processes construct knowledges – in their focus of interest, in what is left out, in structuring data and in writing up (Charmaz 2002; MacLure 2003). At the same time, I was interested in how I myself – as a researcher – participated in the processes of knowledge production and making meaning.

This leads me to the processes of theorisation within the book. As argued by Mason (2002), theorisation is not a stage in the research process; rather, a research study is based on different kinds of theoretical perspectives from the moment of designing research. The role of theorisation in my book is both deductive and inductive. It is a dialectical, deductive (abductive) process associated with the interpretive tradition; I move between everyday concepts and meanings, interviewees' accounts and feminist and other theories (Mason 2002: 180). It also involves an inductive (retroductive) process (Blaikie cited in Mason 2002: 180–181) where I theorise on a pattern that has emerged or that I have constructed from the data. This is called a middle-order approach which provides:

> the empirical circumstances for examining and refining concepts and ideas derived from already existing theoretical frameworks (deductivism). It also encourages the generation of new ideas and concepts from the analysis of new empirical situations or the re-examination of old ones (inductivism).
>
> (de Groot and Maynard 1993a: 169)

Overall, my theorisations take place within the given parameters of the book in terms of timeframes and word counts, and the resulting priorities of my overall conceptual framework. Obviously, large chunks of information and conceptualisations were left out in data organisation and analysis, given the above constraints. There was also a scarcity of published data on some aspects of the topic – despite the multiple data sources accessed.

The final outcomes of my work are both particular to the specific as well as 'generalisable to theoretical propositions' (Yin 2003: 10). Meaning-making here is a combination of medium- or middle-level theorising (Flax 1987; Frye

1990; de Groot and Maynard 1993a; Maynard 1995; Bryman 2004), and strategic theorising as evinced by my proposed methodological framework. Yet, the ultimate aim of the book is not only conceptual unity, but also conceptual contestation (Hughes 2002).

Reflecting on reflexivity as an expression of subjectivity

The above were some of the pertinent issues relating to subjectivity that I highlighted / composed through critical reflexivity. Yet, both in terms of postmodernism and in terms of the philosophy of Buddhism, I could not conceptualise myself as a stable, consistently coherent entity. The research process itself was dependent on aspects of my subjectivity, identity, knowledge and experiences that I was conscious of at the time of researching and writing. Given that focusing on identity in research is a form of self-definition, this chapter is also an expression of self-identity.

I now refer to some of the criticisms of and resistance to the subjectivity of the researcher in research that I experienced firsthand on presenting this chapter as a paper in Sri Lanka. The foremost critiques came from a positivist paradigm that resisted the relinquishment of the idea of the researcher's objectivity on the grounds that it resulted in bias. It was also feared that researchers would misuse reflexivity to provide false accounts of researching which would be legitimised through the writing process. Both these arguments did not recognise the so-called objectivity of the researcher as incorporating some degree of bias as well as being a form of bias, and they assumed that honesty and impartiality were privileges of positivist research. These arguments can be seen as part of the clash of paradigms as theorised by Oakley (2000), for example.

Other arguments include that of considering the relevance of what may be considered as intimate details of research that straddle the private / public divide – such as emotions and predilections. There is some risk of my being exposed to public ridicule and academic belittling from those of positivist persuasions as well as those who may espouse other political agendas: especially when it comes to the revelations of personal illness and emotions during researching (which may be seen as irrelevant or self-indulgent). Equally, it may make me vulnerable to further questioning on the more personal aspects of researching, on the basis that I have introduced it into a public forum.

On the other hand, reflexivity can very easily turn into an overindulgent exercise if the writer is not careful, since the act of theorising and writing the self into research can be a very liberating experience. The researcher can also be thought to be complaining, or providing excuses for methodological lapses in the research process. It is here that self-censorship in writing up becomes a vital control in ensuring that the subjectivity revealed is significant, and linked to the research process.

Finally, there seemed to be a misconception that the issues raised and recorded through reflexivity had to be resolved in writing up. Yet, it is highly doubtful that any research process is able to satisfactorily reconcile some of the methodological questions that the researcher grapples with as they relate to larger ontological or epistemological matters or political / ethical issues that do not have clear-cut solutions (Mockler 2007).

It is my methodological argument and conviction that consciously including the subjectivity of the researcher (however unstable) in the research process promotes a critical / descriptive / evaluative account of the research process from my explicitly subjective perspective. It ensured 'strong objectivity' (Harding 2004c) by exposing the choices and compromises made by me in researching. It may have exposed or acknowledged academic vulnerabilities and powerlessness over some aspects of researching. Furthermore, I compromised delusions of objectivity and authorial authority for what may be a fallible yet more 'accurate' version of the research.

Of course, constructing and focusing on the researcher's subjectivity gave space for possibilities of egoistic diversions and meanderings. In fact, I had to restrain myself physically from exploiting the opportunity to respond to and justify each and every personal perception that I espoused! Exposing and theorising on the self strengthens the political and epistemological value of the research by pre-empting conceptual, theoretical and methodological critiques. It provides depth and insights into the research process – especially by 'deconstructing' positivist assumptions and tenets of reliability, infallibility and resolvability. For me, it was a key means of engaging with the apparent complicities and contradictions of the research process. It provided improved internal validity, and was an enhancement of methodological credibility, despite expositions of the limitations of research.

4 An ontology

Research realities in meaning-making

Ontology refers to the external influences or 'realities' that impact on and are part of the research process (and could be conceptualised as savoir). In this chapter I will make meaning of the multiple 'realities' of researching. In doing so, I will respond to the following questions. What are the 'realities' that are part of and that impact on the research process? How do they do so? How should researchers engage with the implications of these 'realities'? These questions of ontology require consideration, in a research situation where there are recurrent allegations of feminisms on the island being fuelled by Western ideologies and funded by foreign interests (Chapters 1 and 7). It is my intention to address these stale and sour denouncements of feminisms by focusing on the ontological aspects of the issue: such as the politics of imported and indigenous knowledges, the multiple drivers of feminisms, ideology that masquerades as methodology, and interest representation and application.

Ontology and epistemology

By theorising ontology in this way I am striving to create epistemology or a formal theory of knowledge (connaissances). Epistemology tends to become important in any era when new paradigms emerge, and in justifying new knowledge claims against existent ways of understanding realities (Alcoff and Potter 1993). This is pertinent to the situation at hand when you consider women as a new paradigm in research (Chapter 2). Harding (1990) expands on this crucial point:

> Once we note that epistemologies are justificatory strategies, then we are led to ask questions about the hostile environment that creates the perception that one needs a theory of knowledge at all. Perhaps epistemologies are created only under pressure from a hostile environment. After all, why would anyone bother to articulate a theory of knowledge if her beliefs and the grounds for those beliefs were not challenged?
>
> (Harding 1990: 87)

The denigration of feminisms in Sri Lanka has often been based on the question as to where feminist knowledge comes from. This is why it is important for us, as feminists, to consider what knowledge is in specific contexts: who knows it and under what circumstances (Harding 1987a; Stanley 1990a; Letherby 2003).

Envisioning concepts such as ontology and epistemology is a notoriously slippery and complex exercise at the best of times – particularly in an abstract sense. In my book these concepts are conceived of, linked to and seen as emanating from research data and personal experiences, as well as global theorisations. This, however, does not detract from the fact that contemplations on ontology and epistemology are also feats of reflexivity – for both the writer and the reader. One has to distance oneself from considerations of the regular, familiar experiences of life, and from positivist processes of knowledge and meaning-making. Furthermore it requires an appraisal, in turn, of how reality is conceptualised instinctively and normatively by an individual – meta-cognition[1] (Otani and Widner 2005). Even then, there are inherent difficulties in distinguishing, constructing or deconstructing the overlaps and overlays between being and knowing (Chapter 5).

My work is based on the understanding that ontology is a crucial factor in research epistemology and methodology. I conceptualise ontology as a form of politics that is related to the following:

> If realities are enacted, then reality is not in principle fixed or singular, and truth is no longer the only ground for accepting or rejecting a representation. The implication is that there are various possible reasons, including the political, for enacting one kind of reality rather than another, and that these grounds can in some measure be debated.
>
> (Law 2004: 162)

Whitbeck (1989) conceives of ontology as oppositional or dyadic conceptualisations of the self and the other. Ontology for me is not founded solely on the self: rather, my notion of ontology is from a psycho-sociological perspective. It refers to the external as well as internal enactments of competing and complementary realities within the research context that engage with, and are part of, the research act. These include the nexus of various global movements, institutional or structural realities, social / political interests and personal currents that interact with one another. They are understood to be symbiotically linked to the research processes that the researcher is engaged in – consciously and unconsciously. Here, ontology is conceptualised not as grand all-encompassing metaphysical structures, but as concurrent local ontologies or enactments of realities that impact on women-related (WR) knowledge and meaning-making. Likewise, these meaning-making processes (or epistemologies) are seen or conceptualised as influencing research ontologies in a cyclic relationship.

A consideration of the ontological and epistemological politics of research deconstructs the innate tendency to sanitise the ideology that one believes to be above ground politics. It exposes and reconstructs the divergent political pursuits of research, and can thereby prevent existing social inequities and injustices from being reproduced in research.

The attacks and responses

While research is presupposed to establish or construct facts, 'truths' or realities, it has long been the practice of intellectual debate and criticism to question its methodologies in order to undermine research conclusions. Usually, there are hegemonic assumptions about what constitutes an appropriate methodology – particularly from modernist perspectives (Collins 1990; Smith 2008). The findings of counter-hegemonic research can get dismissed on the basis of its methodologies (Smith 2008). Consequently, researchers' ontologies, assumptions about knowledge, theoretical standpoints, conceptual frameworks, and data generation methods can get critiqued.

In Sri Lanka, the attacks on and backlash against local feminisms target the origins of or the impetus for feminist research as being alien (Chapters 1, 7 and 8). The detractors of feminisms have implied that the ideological / political impetus of feminisms renders feminist research flawed and invalid. This is based on the assumption that a problematic methodology (one can read problematic according to positivist paradigms) results in illogical, unstable, subjective and politicised research conclusions. This is because traditional science and social science research methodologies value the seemingly empiricist and objective: since scientific research is understood to have severed its connections with local and historical interests, values and agendas (Haraway 1988; Smith 2004; Harding 2004b).

Attacks on feminisms reflect homophobic, racially purist values (Chapters 1 and 7) as they principally attribute feminist ideologies / research / activism to the West, and condemn them as being culturally alien and decadent. de Alwis (2004b), for example, discusses how feminism is not only portrayed as Western, bourgeois, anti-traditional and anti-cultural, but also as treacherous and anti-nationalist. One of the researchers interviewed for the book, Vivian reinforced this point:

> There is a sort of inherent anti-Western bent in Sri Lanka. I mean feminism is perceived that way. Even by the newspapers on 8 March – while celebrating Women's Day there is also the anti-feminist stuff, right? A couple of years ago they were talking about feminism in Sri Lanka being – what, cigarette-smoking, alcohol-guzzling, lesbians. So that is the kind of image. ...
>
> (Vivian)

As important as it is to engage with these attacks for political reasons, it is equally significant to consider why, how and on what basis these attacks are mounted, especially when other ideologies from Western countries, such as Marxism, have been appropriated without being subjected to the same allegations. There is an implicit denial or condemnation of even the positive effects of certain ontological developments such as postcolonialism, globalisation, transnational labour migration and transglobal media in these accounts. Conversely, there have been selective appropriations of modernisations such as those of Western technologies. Despite the unstable and conflicting standpoints of these attacks, their legitimacy is largely reliant on their supposed indigenousness. This is why these nationalist discourses have the power and evocativeness to be a serious threat to feminisms. They persist, for example, in seeing feminisms in the singular – as a singular political motivation – despite the many strands of women's research activism in the country: spanning from feminist protest to women's advocacy and empowerment programmes. They imply that the espousal of feminism is both a personal and political choice influenced by such identity crosscuts as class, language, Westernization and sexuality; and is therefore not a legitimate choice.

Feminist responses to condemnations of feminisms have usually been strategic. We have, as feminists, engaged with such allegations at face value or only at a literal, political level. This is because feminist research is unashamedly political and ethical research (Chapter 8), and is inexorably part of epistemology. As far as activism is concerned, we have had to negotiate our way through the hegemonic ideologies and dominant discourses of nationalism, parochialism, sexism, heteronormativity, class-ism and anti-globalism. These ideologies have a strong moral tinge, and uncritically valorise the indigenous and reject the foreign. Since the foreign is imbued with negative notions of otherness, the alien, illegitimacy, shame and threat, Sri Lankan feminist research (and more so political activism) has had to strategise to be seen as 'authentic', in order to reach a particular women's constituency, for instance, by appealing to historical examples of women's emancipation and power (Chapter 6). This is because feminists propound a political message, and it will only be seen as legitimate as long as it conforms and is couched in the ideological / political terms that women's constituencies deem to be legitimate.

Aside from these strategic responses to the attacks on feminisms, there is a need for us as feminists to also engage with these condemnations from ideological and methodological perspectives (Flax 1987; Harding 1987b; Alcoff 1988; Butler 1999), especially with the use of deconstruction to expose the superficiality of the attacks. Such methodological approaches (Letherby 2003) can also, through implication, expose the ontological and epistemological foundations of the attack itself.

Ontological research politics[2]

Local ontological politics are highlighted not only as the impetus for feminist research in the country, but also as having a symbiotic link to epistemological and methodological aspects of research (in terms of research focus, designs and objectives) or connaissances. They consist of:

a) Feminist Internationalisms (FI) – the impetus of international influences / standards and resulting epistemologies in research.

b) Feminist Structural Reformative Intents (FSRI) – the influence of neo-liberal forces, structural reforms and the epistemologies of gender main-streaming in disciplines and institutions.
c) Feminist Localisms (FL) – the contemporaneous socio-political develop-ments that provide local imperatives for research epistemologies.
d) Feminist Personal Political Interests (FPPI) – the internal personal poli-tical drive of the researchers and the epistemologies that arise therein.

In conceptualising and considering these multiple and competing realities (ontological politics) that affect or are part of WR researching in the country, it is not my intention simply to situate knowledge in the context of its pro-duction. Nor to propose a categorisation of the ontological enactments of research processes; although it would not be wrong to say that social science research has traditionally striven to assign categories to, and provide causal theories for, the phenomena, group and relations being researched (Harding and Norberg 2005). I conceptualise the ontological politics within the research process as a matrix because it is equally important to account for the con-siderable overlaps and intersections in these enactments – despite the per-ceived exclusions and singularities. Diagram 4.1 illustrates this point.

Furthermore, they are seen as a form of politics because of the tensions that exist between these various strands of feminisms relating to the interna-tional and the local, the structural and the personal. The political intent sig-nified serves to define this research as feminist. This is principally because of

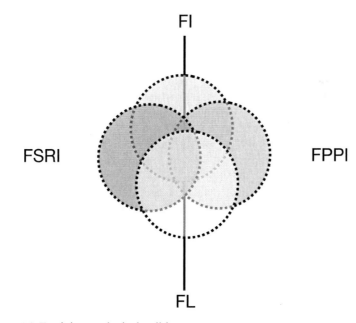

Diagram 4.1 Feminist ontological politics

its impetus and commitment to the identification and transformation of power differentials between men and women (and less explicitly, women and women). This may be in spite of the fact that these studies up to now have been categorised unequivocally as research on women, or that their authors may have rejected the claim of being feminist writers.

Accounting for the ontological / epistemological politics in researching should not be seen as running counter to standpoint theory and intersectionality which marry the text securely to the author (where the author's conscious identity, interest and intention are seen as marking the text [Chapters 2, 7 and 8]). It is perhaps possible to conceptualise the dynamics of research realities as an extension of standpoint theory. Researchers are called upon to position themselves vis-à-vis the ontological / epistemological enactments of research processes and situate their knowledges (Haraway 1988). This is critical in a context where there is more subscription to elements of feminist empiricism (Chapter 6) that thrive on the use of scientific methods, than to standpoint practices (Chapters 7 and 8). Ontological politics are not a continuation of the attempt to ignore or erase the standpoint of the writer, but an attempt to amalgamate into epistemological consideration other factors within the research process as well – so as to situate research / researcher within the wider social / political / ontological climate of its production. This view of ontological politics extends the parameters not only of standpoint theory but also of the concept of situatedness (Haraway 1988; Engelstad and Gerrard 2005). Knowledge is not only situated in reality but is also part of that reality.

I am aware that positioning research / writing into any kind of framework or matrix can easily become an essentialist / structuralist exercise founded on a false sense of totalism. Further, definitions provide closure, certainty and an exhaustiveness that shut down other possibilities, particularly in the light of arguments in the context of postmodernism which highlight the elements of uncertainty, multiplicity, discontinuity and diversity involving the research act. Conversely, a lack of definitions can provoke allegations of imprecision and superficiality. This is why I need to clarify my position: which is that this matrix is not to be seen as watertight, nor conceptualised as having equal or monolithic influences on the research process. Rather, researchers are part of, and forced to engage with these multiple realities and motivations of meaning-making: resulting in what Stanley and Wise (1993) call feminist fractured foundationalist epistemologies. The ontological dynamics highlighted should be perceived as imbuing commonalities, but also disparities; as homogenous to some extent, but also as fragmented; as provisional meta-theoretical groupings, but also as plural and multidisciplinary.

Feminist internationalisms

By feminist internationalisms (de Mel 2001; Basu 2003), I mean Sri Lankan WR research and activism that have global / regional linkages, priorities and patronage (Chapter 1). This ontological strand of feminisms has impinged greatly on the public consciousness due to State, international non-governmental organisation (INGO) and non-governmental organisation (NGO) espousal and correspondingly high visibility in the media. Hence it perhaps contributes to the allegation of feminisms being imported: take the attacks (in newspapers) on the United Nations Convention on the Elimination of all forms of Discrimination against Women (CEDAW) in 2004–2006[3] for being against Sri Lankan culture.

Feminist internationalisms are conceptualised as how international women's agendas are defined by local women's intercessions[4] across nations to global bodies. Conversely, individual women, women's organisations and the State (to some degree) adhere to the standards and aspirations set by these international bodies. For the detractors of feminisms, who see this solely as an imposition, the symbiosis in the interaction must be emphasised. While not mutually exclusive, there are also transnational women's movements[5] (Basu 2003) in NGOs that also form independent coalitions, influence women's mandates and undertake research.

These international and regional initiatives are significant since a considerable section of the research corpus intersects with United Nations (UN) international goals as well as with those promoted by other agencies. However, further research is required to distinguish between the varying research mandates and epistemologies of state-related multi-lateral networks, research undertaken by transnational coalitions and comparative regional studies. For the moment, I refer to the bodies of research literature associated with the celebration of the UN initiatives, beginning with the University of Colombo, and the institution of women's research centres and coalitions such as the Centre for Women's Research (CENWOR) and the Sri Lanka Women's Non-Governmental Organisations Forum (SLWNGOF). These have an unbroken epistemological record and an evolving discourse since 1975 on general issues relating to women (see University of Colombo 1979; CENWOR 1985, 1995a, 2000, 2001; SLWNGOF 1999). A researcher from academia interviewed for this book discussed it as follows:

> The legal issues pertaining to women, general overviews of education, employment, political participation, media, health – again with regard to women are what are dictated by the global agenda. Or they may prioritise areas like civil society and governance and violence against women.
>
> (Dhamani)

Dhamani's comment underlines an important issue pertaining to Feminist Internationalisms. First, epistemologies of these writings centre on empirical data (including first-hand surveys and existing statistics), and were highly influential in depicting general overviews of the status of women as regards these sectors. In many of the studies, women were conceptualised as homogenous and largely in terms of statistics. There is a linear meta-narrative in the research studies which span the over-riding issues in a chosen sector. They depict compartmentalised and totalised pictures of women (Oakley 2000; Ramazanoglu and Holland 2002), which ignore differences amongst women as well as the strategic importance of incorporating men in such analysis (although this is changing). However, they have served the political purposes of recognising and generalising about women's conditions – especially in lobbying for policy change and in creating public awareness. Over the years, some of these publications have also begun to reflect a stronger consciousness of women's oppression or gender inequities and to portray a growing awareness of how other socio-political developments in the country (Feminist Localisms) affect women as a whole (see University of Colombo 1979; CENWOR 1985, 1995a, 2000; SLWNGOF 1999).

Prioritisations of this nature are also related to funding possibilities. While Dhamani goes on to assert that her non-academic research has been constrained by a lack of funding due to contemporary research priorities, this is refuted by other researchers. As argued in Chapter 1, given the diversity of WR research and writing in the country it is doubtful that funders have sole control over the determination of research interests. However, it is possible that more funding is available for particular research subjects depending on what is prioritised by the international research agenda.

On the whole, Feminist Internationalisms (particularly those that have a UN compass) are influenced by liberal feminist leanings, as conceptualised by Maynard (1995), which rely heavily on the State. They hold the State accountable for its women citizens and tend to work within existing structures, in a similar way to elite research in educational policy as discussed by Maguire and Ball (1994). Frameworks of women's rights that centre on policy change are predominantly emphasised. The central objectives of these publications (see University of Colombo 1979; CENWOR 1985, 2001; Ministry of Health and Women's Affairs 1993; SLWNGOF 1999) is to keep the research focus firmly centred on state commitments at the UN Conferences, and to assess periodically the progress made and the lapses in relation to the various sectors identified (see United Nations Development Fund for Women [UNIFEM] / CENWOR 2004). There are also official practices of submitting government reports and NGO shadow reports (on the status of women) to the UN Committee on the Elimination of all forms of Discrimination against Women (CEDAW Committee). In this respect UN-related studies are retrospective, although they are also aimed at providing inputs regarding women into the future national plans of the country. Aside from exposing the lapses of state action (see Soysa 1985; Jayaweera 1985b; Amarasuriya 1995; Goonesekere 2000), the emphasis falls on legislative reform (see Goonesekere 1995), and sectoral reform (see Abeysekera 2000), as well as on increased women's participation in all spheres (see Dias 1985; Jayaweera 1985a; de Silva 1995; Peiris 1995).

As noted in Chapter 1, women's research / activism in Sri Lanka became concretised through UN sponsorship. However, evolving consciousness about women's issues soon triggered researchers to move beyond the continuing UN mandates to other ontological compulsions: institutional reform, local imperatives and personal research interests.

Feminist structural reformative intents (gender mainstreaming)[6]

Research emanating from the ontological currents of structural reformation can be conceptualised into two categories. I make a distinction between gender epistemologies that seek institutional reformation of organisations, and those that envision sectoral or subject reformation through projects. The latter also embraces research-based action projects that carry out gender reforms at grassroots level.

1) Institutional reforms

These are bodies of research that aim for institutional reform through gender mainstreaming (GM), as identified with and promoted by the international Gender and Development (GAD) movement (Moser 1993; Wickramasinghe 2000). One objective of GM is to expose the artificial and misleading 'reality' of objectivity and impersonality within organisations and interpersonal inter- actions, by highlighting the gendered hierarchies and gender biases of insti- tutional structures, mechanisms and practices as well as of the overall work environment and culture (Miller and Razavi 1998a).

The second objective is to sponsor institutional gender reformation through the process of GM. Interestingly, this exercise is geared towards creating a new ontology or reality to replace the existing one within organisations. This is done through the provision of manuals and guidelines for organisational policy or strategy formulation to mainstream gender into work structures and practices. It is also attempted through evaluation research on GM in organi- sations and projects; and through gender-based technical research such as 'gender auditing'. Carried out by gender 'professionals' (including myself), much of this research has a practical orientation, is specific to the objectives of the institutional context for which it is undertaken, and is retained within those institutions for internal usage.

Having identified that institutional structures / practices / micropolitics are unequal and unjust to women, GM attempts to change these ontologies. Particular procedures and instruments are devised for this purpose, such as gender theoretical frameworks[7] or specific gender-related tools[8] to provide a strong methodological base to de-institutionalise gender bias in the public sphere of work organisations or subject areas. The overall aim here is to promote the 'consciousness' of gender disparities, women's access to decision- making levels, gender-sensitive mechanisms, practices and organisational cultures, and the increase in both men's and women's participation in non- traditional fields. It is assumed that this leads to the overall redefinition and reorganisation of gender relations and the existing division of labour in the workplace.

2) Project reforms

The second category of feminist reformative research refers to research projects that mainstream gender into the realities of disciplines and subjects that
have been identified as androgynous or which have taken the male as the
norm. Examples include education and training (see Jayaweera 2000; Mendis
2002; Gunawardena 2005), disaster management (see Ariyabandu and Wickramasinghe 2003), or the private sector (see Wickramasinghe and Jayatilaka
2006). There are also gender research projects that are undertaken (particularly at grassroots) as background studies, which are then followed up by
action interventions. One of my interviewees described such an intervention:

> Our organisation went in to do a project with the women but realized
> that the main problem in the community was alcoholism – this led to
> family disharmony, violence against women. After the Needs Assessment,
> we got in another organisation to reduce alcoholism – they are not only
> working with the men and women but also the children to create con-
> sciousness, closing the taverns ...
>
> (Jalani)

Jalani, who works for an independent research organisation, referred to a
research epistemology which involved action (that of researching to assess
women's and men's gender-based needs and designing interventions to address
a specific community). The action component of this developmental intervention was part of an overall project aimed at gender reformation.

There are many doubts pertaining to structural reformative research or
GM at both institutional and project levels. The fundamental objections are
ideological. Research is seen as imported from the West and sponsored by
foreign funding. It is also seen as an approach that is centred on compromise,
mutuality and joint gender responsibilities (necessarily dependent on the
goodwill of power-holders in the institution, discipline or community). It then
becomes questionable whether GM research has the power to effect realistic
social transformations, and to what extent. It is acknowledged that the
'professionalised' terminology of GM legitimises women's knowledge and
experience, and clinches its position within the mainstreams of research epistemologies and institutional practice. However, it conceptualises one overarching institutional reality for all women, thereby fundamentally undermining
the very notion of women's different 'realities'. Furthermore, GM can be seen
to interpret women's realities in male terms. Mainstreaming women's experiences in any form other than on women's own terms can defeat the purpose
of GM.

There is criticism of GM that it is not informed by feminist theory and that
it presents gender as a methodology, rather than an ideology. GM epistemologies
are problematic in some researchers' conceptualisations. Researcher Wishva
described it as 'an instrumentalised process' or 'a methodology'. This is because

specific formulas or theoretical frameworks and methodological tools are applied to an organisation / project for a predetermined purpose. Consequently, the research process and outcomes may become instrumentalised – perhaps to the detriment of research objectives. Equally, strategic linking of gender equity with development and other goals such as efficiency, peace, environmental sustainability and poverty alleviation may dilute the political implications of the process, resulting only in superficial changes (Wickramasinghe 2000).

Proficiency in the instruments of GM and the associated jargon of the related gender discourse could also result in those who do not have a commitment to feminisms undertaking such research. The concern of feminists as to who should undertake feminist research comes to the fore in the light of this perception of commercialisation associated with GM research (Chapter 1). This is critical, because emancipatory research needs to engage with the wider ontologies of organisations – beyond the research circuit and women's movements. Consequently, GM may not always have the specific political purpose or outcome of empowering women in a wider sense.

Furthermore, as far as organisational research is concerned, this research is 'owned', and remains within the institution for which research is carried out: it does not enter the public realm for discussion or debate. Consequently, the exercise can halt at different ontological levels – at the stage of policy, for example – becoming a form of 'lip service' paid by the organisation concerned. It may not necessarily address the micropolitics within organisations. Because research and its outcomes are confined to the organisation, they may not have the ability to activate structural changes or changes in the private sphere that go beyond an institutional or developmental intervention.

My experience of doing reformative research or GM has involved extensive negotiations and interactions between myself (the researcher) and those in the particular organisation / sector / community. Sometimes, I have been successful in converting organisations to adopt wholesale GM. At other times, I have had to balance my commitments towards gender equality / equity with the extent to which the organisation or participants were willing to adopt and adapt GM. I have had to negotiate the realistic extent to which institutions would take on gender concerns or activate a GM policy. This has been with the strategic and pragmatic objective (Chapter 8) of making some headway in instituting gender concerns in the short-term, with a more long-term plan in mind. Here, a great deal was dependent on the capabilities of individual women and men to drive the policy into practice within an organisation / sector / community.

Yet, in spite of these drawbacks, gender reformative research has been successful – at least in creating 'organised consciousness' of gender ontologies within communities, and at most in institutionalising gender concerns within organisational and wider structural policy and practice. The ontological possibilities of feminist reformative research in Sri Lanka are evident: what is required is the continuing development and refinement of its epistemologies to overcome the shortcomings.

Feminist localisms

As argued by Wanasundera (1995), another determinant of what is researched / written is the over-riding imperatives of the times. These can be configured as the war and natural disasters, development processes, neo-liberal forces and social currents. This contingent characteristic of local feminist literature can be traced back to sporadic inputs during the debates on women's education in the latter half of the nineteenth century, and the lead-up to universal franchise in 1931 (Jayawardena 1986, 1995a; de Alwis and Jayawardena 2001; Jayawardena and de Alwis 2002). Tracing and conceiving such a history (Chapter 1) contradicts the assertion that feminist research is alien – even though researchers use theoretical approaches associated with development / gender / UN standards and socialist frameworks. One objective of Feminist Localisms is to highlight the many facets, specificities and complexities of women's material ontologies: not only in terms of these women's engagement with local socio-political, economic and cultural imperatives, but also in terms of their experiences of oppression relating to structures and the micro-politics of day-to-day interactions (Morley 1999).

One example is research that focuses on the liberalisation of the country's economy in 1977 as part of Sri Lanka's original Structural Adjustment Programme (SAP), which involved the relaxation of restrictions on imports; the promotion of large-scale foreign investment in the private sector within and outside the newly established Free Trade Zones; the privatisation of state-owned enterprises; expansion in the service sectors such as tourism; the institution of large-scale hydro-power schemes in the form of the Mahaweli project; and the export of labour. This resulted in women entering the factories in the Free Trade Zones (FTZs) and being exported as labour to the Middle East, and later to other countries.

However, these new neo-liberal, women-specific economic opportunities were problematic. Research and writing illustrated how women were under-employed in relation to their educational qualifications and how their employment / wage expectations were not met. In fact, there was a conflict between the degree of liberation and economic empowerment usually associated with waged work and the new forms of oppression faced by women within these employment structures. These included poor working conditions, barriers to unionisation, and sexual harassment within the Zones as well as the low moral standing attributed to these women workers (see de Silva 1981; Jayasinghe 1981; Rupesinghe 1981; Dias 1983; Goonatilake 1986; Kottegoda 2004b).

Another objective of Feminist Localisms is that of filling the gaps in knowledge about women when it comes to specific areas of interest and categories of women. This dispels the so-called neutrality and objectivity of hegemonic knowledge banks – especially at national policy levels. Like Feminist Internationalisms, these studies grappled with the authority and outcomes of state action, and tried to pose alternative visuals centred on women.

Spurred on by the international neo-liberal focus on development, these texts looked at the various developmental programmes vis-à-vis their impact on women. Studies identified the gender blindness of early development planning and the need to take women into consideration in the planning process (see Jayaweera 1979; Jayawardena and Jayaweera 1985; International Labour Organisation 2000). Others concentrated on how development projects either completely ignored women, or conceptualised women as dependent housewives, despite their economic contributions (see Ulluwishewa 1991; Schrijvers 1993).

Bandarage (1988) presented an overview of how the capitalist development model since 1977 both incorporates and subordinates women. Researchers also looked at the impact on women of specific development programmes such as the Mahaweli Development Scheme and the District Integrated Rural Development Schemes (Lund 1989). For instance, women have lost their land rights during re-settlement programmes (de Zoysa 1995). Since the 1980s the overall focus in the country has turned to poverty, and this is also evinced in WR research (see Kottegoda 1999; Kottegoda 2003; Kottegoda 2004a, 2004b; Ruwanpura 2006). The principle insight given is that poverty alleviation schemes still tend to relate to women as secondary earners or as dependent on men – despite the increased burdens placed on women in poverty due to social, political and economic developments. This includes the phenomena of female single-parent families and heads-of-households and their negotiations with poverty. The assumption here is that these research interventions will eventually lead to ontological changes – particularly since some of these studies are utilised for lobbying purposes[9] (Chapter 8).

Another crucial ontological factor prompting research has been the violence that has engulfed the country during recent times. The protracted ethnic conflict has affected the North East of the country and the capital, Colombo, for over twenty-five years. In addition, the late 1980s saw the island-wide terror of the Janatha Vimukthi Peramuna (JVP) uprising and its suppression by the State. Some of the first oppositional action against terror, violence and militarisation was from women's movements both in the North and the South. Women for Peace was a women's organisation that campaigned against war from the 1980s onwards, in a hostile ideological environment that promoted militarism as a solution to the ethnic conflict in the country. Another response was the political mobilisation of motherhood (Jayawardena and de Alwis 2002) through the Mother's Front movements (of the late 1980s and early 1990s), led by women (Chapter 6). The Northern mothers were protesting against the arrest of their sons, and the Southern movement were marching against the disappearances of theirs. Later, the Northern front was made to conform to the Liberation Tigers of Tamil Eelam (LTTE),[10] while the Southern was co-opted by a dominant political party.[11] The activities (opposition to war and the demand for accountability) of both these groups, Women for Peace and the Mother's Fronts, were based on women's apparently normative role of caring and nurturing. Conversely, there was the militarisation within the LTTE of women who not only fought in armed combat, but also pioneered and perfected the gruesome act of martyrdom through the concept of female suicide-bombers (de Mel 2007). Belying these extreme positions, during the negotiations between the LTTE and the Government in 2002, a Joint Gender Committee comprising state and LTTE nominees was established to look into gender and women's issues.

The research frame expanded accordingly in the 1990s, to include concerns that emerged from women's experience of civil war and revolt – war victims, women militants, psychological trauma, displacement, refugees, war widows and female-headed households. Furthermore, after the Asian tsunami of December 2004, similar concerns of gender in disaster relief, mitigation and rebuilding came to the fore (see Abeysekera 2005; Ms. 2005a, 2005b). The practical concerns of war in relation to women's livelihoods and displacement were seen as processes which might blur traditional distinctions between the private and the public, but at the same time expose women to alternative conditions and forces of oppression (see Rajasingham-Senanayake 2001; Zackeriya and Shanmugaratnam 2001). In analysing war protest, de Alwis (de Alwis and Jayawardena 2001) posed that the Mother's Front, though creating a space in which to protest against an oppressive regime, defies a simple categorisation as either victimised mothers or idealised mothers. The complexities and paradoxes of women's involvement in conflict resolution were considered by Samuel (2001).

It is important to note how the material alternatives or marginal activities of women are given epistemological value in Sri Lankan research. On the one hand, they are posited as an implied binary opposite to the dominant male action (for instance, male fighters against women victims) but on the other hand, they are not essentialised despite being brought forward as opposites. In fact, women's activism and engagement with socio-political currents are represented in all their complexity and contradictions through a number of theoretical concepts such as women's victimisation; agency; embodiment; capacity; gender identities and relations; and the public / private divide (Wickramasinghe 2009).

The research epistemologies of Feminist Localisms centre largely on empirical data. There is, however, a strong qualitative aspect to many studies which tries to illustrate how a particular group of women were part of a particular ontological enactment. This epistemological perspective involves the construction of the realities of women's oppression, the filling of knowledge gaps and the provision of alternatives about women for the country's collective knowledge base. Here too the political objective of promoting social change is given. Women's voices are represented in research / writing to some degree, though issues of representation argued by feminist researchers (Stanley and Wise 1983b; Fine 1994; Maynard and Purvis 1994a; Skeggs 1994) are not extensively contested or theorised.

As in the case of feminist internationalisms, there is a dearth of theorisation on the personal standpoint of the researcher. Some studies 'begin theorisation'

(Chapters 1 and 7) through a combination of deduction and induction on topical subjects. In these, women are not conceptualised as a universal, as in feminist internationalisms. Rather, women become segmented into specific ontological / epistemological categories of a lesser universality: 'estate women', 'migrant women', 'low-income women', 'conflict women', and latterly, 'tsunami women'. Although the implied homogeneity within these segments remains, the experiential realities of these women are recorded for the purpose of consciousness-raising, grassroots developmental interventions and policy change. But feminist localisms also clearly incorporate a degree of personal political interest.

Feminist personal / political interests

> I sort of came into feminism – I think it is a very personal thing for me. I think I was unconsciously a feminist even before I encountered the discourses of feminism and to this day that is what motivates me ... I write on the things that pertinently interest me so I think I do have a very personal politics and also in general I see a lot of injustices basically against women in Sri Lanka and some of these injustices against women are things that I see in my own life and in the lives of people around me and I've seen the suffering as a result and I think that I want to make life better for women.
>
> (Vivian)

This quotation from Vivian – an academic / NGO researcher – encapsulates and conceives of another factor that directs research: the personal and political interests of individual researchers.[12] Here, she was unable to pinpoint what made her a feminist, but her experiences seem to have confirmed her ideological standpoint (I discuss researcher standpoints and intersections further in Chapter 7).

Researcher Jayani, on the other hand, spoke of the tensions between her commitments to feminism and class struggle – from the perspective of her colleagues:

> There is the class struggle which I am always conscious of in women's work. Coming from the Marxist tradition ... when I started writing feminist stuff there was this thing – the comrades and others used to say – what happened to her, you know, she had potential – she used write about labour – she was going in the right direction politically and she could have been a professor, but then she dumped it for feminism – like you went on drugs or something.
>
> (Jayani)

At the ground level, Jayani's colleagues demand an over-riding commitment to labour politics. They see her passion for feminist research as compromising her Marxist stand. This conveys the antipathy and contradictions between what have traditionally been perceived as progressive labour politics and women's politics. Feminist personal politics relate to research undertaken for the politically specific and strategic purpose of presenting ideologically and politically feminist viewpoints. Research has the aims of:

a) resisting the negative ontologies affecting women (epistemologically con-ceptualised as patriarchal ideology and structural biases, the Marxist concept of the oppression of women or postcolonial notions of multiple oppressions, inequitable gender relations, absence of rights, politics of embodiment, or personal self-censorship);
b) posing contentious alternatives;
c) countering the attacks and the backlash against feminisms.

It is assumed that these personal / political interests arise from the researchers' internal ontologies in terms of the multiple aspects of their sub-jectivities; their identities and personal experiences; their professional / aca-demic training and discipline; and their exposure to feminisms, and women's studies and action, locally and internationally (Chapter 7). It is, quite possibly, the epistemologies arising from personal politics that irk and provoke many detractors of feminism. This is not only because their compass goes beyond the socio-political to the more contentious reaches of history, culture, psyche and sexuality; but also because of the ethically / politically assertive tenor of these writings (Chapter 8). Thus, the primary motivation for research is political.

My overview of WR research conveys that the personal politics of research are especially evident in historical research, research on Sinhalese / Tamil / English literatures, on sexualities, and on cultural topics of individual and multidisciplinary interest (spanning the Humanities, Liberal Arts and Social Sciences). One epistemological aim of personal politics, as indicated earlier, is to present a feminist viewpoint or gender perspective. This is evident in the work of such writers as Wijayatilake (2001), Thiruchandran (2001), and the edited collection of writing by de Alwis (2000) that address a range of issues, predominantly cultural, of day-to-day existence (micropolitics).

Another strategy, as discussed earlier, is to fill the knowledge gaps con-cerning women by submitting alternative trajectories of women's activism. Researchers put forward feminist epistemological trajectories in mainstream political activism, in literature written in English, and in history (see Jaya-wardena 1986, 1993, 1995b; Ranaweera 1992; de Alwis and Jayawardena 2001; de Mel 2001; de Mel and Samarakkody 2002; Vimaladharma 2003; Feminist Study Circle undated). These are different from some existent nationalistic, as well as religious, contentions that give Sri Lankan women a high status – largely based on wifehood and motherhood (Dias 1979) – or others which value women as cultural signifiers / guardians (de Mel 2001), or as moral custodians of the family.

In this context, it is important to focus on formal epistemological projects aimed at constructing or resurrecting women's history (Chapter 6). My respondent, Sadia, primarily an activist, talked of the critical significance of constructing lost history:

> I wanted to record women's histories – of our grandmothers – in the women's movement. These were working-class women and some of them came from the left parties. And they have been working throughout … for women. In the forefront of mainstream political agitation (sometimes providing fodder for the boys' circuit), but also, they had been protesting against the war, the cost of living, been in the Zones …
>
> (Sadia)

Research has established waves of women's activism during the nineteenth and early twentieth centuries (Chapter 1). Over the years it has successfully counteracted some of the attacks against feminism as being a 'Western import'. It has also engaged with global perceptions, and the remnants of colonial assumptions, as well as some Western feminist perceptions of non-Western women. Research has challenged the stereotyped images of passive Asian women, bowed down under such economic, patriarchal and cultural burdens as sati, purdah, dowry, poverty, and endless suffering, and in need of liberation (Jayawardena 1995b).

The third epistemological aspect of feminist political and personal interests that I cover is its response to the local backlash against feminisms, which tends to portray feminism as a foreign ideology (Jayawardena 1995a), or as a 'modern concept' and therefore alien to local women. While there are similar fundamentalist currents in the country against other 'foreign imports' such as INGOs, foreign-funded NGOs, the new Christian Churches and the World Bank – depending on political expediency, feminism has been derided and discredited throughout recent history, at the whim of political expediency. As indicated earlier, the backlash consists of accusations that feminists are 'fast and loose', 'smokers and drinkers', 'English-speaking', 'Westernised', 'urban', 'upper-class' and 'elitist', 'home wreckers', 'hairy male bashers', 'anti-nationalist', 'treacherous', 'prostitutes and lesbians', 'who lead village women astray': accusations that have been made by members of the public, and by editors of newspapers (Abeysekera 1995: 375; 2000: 158; Cat's Eye 2000a: 291–292; Jayawardena and de Alwis 2002; de Alwis 2004b).

The status, orientations and activities attributed to feminists are, of course, intended as a form of derogation. In fact, these charges echo some of the indictments made against women during the lead-up to universal franchise (de Alwis and Jayawardena 2001; de Mel 2001), as discussed in Chapter 1. The contemporaneous attacks on feminism are imbued with the same ideological strands of nationalism, distorted Marxism, homophobia, parochialism, and patriarchy that seek to contain women within a normative framework. What is particularly striking here is the appeal to a shame factor in the demonising of feminists. This is achieved by highlighting women's heterosexuality or homosexuality, in a context where women's sexuality is kept concealed, and heteronormativity valued; or by attacking the privileges associated with urbanity, class and language; or by portraying a 'deviancy' in behaviour, in order to make women conform. 'Normalcy' on the other hand, is apparently based on the myth of woman as heterosexual, chaste, Sinhala or Tamil-speaking, and living in the village. This tendency to polarise feminists and 'normal' women, and to portray feminists as 'other' (in opposition to local cultures and in juxtaposition to ideologies of nationalisms), has been a continuing and common feature of the challenge faced by feminisms (de Mel 2001; Jayawardena and de Alwis 2002).

We feminists have responded to this anti-feminist backlash by highlighting it (see Abeysekera 1995, 2000); by counter-attacking in feminist columns (see Cat's Eye 2000a); enlightening detractors by tracing feminist historical trajectories (see Jayawardena 1986); and rationalising feminisms by linking women's rights to human rights (see Gomez and Gomez 1999, 2001; Goonesekere 2000). Of note here is how WR researchers have also looked at and critically evaluated WR research activism and outputs. Examples include Emmanuel (2006), who analysed the representation of women's militancy in feminist discourses, and Bandarage (1998), who established a theoretical framework to legitimise WR research in the country. This book is also an example of such an epistemological exercise.

However, a lot more needs to be done, especially in responding to attacks on the class and sexual orientation of feminists. In particular, feminists need to use as many political stands and tactics and, as has been argued, methodological angles, as possible. There is a need to meet some of the attacks head on – not only through strategic means but by engaging with the ontological and epistemological concerns of research – if feminisms are to attain legitimacy in the long run.

The matrix of ontological politics discussed so far shows that the relationship between ontology and epistemology is conceptualised as one of some complexity. The contention that WR research is fuelled by foreign funding, according to global interests, is a simplistic argument. Sri Lankan WR epistemologies result from many ontological politics, including local developments and personal / political interests.

Ontological / epistemological politics are summarised in Table 4.1 for further clarity.

The competing enactments of some of the dominant realities outlined (FI, FSRI, FL and FPPI) were conceptualised as giving rise to related epistemologies. The interface between epistemological and ontological politics was actually hard to distinguish, and was conceptualised in an abstract sense.

Diagram 4.2 illustrates the relationship between ontology and epistemology.

At the same time, these local epistemologies were conceived as arising from and spanning a number of ontologies simultaneously. Take the work on violence against women that is part of the international agenda, and of local imperatives. Then there were epistemologies that impacted on multiple ontologies. Take the epistemology of GM that has the opportunity to

Table 4.1 Feminist ontological / epistemological politics

Ontology (Savoir)	Ontology constitutes	Epistemology (Connaissances)	Epistemologyinvolves
Feminist Internationalisms (FI)	UN initiatives Multi-lateral alliances Local women's representation in global bodies NGO regional co-operation Local interests Personal / political interests	Feminist Internationalisms Research	A UN compass Liberal Feminism Mainly empirical data (Quantitative / some mixed methods) Homogenous pictures of women Mainly women-centred analysis Sectoral work Policy initiatives Consciousness-raising
Feminist Structural Reformative Intents (FSRI)	INGO inputs Local interests Gender experts Personal / political interests	Feminist Structural Reformative Research	Objectives of gender equity / equality Gender policies / frameworks of analysis / methodologies / evaluations Action interventions for institutions / sectors The inclusion of men Dangers of instrumentalisation A confinement to organisations Policy / action research
Feminist Localisms (FL)	The impact of development on women Other realities (Poverty / Ethnic Conflict / Tsunami / etc.) Personal / political interests	Feminist Localisms Research	Empirical data (Quantitative / Qualitative / Mixed methods) A focus on specific categories of women (Migrant / garment / estate / women-headed households) Consciousness-raising
Feminist Personal Political Interests (FPPI)	Feminist understandings of realities Women's oppression / attacks / backlash against feminisms Future feminist alternative visions	Feminist Personal Political Research	Multidisciplinary work (including History / Cultural Studies) Contentious issues (Sexuality / culture / etc.) Consciousness-raising Political activism

Epistemology

Ontology

Diagram 4.2 Ontology / epistemology

influence and reproduce the ontological perceptions of researchers. This sym-biotic relationship between ontology and epistemology is part of my overall argument in the book that aspects of research methodology are interlocked, but can simultaneously be conceptualised as conditionally detached cate-gories. These multiple understandings are vital for research praxis not only in terms of feminist politics but also for feminist methodology.

5   An epistemology

Making meanings of being / doing gender[1]

Gender is an important criterion in identifying ourselves and is central to the way we perceive and structure the world and events in which we participate.

(Jarviluoma et al. 2003: 1)

In this chapter, I will be examining gender as conceptualised and applied in Sri Lankan women's studies discourses, and arguing that gender is, in effect, an epistemology (connaissances). This is a sharp departure from existing understandings within the local context of gender as a category of research alongside the categories of women and feminist. To argue the point I will pose the following questions concerning gender. How does gender generate / construct / deconstruct knowledge? What is the relationship between gender and subjectivity? How does gender operate in research praxis? In responding to these questions, I hope to uncover, compose and problematise epistemologically what it means to 'do' gender research in the local context (as well as what 'being' or becoming gender means).

The concept of gender

It was with an element of trepidation that I wrote this chapter on gender. This is because gender has become one of the most incessantly theorised concepts in global Women's Studies discourse. Feminist theorists and methodologists have broached the concept of gender through numerous disciplinary lenses and from many theoretical angles (Chapter 2). As far back as in 1953, de Beauvoir conceived of the idea that one is not born, but rather becomes, a woman (de Beauvoir 1972). Oakley (1972) was one of the first feminists of the second wave in the West to make a distinction between sex as a biological term, and gender as a psychological / cultural term. Minimising gender differences was a strategic move in the demand for political equality, by separating sex from gender and thereby distancing gender roles and responsibilities, gender characteristics and behaviour patterns from biological determinism.[2]

Since then, the meanings, counter-meanings and debates attached to gender have gained multifarious political and theoretical significances. For instance, gender has been aligned with the human psyche, corporeality and sexuality. Social constructionist theories (Hepburn 2006) have argued that gender is not a noun, but a verb (gendering). The gender we are / think / do requires an understanding of gender as a process and not as a static entity (Adkins 1995). On the other hand, Stanley and Wise (1993) have argued that a feminist consciousness is both a state and a process. So too, I would argue, is gender.

The prioritising of gender to the exclusion of the other facets of identity such as race, class, and sexuality has also been questioned (Rich 1980; Mohanty 1988; Skeggs 1997; Reay 1998). Moreover, the notion of gender as a materialisation involving anticipatory, repetitive and ritualistic performances of individuals (Butler 1993) has surmounted the previous constructions of gender as restrictive, and exclusive to biologically defined men and women. Yet, theorisations of gender have also been gravely problematised and destabilised by the view of biology as being a social / cultural construction as well (Oyewumi 1997; Moi 1999), and by the naturalisation, as Wittig (1981) exposes, of corporeal / physiological differences (Chapter 2). In a sense, the earlier theoretical debates on gender, which swung between seeing gender as primarily biologically defined or socio-culturally and psychologically constructed, now need further re-visioning.

But it is not my intention here to provide a comprehensive review of the directions and debates concerning the concept of gender within international feminist discourses. Rather, in my response to gender within the local context, I wish to move the direction of the debate from ontology to epistemology (notwithstanding the sophistication of some of the current theorisations on gender and the deconstruction of others). I argue that this is the most appropriate way to frame the concept of gender: despite its predominantly unreflexive usage in Sri Lankan discourses.

In Chapter 1 I reflected on the researcher's subjectivity, with the understanding that subjectivity can also be conceptualised as part of ontology. In Chapter 4, I discussed / constructed gender as one form of the ontological politics that directs epistemology within Sri Lankan women's studies research. Here, I take this argument further and discuss in depth the exact ways in which researchers' perceptions / apprehensions of gender as an aspect of reality form the basis for knowledge / meaning-making in an attempt to respond to Maynard's question 'who knows what about whom and how is this knowledge legitimized?' (Maynard 2004: 467). Epistemology involves such considerations as whose knowledge is represented / constructed and how; and what gives confidence / authority for that knowledge. It has been conceived of as an explanation of ontology, or as providing a theory or justificatory strategy (Harding 1989), or evidence for knowing. It is my basic contention that gender epistemology originates from gender ontology. By epistemology, I refer to a premise of what constitutes knowledge and how much confidence we can have in it. Mason puts it more tellingly – as follows:

A theory of knowledge should therefore concern the principles and rules by which you decide whether and how social phenomena can be known, and how knowledge can be demonstrated.

(Mason 2002: 16)

In the final analysis, my definition of gender epistemology encompasses the following: knowledge theories and practices; the origins of the conscious and unconscious world views of researchers; and the political objectives and justificatory strategies that go into the construction / generation / deconstruction of knowledge.

Immanuel Kant was one of the leading eighteenth-century philosophers to theorise that ontology is epistemology, and he situated such thinking in the Enlightenment movement in Europe. Likewise, for feminists, adopting an aspect of being / doing into a way of knowing or meaning-making has been a foundational theorisation. It is being / doing women, which gives women privileged knowledge about gender as a construct / concept (savoir). If one constructs a history of feminist research worldwide, there are many testimonies as to how aspects of women's experiences and interpretations of realities (though often contested) form the foundations for feminisms, feminist knowledge and meaning-making (Chapter 2). This is because feminist research, by its very nature, aspires to political and social change (Mies 1991). In fact, to use the erstwhile feminist maxim, 'the personal is the political and the political is the personal'. The political authority and validity of research, for feminists, often lay in a prioritisation of such aspects of knowledges: as personal lived experiences; as notions of women's experience as universal; woman-specific standpoints; and researcher reflexivity. This is why feminists (Stanley and Wise 1983a; Smith 2004; Harding 2004b) have argued for the legitimisation of such multiple, unacknowledged knowledges, or what have been called 'subjugated knowledges' by Foucault (1980b: 81–82), in the face of challenges posed by positivist / empiricist paradigms.

Justification for an epistemology of gender

The justification for an epistemology of gender is situated in its ontological 'origins' / perceptions – not to mention its theoretical constructions, political aspirations, methodologies, analytical categories or variables. While from the modernist structuralist[3] perspective it is possible to isolate these aspects of gender epistemology, from a postmodernist perspective these components are diffused and often not distinguishable from one another. Moreover, as discussed in Chapter 4, pinning down conceptualisations of ontology and epistemology is exceedingly difficult at the best of times.

Realities that are represented / composed into research are always filtered and mediated in one way or another (Kuhn 1970) according to the writers' ontological perceptions. Gender ontology is conceptualised as a sense of being / doing: internally – in terms of self-presence, self-awareness and self-performance

of one's identity; and externally – in terms of one's perceptions and relationships with the outside world. It is both an external and internal operation. A
sense of being / doing is part of one's personal ontology or how one conceptualises / engages with the forms, nature or aspects of reality. However, one's
ontology is not always completely apprehended; nor are ways of making sense
of such ontology always clear to the individual. This is because the individual
is part of ontology, and the way in which ontology is conceptualised is a
simultaneously unconscious and conscious process. Furthermore, one's sense
of ontology (and identity) incorporates many aspects of being / doing – such
as sexual divisions, class, status and sexual orientations, gendering, racial and
ethnic classifications, religious and language factors, bodily incorporations,
age and physical ability / disability (Chapter 7).

Butler's ontology of gender decentres the agency of the subject in favour of
a priori, performative acts that are discursive, social, cultural and psychical
(Hey 2006). Although I do not disagree with this, I seek to rehabilitate the
emphasis on the agency of subjectivity too, since change is also reliant on
conscious individuation. My ontology of gender takes off from Scott's (1991)
analysis of gender, and refers to a vision of the self and the world which has
been sharpened as a result of political, ideological and ethical sensitivities.
Attempts at conceptualising ontology are attempts at clarifying and making
meanings of the ways in which the world is perceived or conceived.

Knowing can be conceptualised somewhat broadly in terms of embodiment,
emotionality or apprehension, deliberate imprecision and situated inquiry
(Law 2004). In this book, the state of knowing refers predominantly to the more
formal process of researching or meaning-making (connaissances). I make
linkages between the formal processes of researching, and the perceptions /
assimilations of the self and realities, to argue that being / doing is knowing. I
have formulated Diagram 5.1 to clarify this argument with regard to gender.

Gender as an aspect of being / doing (ontology)

My research into women-related (WR) discourses surfaced / resulted in some
of the following states of being / doing gender. Or rather, I have identified /
composed the following ontological uses of the concept of gender. Here, I am
conscious of the likelihood that I have extracted or construed these particular
aspects of the realities of gender from amongst other possibilities that may
not have struck me as pertinent at the point of researching.

1) The dominant underlying assumption of gender amongst researchers is as
   a heterosexual distinction between men and women – as identified by
   Wittig (1981). de Alwis (1994a) argues (with regard to film criticism) that:

   > what is required … today is an understanding of the articulation of gender,
   > of feminine as well as masculine subject positions that are on offer …
   >
   > (de Alwis 1994a: 23–24)

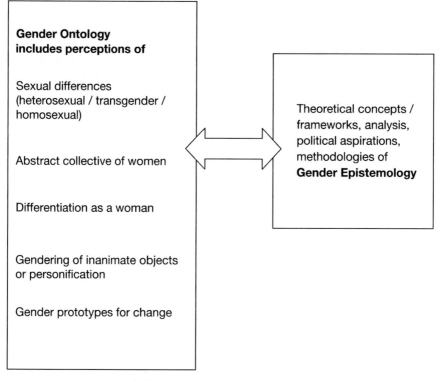

Diagram 5.1 Gender ontology / epistemology

An understanding of gender as relational constructs / performances of masculinity and femininity dependent on one another is undermined, however, by the challenges posed by gender processes such as transgendering and gay / lesbian orientations: as exemplified in the work of Abeysekera (2005) and Wijewardene (2007).

2) Gender is also insentiently conceptualised as the universalised state of women (Wickramasinghe 2009). Studies that purport to examine gender often end up with a homogenous worldview about women, and gender thus becomes simply a synonym for women. These unconscious and conscious contradictions in researcher world views may be described as 'ontological slippages' in writing. Focusing only on women not only compartmentalises women, but it also leaves men and their situation unquestioned. They are assumed to be homogenous: their gender and accompanying institutional power positions are left unquestioned (Collins 1991).

3) Alongside this process of identification with women is the process of differentiation as a woman in regard to, for example, the intersections of class, sexuality, ethnicity and language (Chapter 7). The action of differentiation is designed to establish subjectivity for the feminist cause. From

an ontological perspective then, gender is seen as a process of collective identification (an earlier point), or individual differentiation.

4) Other forms of ontological abstraction also occur. Concepts, objects, institutions and processes are often personified into either male or female. Take the notions of 'gendering the nation' or 'feminising poverty'. This inherent practice of attributing what are considered to be male or female characteristics to concepts and inanimate objects is another conceptualisation of gender. Such ontological perspectives serve to stereotype, naturalise and normalise gender (since gender characteristics, roles, responsibilities, behaviour and performances thus become solidified as male or female).

5) There are ontologies of gender that are aspirational, such as gender as a proto-type for future change (Chapter 4). Take the assumed outcome of incor-porating, integrating or mainstreaming women into conceptualisations of realities — gender mainstreaming. Researcher Rasika, from her vantage as a social scientist, subscribes to the view that 'gender issues are part of the larger social makeup. One cannot simply address women – you have to look at the larger picture' (Rasika).

> Unlike other gender world views, the ontology of gender as a prototype is founded on the realisation of certain political objectives. Examples of these include women's rights and gender equity / equality or justice.
> (Rasika)

I have conceptualised / mapped the dominant gender ontologies pertaining to the self and the world as being at the root of a gender epistemology. However, these representations / constructions of gender realities (or their assumed objectives) are not posited as mutually exclusive of one another. Gender ontology is conceptualised as a foundational concept and therefore a justification for gender epistemology. I do not – in considering these gender states of being – foreclose on the possibility of gender as a constant process (of becoming). For this reason I express gender realities as being / doing gender – to demonstrate the agency in as well as the inconclusiveness of the condition / act. As noted earlier, this aspect of being, or existence, or enact-ment is seen as concurrent with other states of being: such as race, class, age, religion, sexuality and language. Gender as identification, difference, compar-ison, abstraction, personification and prototypes is identified / constructed as a means of defining gender ontology. Here, not only is gender conceptualised as a particular form or aspect of existence, but each aspect of reality can also be conceptualised as gendered (Sangari and Vaid 1989).

It is possible that one is conscious of this at some level, although not necessarily able to articulate a comprehensive personal ontology as regards gender. While the lack of such an awareness of gender has been argued to be a capacity to transcend gender (Meerachakravorthy 1998), I contend that what is important for feminism is not whether one is conscious of the state of gender, but whether this state of being is politicised or not. Similarly, Harding

(1987) contends that feminist research arises not simply from women's experiences, but from women's political struggles – from the bedroom to the boardroom. Because gender is usually conceptualised in relation to the accumulation, deprivation and negotiation of power between and among the sexes, it becomes a powerful ontology in the demand for change by feminists, across a spectrum of ideological and political interests. Gender is then a conceptualisation of ontology apprehended / created for political and methodological purposes.

Postmodern contributions to discussions of ontology and epistemology unlocked the false sense of stability, totalism, essentialism and universality that imbued the early theoretical / ontological debates of feminism (Flax 1987; Weedon 1987; Fraser and Nicholson 1990; Maynard 1993). They also revealed that conceptualisations of ontology were highly dependent on numerous variables such as time, age, location, class, race, sexual orientation, transgender status, external conditions and events. When it comes to conceptualising of gender as ontology, postmodernist tendencies do not emphasise universality or commonality, but concentrate on differences and discontinuities. In conceptualising gender as ontology, one has to take into account the varied aspects of being / doing gender as well as the gendered aspects of being / doing – as noted above. Consequently, gender as ontology must be envisaged as fundamentally relative, fluid and in a state of flux.

An epistemology of gender

I will now focus on how the above ontological assumptions operate within an epistemology of gender. At this point my book therefore spotlights what constitutes an epistemology of gender.

Gender theoretical concepts

To begin with, my interest lies with the theoretical concepts of gender used in knowledge and meaning-making. These can be seen as foundational conceptualisations of gender identities, roles and responsibilities; gender relations and subject positions; gender hegemonies and ideological systems such as patriarchy; and structural interactions such as gender micropolitics and gender-based violence. These concepts help in the visualising and understanding of realities. To be reflexive in this exercise, what I classify as gender theoretical constructs fuel my conceptualizations of gender, in the final analysis.

The gender-related concept of patriarchy is one that occurs frequently in WR research and writing (Chapter 2). de Mel (1994) conceptualises / exhibits exactly how women writers are situated as gendered subjects within the literary tradition in Sri Lanka:

> Just as the West imposed an identity for the Orient, patriarchy constructs woman as the gendered subject, and within the hegemony of a patriarchal

literary establishment and tradition, women writers have been given a particular space – that of autobiography and domestic life ... the auto-biographical nature of women's writing resulted in its marginalization by a literary critical establishment dominated by males, for its perceived inconsequentiality in terms of public-world affairs and its inability to contribute to great debates on culture and morality.

(de Mel 1994: 117)

de Mel argues that the patriarchal structures / ideology of the literary establishment have demoted, marginalised and compartmentalised women's writing. This argument is founded on the following ontology. Gender, in this instance, is assumed to be a collective of women, in the form of women writers. Gender is also by implication a comparison and contrast between men and women writers. Yet, in this comparison, male writers are the norm while women are visualised as the other[4] (Said 1978), occupying a different space.

Similarly, Wijayatilake discusses the construction of gender ideology / practices – especially as a form of social control over women's subjectivities – in a three-generational study of women. 'In other words, it refers to beliefs, behaviour, language or other actions of the sexes which projects the exhaustive, established, and institutionalized view that women are inferior ... ' (Wijayatilake 2001: 26). She identifies some of the cultural practices relating to menarche, marriage, dowry, virginity, pregnancy and childbirth as being instrumental in limiting / liberating women's identities. Gender ideology is conceptualised as sexism and patriarchy in cultural practices. And it 'needs to be viewed in relation to other forms of oppression such as class, race, sexual orientation and caste' (ibid.). The central argument is that gender ideology exerts social control through social institutions such as the family, religion, culture and tradition, media, state policy, laws and regulations, education and the economy. She further conceptualises of the way in which gender ideology operates in societies – not necessarily through external forces but through internalised censorship. Gender ideology is a foundational theoretical concept for many research studies to explain issues of gender inequality and women's oppression.

Another generalised concept – gender identity – is seen as constructed with reference to the norm and exceptions in gender roles, responsibilities, skills, occupations and relationships, gendered characteristics, behavioural patterns and sexual orientations (Wickramasinghe 2002b). Gauri, one of the interviewees in my study, made the point (from her own work on socialisation processes within the family) that gender identities are a result of 'socialisation through the lived experiences of gender'. While the idea of socialisation[5] is seen as crucial in the fashioning of gender identities, it would be dangerous to conceive of the effects of socialisation as a homogeneous model (that precludes exceptions and change), or to ignore the roles of the human unconscious and the play of free will on gender identities.

Alongside the commonality implied in the construction of identity come the differentiations regarding identity in terms of class, race, sexual orientation, language, caste and transgender. Respondent Rasika, the product of an inter-racial marriage, made the observation that 'one's cultural or national identity may prompt one's gender identity'. The interplay of the various socio-political, cultural and ideological facets of identity politics was highlighted by her.

An example of collective identity politics is found in Jayawardena (1994), who focuses on the popular ideological construction of Sinhala Buddhist womanhood as an identity marker in the Buddhist revivalist discourse of the late nineteenth century. She argues that such a construction was committed to the maintenance of Sinhala Buddhist hegemony over other ethnic groups (especially Christian and Burgher women):

> The construction, within this framework, of a specifically Aryan Sinhala Buddhist woman pervades ... the early nationalist discourse on the writings of Sinhala novelists and poets. The correct way a Sinhala Buddhist wife / mother should behave, dress and conduct herself in society was categorically defined. Women followers of the Buddha and the queens and heroines of early Sri Lankan history were projected in the nationalist press as role models. While being exhorted to follow the patterns of conduct laid down in the discourses of the Buddha, women were given the added roles of guardians of the Aryan Sinhala race and inspirers of their men – dissuading them from alcohol, meat-eating, immorality and imitation of the despised foreigners.
>
> (Jayawardena 1994: 116)

In a similar study on identity and implied difference, Thiruchandran (1997) considers the gendered constructions of Tamil women within the status quo, and the modernising forces of colonial Jaffna.[6] In both cases, gender is a collective of women, generalised in terms of race / religion. The two researchers emphasise how the differences within gender centre on the prevailing notions of mythology, history, racial and religious ideals, and cultural and social practices, to create differences.

Theoretically, gender as espousing the normative female has been largely destabilised by the dynamic international debates on transgendering and Queer theorisations. Butler (1999), for example, deconstructs the idea of gender as a normative heterosexual polarity between male and female, and conceptualises of gender as performativity (Chapter 2). Within the Sri Lankan context, research contributes to the construction of differentiation through the formation of transgender ontology.

Wijewardene (2007) documents the psychological crisis of transgender people within the Sri Lankan context, where there are limited points of references for such identities within the community. She argues that creative self-assemblage is a strategic means by which individuals understand transgender realities. However, she points out that this exercise is limited by the possibilities for trans-expression within a particular culture as well as the specific trans-performance of the individual. The complexity of transgender ontology within this context is evident in the lack of:

> resonance for the transgender individual in the culture he / she is situated; and the continuous pressure and striving to define and control the gendered state of being in a situation where gender is constantly checked and rechecked by society.
>
> (Respondent Wadhani)

What can be seen as slippages in being transgender is illustrated by de Mel (2001) when she argues for the undecidability of gender signification, in looking at the convention of female impersonation in Sri Lankan theatre. These theatrical enactments of women as imagined by men, played by men, for the primarily male-dominated audiences of the times, did not pose a challenge to existing social cultural norms of femininity (de Mel contends). In effect, these exaggerated and voluptuous on-stage portrayals of femininity were fetishised, and de Mel illustrates how they later influenced the construction of a particular type of femininity amongst women spectators and within popular culture.

In both the above representations, gender is conceptualised as androgynous, individual constructions of the self, which combine the existent sexual identity with what can be seen as conscious performances of either femininity or masculinity, in becoming new selves. The individual's sense of agency is uncompromised in these constructions, despite the fluid and irresolute nature of the gender identities enacted: one for theatre and the other for 'real'. The transgendering of women to men is posed as not having any reference points in contemporary Sri Lankan society. It is a challenge to the existing expectations of gendering. On the other hand, cross-dressing in the context of female impersonation is seen as possessing the capacity to institute new role models, not only in the theatrical tradition, but also in terms of an image for women to emulate more widely.

In this instance, the ontology of transgender is essentially a process of differentiation, or even of internalised homophobia. When composed in research, it not only strives to fulfil feminist objectives of consciousness-raising, but also to give epistemic legitimacy to the process of transgendering and to transgender identities. Despite these efforts, transgendering remains an auxiliary concept to gender, which is constructed as the normative.

Gender analysis

Epistemology involves the consideration not only of the theoretical tools of meaning-making but also of its practices. Accordingly, I will discuss the practice of gender analysis as an epistemological issue. The practical use of the conceptualisation of gender as a form of investigative method in research can be seen in gender analysis. It is believed to lay bare or compose the vicissitudes and variations of gender realities: even though the perceptions of these realities themselves determine the types of analysis utilised by researchers / writers. In fact, ontologies of gender can be constructed and deconstructed through gender analysis, and in this sense it forms a principle and tool of knowledge and meaning-making.

I turn to studies on local development efforts for common examples of gender-specific concepts, discourses and methods of analysis. Work by Schrijvers (1993, 1998) and Rajapakse (1995) for instance, included critiques of policy hegemony through the exposé of gender inequality, in developmental concepts such as 'heads-of-household', 'breadwinners' and 'secondary earners'. Other studies included the usage of lately constructed gender concepts such as 'doubleday', 'gender segregation', and 'female-headed households', and the incorporation of gender-prescribed methods of analysis such as 'time use research' and 'social relations framework'. These serve as new ways of analysing the world – according to gender – through concepts as well as methods.

Gender as analysis in local research captures / constructs epistemologically the facets of gender as a state of being / doing. One particular success of gender as a quantitative and qualitative analysis needs to be cited here. This is Jayaweera and Sanmugam's (2001) study researching the impact of macroeconomic reforms on formal and informal sector women workers, in the garment and textile industries. It does this through a theoretical lens of gender roles and relations:

> Even though it is not possible to establish a clear association between changes in employment and the less tangible changes in gender roles and relations, the study documents facets of change and resistance that take place in the context of macroeconomic policies and social construction of gender.
>
> (Jayaweera and Sanmugam 2001: 501)

Interestingly, researchers combine survey techniques with case studies in delineating gender roles and responsibilities, the gender division of labour, and gender relations within lived experiences. What are usually considered to be numerically invisible concepts, such as gender roles and relations, are statistically analysed. The researchers attempt this by numerically deconstructing such ontological indicators as: the control of labour; the control of economic resources and the allocation of other resources pertaining to education and health; gender division of labour within the household; gender relations in terms of marriage, reproduction and sexuality; household decision-making; and violence in the family. The state of gender reality is analysed according to a conceptualisation of gender ontology that focuses on gender roles and relations as an abstract collective identification of all women workers. By claiming to construct and represent the breadth and depth of gender roles and relations qualitatively and quantitively, this study makes wider claims of prevalence for policy purposes which have the potential in the long-term to impact on these women workers themselves.

Researchers also utilise formal gender frameworks. For instance, we (Ariyabandu and Wickramasinghe 2003) applied a gender vulnerabilities and capacities framework in our work. Natural disasters, management practices and the micro-politics of development initiatives in several South Asian countries were examined by us (the writers) from this perspective of gender vulnerabilities and capacities. Gender analysis hinges on an a priori understanding of gender in the particular context of disaster management. Through the application of a common gender framework, it became possible not only to compare and contrast common perceptions of gender differences, but also to analyse comparatively the commonalities and differences in gender across countries. This belies the conventional criticism of policy research as being too overarching and generalised to engage with the specificities of individual contexts. Consequently, the last section of the book provided ontological guidelines on what one should strive for in terms of gender mainstreaming. This was a prototype of gender, founded on the realisation of certain objectives of women's rights and gender equality / equity and justice.

Other informal forms of analysis are based on the personification of gender for political reasons. In many instances, gender could simply refer to the dominant presence or participation of either men or women. Take as an example the expression from the discipline of Economics – 'feminization of poverty' – which has captured the popular feminist imagination by denoting the predominance of women in poverty statistics, especially after economic restructuring, in Sri Lanka.

In another example, Jayaweera writes that:

> the most significant of these was the handloom industry, which was *virtually feminized* [my italics] in the mid-1960s by the distribution of a large number of looms to women producers and the establishment of handloom training and production centres in villages.
>
> (Jayaweera 2002: 109)

Conceptualisations of gender as personification in research also relate to the characteristics and embodiments of masculinity and femininity. de Mel's (2001) conceptualisation of 'gendering' as a personification means 'feminising'. She constructs a comprehensive embodiment of gender when she writes of 'setting the stage, gendering the nation' in Sri Lankan theatre. First, she refers to the entrance into, or peopling of, the theatre by women – in terms of actresses, audiences and the representation of women in drama. Second, she talks of the enactment of gender, denoting not only the presence of female impersonators, but also their gender performances, as well as the construction of particular forms of desired femininities for the nationalist project. Third, there is the specific construction of the image of the Arya Sinhala[7] woman as a dramatic persona (and preferred normative image), as well as the popular ideal of the first Sinhala actress. For de Mel (ibid.) the gendering of theatre is significant in the larger equation of gendering the nation, through the crucial role of the theatre in forging a sense of community and a shared national consciousness.

I see gendering as an ontological / epistemological / methodological exercise deliberately carried out by feminists to highlight the forms of structural hegemony found in societies, or to expound an alternative world vision. The danger here is that such personification further fuels the schism in gender as being a heterosexual male and female one, leading to further stereotyping of men and women. This can, paradoxically, lead to an inertia which precludes conceptualisations of social changes within gender epistemology.

Gender political aspirations

My personal experience as a researcher gives testimony to the fact that an epistemology of gender has political objectives. I have worked on gender research pertaining to institutional mainstreaming, devised gender frameworks for developmental contexts and formulated gender policies for the Sri Lankan private sector and for disaster management. The political intent of such work drives the epistemology of gender research; whether in the ultimate interest of consciousness-raising, action researching, policy change, institutional change, attitudinal change or far-reaching social change (Chapter 8). These goals are sometimes clearly articulated and striven for – in terms of overarching objectives of gender equity, equality or justice or in terms of equal representation, women's participation, women's rights, or fair work cultures.

At an individual level of redressing women's oppression, empirical research highlights and recommends possibilities and strategies. For instance, Wijayatilake and Zackeriya (2001) write the following, after recording the responses of women workers, trade unionists, activists, development workers, employers and state officials while addressing the problem of sexual harassment in the plantation sector:

> Actions for dealing with sexual harassment cases still remain weak. Much needs to be done for evolving proper policies and procedures to raising awareness and creating 'a safe enabling environment' for women victims to talk about it. Trade unions need to rethink their role and rights of women members so that issues could be addressed within their normal mandate using precedents already in place. Management companies could formulate a code of ethics incorporating specific policy guidelines and orient staff on actions violating such standards.
>
> (Wijayatilake and Zackeriya 2001: 24)

These researchers aspire towards policy changes, the institutionalisation of a safe and enabling environment, and the integration of women's rights in trade union activism, as well as the formulation of a code of ethics. It is assumed that the collective of women workers / victims in the plantation sector can be addressed through this intended prototype. Yet, as proposed here, these aspirational ontologies need to be operationalised through decisive gender methodologies – as will be argued in the next section.

In conceptualising gender equity / equality in Sri Lankan private sector workplaces (Wickramasinghe and Jayatilaka 2006), we, the authors, designed concrete policy measures to change existing work cultures and practices on the basis that:

> the concept of gender equality means that women and men should have equal opportunities and conditions for realising their full human rights and potential to contribute to the work organization (especially at management levels) and to benefit from the results. On the other hand, the concept of gender equity means the recognition and equitable valuing by the work organization of the differences between women and men, as well as the social expectation of the varying roles / responsibilities / status / relationships of men and women. Instead of demanding that women be similar to men, gender equity requires women's empowerment through specific measures designed to eliminate barriers to gender inequalities and actively promotes the recognition and participation of women – resulting in gender justice.
>
> (Wickramasinghe and Jayatilaka 2006: xiv)

We distinguished between the aspirations of gender equity and equality, the fulfilment of which would eventually lead to gender justice in the workplace. Our ontological vision at this juncture was of gender as something to be achieved through interventions in people's attitudes, institutions, practices and processes. Of course we were cautious as to the extent to which this was possible.

The incorporation of gender aspirations and ideals into institutions, processes and social practices is usually termed gendering, or engendering. Take the example of Coomaraswamy (2004), who refers to gendering and engendering intermittently in her piece 'Engendering the constitution-making process'. Her concluding remarks conceptualise of gender as a model, as follows:

> Throughout history, constitutions have been a male preserve. Men struggled with the issues, wrote the constitutions and interpreted its provisions. Women operated within the structures determined by male attitudes and concerns. Today, there is recognition that women's voices must be heard in constitution making, constitution drafting and constitutional interpretation. Women appear to have different visions of the state though even within the category of 'women' there is diversity. There appears to be more emphasis on security in everyday life, social and economic rights and the need for equality. Women's participation in political life of the country also needs to be encouraged and actively supported. Unless this

is done, women's alternative formulations for the State and their demands on State structures will not be met with adequate response. These different visions must now find expression and the constitutional life of any given society can no longer ignore their concerns ...

(Coomaraswamy 2004: 204–205)

Here too, engendering is visualised as a comprehensive process. First, it involves increased political participation by women. Second, it requires gender sensitivity in law enforcement so as to recognise everyday criminality, as opposed to the greater emphasis given to national security. Aside from which, equality, through affirmative action and other legal standards and mechanisms, is also referred to along with economic and social rights. The need for the recognition of diversity amongst women is also accentuated, in light of the ongoing conflict on the island.

The ontology of gender as a prototype aims towards social transformation through adherence to specific policies and measures. The world is perceived as socially constructed, capable of being transformed through specific interventions. In fact, 'gender can be institutionalized', argued my interviewee Rasika, through such institutional interventions as gender mainstreaming.

Gender methodologies

When the theoretical frameworks, political aspirations, and analysis of gender are accompanied by concrete measures of redress, then epistemology turns into methodology (Chapter 4). Granted, these aspirations are generated from gender ontologies that are based on lack, disadvantages, biases and gaps pertaining to women: 'one can't simply address women – one has to look at the larger picture' (Rasika).

Gender is not confined to identity politics but expanded into an institutional or social context. The most tangible method of realising the political aspirations of gender is through gender mainstreaming (Schalkwyak et al. 1996; Miller and Razavi 1998a; Kabeer 2003), as discussed in Chapter 4. Gender mainstreaming can be defined as a practical methodology for institutionalising structural change in social configurations, policies, organisations, disciplines and programmes through attitudinal changes. When it comes to research praxis[8] (Stanley 1990a) in Sri Lankan writing, gender has utility value. Gender mainstreaming can be seen as extending knowledge-making or epistemology into institutional / individual practices (Chapter 4). Efforts at gender mainstreaming include methodologies such as a Code of Ethics on Gender Representation for the Electronic Media (Women's Education and Research Centre 1998) and Guidelines on Company Policy for Gender Equity / Equality (International Labour Organisation and Employers' Federation of Ceylon 2005), as well as a Guide for a Code on Sexual Harassment for private sector companies (Employers' Federation of Ceylon 2003).

As I have already reviewed the pros and cons of gender mainstreaming as a feminist reformative ontology / epistemology in the previous chapter, I will limit my discussion here. Suffice to say that gender methodologies aspire to institutionalise the political aspirations of gender in organisational policy and practice.

Gender ontology as epistemology is gender epistemology as ontology

To recap, gender epistemology as theoretical constructs has the capacity to encapsulate, reconstruct or deconstruct gender within research discourses, ideologies, disciplines, institutions and social structures. As an analytical category or variable, it has clarified and defined the ways in which the state of being gendered was 'taken up, regularized, resisted, contested and transformed' (Jarviluoma et al. 2003: 7). As a political aspiration it has the potential for promoting individual and social change in the state of gender. Finally, as a methodology that is not confined to research alone, it has the capacity to provide concrete approaches for the transformation of institutional states of gender (though it may not guarantee attitudinal changes).

These facets of an epistemology are not conceptualised as in any way providing a sense of closure or boundaries. Nor are these understandings of gender epistemology mutually exclusive. In fact, as argued before, it is possible that for many feminists, the political intent or aspiration of gender vis-à-vis individual and social transformation underpins all epistemological usages of the term – irrespective of the other strategies undertaken to create knowledge.

Moreover, these ways of knowing (gender epistemology) also influence the ways in which one experiences or apprehends life (gender ontology). For instance, gender as a methodology is an aspect of epistemology that can reproduce 'better' gender ontologies. Gender analysis that is a key tool in empirically portraying gender concepts is also part of ontological assimilation. This clarifies the argument that theories and justifications of gender-based knowledge-making give rise to the conceptualisations of gender realities themselves. To reiterate: gender as epistemology is also gender as ontology, and gender as ontology is also gender as epistemology. This is essentially a circular explanation of gender; gender as ontology (savoir) is gender as epistemology (connaissances) is gender as ontology (savoir).

Perhaps it is necessary to refer to a hypothetical example to further clarify this conclusion. Because we (as researchers) conceive of women as an abstraction (ontology) in the national context, we undertake research on the status of women. The conclusions in such research reports (epistemology), with regard to the status of women's health or education, affect the way we conceive of women's health concerns or access to education (ontology). Or, to simplify the issue, research findings on the social construction of men and women within the urban nuclear family in Colombo (epistemology) may influence the way we conceptualise gender relations in general (ontology):

which may in turn lead us to research on gender in low-income families in Colombo (epistemology).

As noted before, the conceptual slippages, ambiguities, inconsistencies and contradictions pertaining to the discussion of abstract concepts such as ontology and epistemology, have made this chapter one of the most difficult to write. It is possible that the conceptual difficulties and murkiness in articulating my arguments arise from the fact that both ontology and episte-mology are, after all, abstract academic concepts from modernist perspectives. Whilst working with the meanings and assumptions associated with modern-ism, I have also deconstructed these social constructs of research and writing processes from postmodernist standpoints by contextualising them. However, I have kept in mind that contexts too are unstable (Butler 1999), and open to forms of change.

6 A method

Literature reviewing as making meaning

In this chapter I reflect on the method of literature reviewing rather than other available methods of data generation / construction (such as interviewing, observation, textual analysis, surveys, etc.). One reason for this choice is because literature reviewing is generally neglected in many books on research methodology because it is conceptualised as a way of contextualising research rather than as a research method. In Sri Lanka, when it comes to women-related (WR) research, the reviewing of local literature is not always practised even though there are global literature appraisals. What is the role of a literature review? What significance does literature reviewing have for feminist research? How does literature reviewing make meaning? These are some of the questions that will be considered in this chapter.

In order to do so I will focus on a literature review of feminist research methodology in Sri Lanka, spanning from 1975 to 2008. This review focuses on work that explicitly concentrates on WR research methodology, and on work that discusses methodological concerns as an auxiliary issue in research. As an epistemic[1] project, it identifies / constructs a corpus of local literature on research methodology that is based on my subjective selection of research examples, on researchers' textual deliberations and on my application / deconstruction of theoretical approaches. While Derrida's (1998) understanding of an archive is of value, in legitimising informal knowledges (savoir) as applied by de Mel (2007) in her work on archiving the testimonies of war-affected women, Foucault's (1998) concept of connaissances or formal knowledge is more useful in literature reviewing. The literature review is a feature of connaissances, since the researcher is called upon to discover / construct formal knowledge from formal knowledge. This can be contrasted to the way that I construct / capture savoir (informal knowledges) in Chapter 7, in particular where I rely on experiential, everyday theory and practice for research evidence and authority; or conflate savoir and connaissances, as in Chapter 1.

Constructing formal knowledge may also involve an element of theorising, and as argued by Letherby:

> Historically, legitimate theory has been bound up with legitimate beliefs and secular and sacred knowledge has often been difficult to disentangle.

There has been constant tension between theory based on experience and / or observation and abstract or universal theory.

(Letherby 2003: 24)

She points to the difficulties of distinguishing between theories arising from universalised beliefs, everyday beliefs and religious beliefs. Literature reviewing is a problematic attempt at theorisation (or epistemology) and the establishment of academic credence. Here my review incorporates textual discussions of research praxis as well as instances of 'actual' research praxis in texts. In this chapter too, I pursue my theoretical approach of combining modernist and postmodernist approaches. In literature reviewing, I make meaning by representing and constructing the epistemic evolution of feminist research methodology. This is done by charting (partially) its origins, classifications, definitions and types. Simultaneously, I make parallel meanings – by focusing on the difficulties of origins and discontinuities, as well as on the contradictions and overlaps of such a project.

The method of literature reviewing

As argued by Mason (2002: 52), method in qualitative research is 'more than a practical technique or procedure for gaining data. It also implies a data generation process involving activities that are intellectual, analytical and interpretive'. A method is part of the complex process of data generation and construction on a research topic that is therefore subjective. Literature reviewing, when taken as a method, is an aspect of research methodology that is integral to any research study. Hart (1998) identifies the literature review as the methodological starting point for a research project, as it gives an idea of the methodological traditions, assumptions and research strategies of previous research, which undoubtedly influence a researcher. He defines methodology as:

a system of methods and tools to facilitate the collection and analysis of data. It provides a starting point for choosing an approach made up of theories, ideas, concepts and definitions of the topic; therefore the basis of a critical activity consisting of making choices about the nature and character of the social world (assumptions).

(Hart 1998: 28)

Keeping in mind that origins are highly arbitrary, unstable and largely subjective, methodology is not only a starting point in terms of choice, as pointed out by Hart (ibid.); in fact, it permeates the entire research process. This is because the partialities, directions, rejections and selections continuously made within the research process are based on a methodological standpoint. This involves not only preliminary questions like why the researcher chooses to focus on a particular aspect of the research topic, or why the researcher argues that a particular method/s is the best in data generation as opposed to other methods. It also involves progressive questions in research, such as which theoretical frameworks should be applied, or what type of theory can be generated from the research data collected / composed. Therefore, literature reviewing is a constant in researching and may result in several reviews: on the specific topic, on research methodology, or on related fields of interest. Consequently, it cannot be seen as a sanitised exercise that can be strictly classified, with no loose ends.

Studies on literature reviewing have hitherto emphasised the practical advantages of the exercise: such as identifying knowledge gaps, clarifying research questions, improving researchers' methodologies, providing a grasp of the issues relating to the topic and establishing validity (Hart 1998; Barron 2006). It may also provide background and therefore help contextualise the research process. Aside from which, I reiterate that reviewing is a distinctly epistemic project. It makes meaning by relying on knowledge established through the privilege of a priori publications; through the delineation and composition of historical trajectories of the research topic; through classifications and ordering; and through the review of research issues. However, it does not always take into consideration the analogous existence of other forms of knowledge and meaning-making (savoir) that are imperative for a holistic or more profound understanding.

Literature reviewing is a subjective process of knowledge production and meaning-making (as is any other method of data generation in the final analysis). It is based on selective reading and understanding and is reliant on the researcher's subjectivity and standpoint of the moment. In this context, the systematic literature review has been proposed (Oakley 2002) as a method that can circumvent the failings of the individual literature review – by democratising the process and refining the central objectives and design of a review. Yet, aside from formalising the research process through a strict adherence to method, even systematic reviews do not consider tacit / implicit knowledges (savoir) that are apprehended / understood in different ways.

Undertaking a historical review of WR research methodology in Sri Lanka has not been easy – for empirical reasons, apart from the theoretical issues. For, as noted in the introductions, literature focusing exclusively on research and methodology is sparse in Sri Lanka. Further, it is my contention that research is widely influenced by researchers' intuition, and is sometimes an instinctive rather than a formal, theorised, methodological process (Chapters 1 and 7). Due to these empirical and epistemological constraints on constructing / generating formal knowledge on feminist research methodology, this literature review is partial, provisional and contingent. It is partial in its subjectivity and inherent incapacity to encompass all knowledge; provisional until more knowledge on the matter is generated / constructed; and contingent above all on texts and the written word, rather than on other forms of discourse.

Within international Women's Studies research, methodology has now become an area of feminist specialisation, with its own academic specialists, focal points and lineages. Researchers like Mary Margaret Fonow and Judith Cook (2005) and Louise Morley (1996) have used literature reviews to map the diverse methodological issues, implications and directions of the topic.

Constructing a historical trajectory?

Composing / depicting a historical evolution of a research topic is one of the foremost methods of making meanings in literature reviewing. By giving a history of ideas, as opposed to a genealogy[2] (Foucault 1991) and insights into previous work, possible 'origins' can be provided, directions traced, and depth / scale of meaning given to a research topic – despite the questionability of such epistemic evolutions.

Given the dearth of consistent writing on feminist research methodology, the objective of depicting / constructing a historical trajectory was constrained here. Goonatilake's (1985) article 'Research and Information on Women' sketches a historical trajectory of women's research in the social sciences, and reviews research activities and demographic data in Sri Lanka up to 1985. She makes a distinction between research and information, and discusses the influence of the United Nations (UN) International Women's Year (1975) in providing the crucial boost for research on women. Wanasundera's (1995) paper of the same title 'Research and Information' is a literature review that continues to look at the growth of research literature from 1986 to 1995. It considers the institutional contribution to the growth of research, as well as efforts to improve gender-specific data and to disseminate research findings. There are three distinct areas of research activity identified during this period, as a result of the social changes of development and globalisation. Research that deals with women and work; research that argues for the need to promote legislative changes for women; and finally, research that supports ideological change by highlighting the social construct of gender. These categories of research reflect early feminist neo-liberal critiques of the gender blindness of development policies, as well as women's lack of access, participation, and staying power in different and shifting fields of employment. Similarly, her section on law traces the various liberal currents in legal research that highlighted women's failure to challenge discriminatory laws and to further women's rights through legal precedents.

Wanasundera (1995: 344) also looks at later research that specifically identifies the structural causes of subordination as based on the 'social construction of gender'. Though not expressly argued out, Wanasundera's selection of research studies reflect mono-causal understandings of the historical, social construction of gender – despite its various faces. Examples include the feminist appropriation of Marxist ideological superstructures to convey women's subordination as cheap labour; the identification of 'social backwardness' or traditional cultural ideologies; and patriarchy (with its attendant concepts of shame and evil), as forces that oppress women. I see Wanasundera's (1995) overview as a very promising start to the consideration of WR research.

Leaving a trajectorial approach behind, she categorises the first two groups of WR policy research on the economy and legislative frameworks based on their subject matter, while the social construction of gender is not only a topic of research but also construes a theoretical framework that may span the other two categories. Wanasundera (ibid.) identifies her categorisations of research as arising from the UN agenda at an international level, as well as from the local socio-political imperatives of globalisation as they manifested themselves in Sri Lanka. This is a variation on the informal conceptualisations of WR research as constituting literature on women, gender and feminism (Chapter 1) in the local context. But I take Wanasundera's (ibid.) categorisation of gender a step further, to argue that gender is also a method of analysis, a political objective and a methodology (Chapter 5) and therefore constitutes an epistemology. While Wanasundera's classifications cannot be seen as isolated categories they are acceptable ways of making meaning, as will be argued further in the next section.

Classifying types of approaches

The classification and ordering of methodological issues found / composed in WR literature is then another way of making meaning through literature reviewing. Such an exercise clearly calls for the identification, selecting, composing, and ordering of categories or the highlighting of issues by the researcher, based on what she considers to be of significance. Classification according to a particular schema or pattern leads to theory at a simplistic level – as called for by positivism. Stanley and Wise (1993) talk of this as a form of inevitable caricaturing of typologies[3] of research based on differences. The following categorisations have been selected primarily on the basis of their feminist political aspirations, and for their value as methodological types of feminist research (even though the classifications are not exclusive to one another). They have also been chosen for their predominance (in the cases of feminist empiricism / theoretical research / mixed-methods research) as well as due to researchers' textual discussions (in the instances of action research / theoretical research).

The empiricist bent

One of the predominant epistemologies within Sri Lankan WR research can be identified / constructed as being feminist empiricism. The founding assumption of empiricism is that social realities can be represented in research through empirical data collection – based on scientific, and through implication value-free, objective methods (Haraway 1988; Harding 1990, 2004b). Feminist empiricism in the country involves meta-narratives of social realities that are composed / represented through surveys and interviews (Chapter 4). These relate to women and abstract social structures, such as women in education, or women in the media, or women and work (see CENWOR 1985,

1995b, 2000), or women and meta-narratives of issues such as violence against women (Samuel 1999). Research converges on women and evinces a partiality towards women, even though the opinions, standpoints and colla-boration of the researched women may not be part of the research process.

Many of the epistemological / methodological assumptions shadowing early research texts were simply those of filling a gap or re-integrating women under a non-male norm (Chapter 4). In this effort, researchers construct panoramic pictures of the research subject through quantitative data; how-ever, they do not consciously express their standpoints or situatedness. Har-away (1988) considers such research to be a view from everywhere. But as Harding (1990: 93), one of the main critics of feminist empiricism, concedes, the researcher needs to be conceptualised as 'a knowing mind' located 'in the environment of the present women's movement' and the everyday experi-ences of individual oppression. Consequently, the so-called 'objectivity' of the researcher is questionable; even feminist empiricism has political / ethical motivations.

Quantitative sources and methods (of macro- / micro-surveys, census data and statistical analysis) form the bulwark of feminist empiricism. Both Wanasundera (1995) and Goonatilake (1985) focus on statistical information in their work, and call for adequate sex disaggregated data, as well as data compatibility and timeliness, in order to maximise on the needs of women. In this context, both writers assume a linkage between data, its effectiveness and its usage. Goonatilake identifies bibliographic and statistical data as infor-mation which is:

> a resource, a production factor, which forms the basis of research while research is the process of converting information, which starts at a given level, by processing, organising and analyzing it to generate new infor-mation as its output, to be utilized for a variety of purposes
>
> (Goonatilake 1985: 38)

She makes a distinction between research and information, by identifying information as the basis of research, while research itself is the process of converting information in order to generate new information. This was per-haps an important point to make during the relatively early stages of WR research, when there was a tendency to present statistics without a thorough accompanying analysis. Goonatilake (1985) goes on to list the types of data, surveys and statistical reports, and their parent institutions, that would be relevant to women's research and the purposes for which they could be used. Given that information alone does not necessarily reflect the differences between women, their work, their changing roles, their needs and hidden areas of women's participation, she argues for attitudinal, policy and metho-dological changes that accept the centrality of women's role in society. This establishes further that even feminist empiricism is fuelled by some form of feminist standpoint.

From a positivist perspective, Goonatilake's (1985) article and Wanasundera's (1995) brief reference to gender statistics are useful in indicating the progress made at that time in data collection and dissemination. Today, the situation has improved marginally; as there are occasional statistical visuals of women's roles and status portrayed by government agencies under special projects (see Department of Census and Statistics 1995, 1997; Ministry of Women's Affairs 2003).

However, as pointed out by feminists (Harding 1990, 1991, 2004b), and Goonatilake (1985), the objectives of feminist empiricism are limited. Despite advocating changes for women, it does not conceptualise the required changes in epistemology and methodology to incorporate research subjects as actors in the research process (so that they could initiate and direct changes for themselves). The researched themselves remain powerless. Indian feminist Narayan (2004) differs from this position when she points out the capacity / authority of empiricism to challenge forms of cultural hegemony from the privilege of a scientific perspective.

In Sri Lanka too, the value of feminist empiricism within the local context lies in its ability to provide justification for the political project of feminism. The bulk of research, lobbying and activism directing national legislation, governmental and other policy changes are founded on feminist ontological politics (Chapter 4). Take the example of research activism concerning government land allocation schemes that discriminated against women in the allotment of state lands, which led to administrative changes in the public sector. However, further research is necessary to track / establish these linkages between research and institutional changes.

Action research

There are uncritical assumptions in WR research about the approach / objectives / outcomes of research. Action research[4] is one area that requires attention. Many controversial issues have been raised internationally about action research, as recorded by Reinharz (1992), for example. These include the vagueness of research objectives and outcomes, the capacity of action or emancipatory research to empower the researched, and the extent of participation / collaboration between the researcher and researched (Lather 1986; Stanley 1990a; Letherby 2006).

A fleeting reference to action research was made in an article on the rural economy in 1976 (Economic Review 1976a). It conceptualised action research as a top-down approach by the researcher, identifying opportunities for a developmental intervention (via new skills, training and infrastructure changes), based on an analysis of the division of labour in farm households. Here, social change meant economic empowerment.

Citing Mies on the necessity of 'research objects to be viewed from below', Goonatilake (1985: 37) argues for a version of action research that places the researcher on an equal plane with those studied, although in her opinion researchers are 'technicians at the service of others, not far removed from the masses' (ibid.). Goonatilake conceptualises research as a service to the community under study: a Marxist standpoint, but one which could equally cover other stances including those of welfare, Christian and Muslim charity, Buddhist altruism, class condescension, or gender inequity (Chapter 8). In this context, Schrijvers (1993) strikes a cautionary note by arguing that simply using a bottom-up approach does not guarantee that the interests of those at the bottom are incorporated into the analysis. There also needs to be a moral stand on the part of the researcher – perhaps 'a conscious partiality' – as advocated by Mies (1983: 68) and others (Smith 1974; Stanley and Wise 1983a; Jagger 2004), using different terminology and other discerning arguments.

Though not cohesively argued, Goonatilake (1985) makes a case for the researcher as being mandated to create consciousness of women's oppression from a theoretical perspective, and thereby stimulating the researched into action. While she does not make references to global theorisations (Mies 1983; Stanley and Wise 1983) on the consciousness-raising aim of feminist research, she nevertheless sees research as being both theory and action based. An interactive methodology is advocated where the women being studied would decide on the object and procedures of research. Although she makes the point that women are not a homogeneous group, the possible power dynamics of the researched within their social context is not addressed in her conceptualisation.

Schrijvers (1996) refers to a research experience with internally displaced peoples (IDPs[5] mainly Tamil and Muslim women), which is similar to the model promoted by Goonatilake. Schrijvers explicates a 'feminist-inspired transformative' (1996: 19) research approach, where the research agenda was determined by the researched women themselves. It involved a bottom-up movement for change – through advocacy about the situation of displaced people among the relevant authorities, so as to influence the decision-making process from the viewpoint of the affected. Schrijvers' compact and essentially descriptive article does not indicate the methods used in her interaction with either the displaced women or with the authorities, although she refers to the power play experienced in a situation of displacement and civilian interaction. However, her insights from this research show that the above methodology was able to benefit from:

> feminism's appreciation of the heterogeneity of experience of people in particular categories, yet their shared positioning in systems of domination. And to provide a perspective on systems of domination which is relevant in studies not just confined to women.
>
> (Schrijvers 1996: 20)

At the same time, Schrijvers (1993) wants to develop a research methodology that can analyse the interflow of power (top-down and bottom-up) within the research situation.

However, neither Goonatilake nor Schrijvers elucidate the exact means by which, and the extent to which, the activist / researcher can collaborate with the women researched to determine the research process; or the different aspects and levels of action possible. Further, they do not indicate whether the action involved is feminist consciousness-raising, or educational interventions; or whether other forms of activism such as policy-making or lobbying, demonstrations, community-based welfare projects, or grassroots development schemes are conceptualised. It also assumes that the researcher is equally trained in such areas as facilitation, to be able to ensure that there is constructive and equal participation of the women concerned, especially if these are instances where communities are handicapped by illiteracy.

Further, in Schrijvers' (1995) approach, the researcher also needs skills and strategies of advocacy that expand the role of the researcher into that of a political activist. Action research is assumed to have linear aspirations that are based on a rational theory of change, where the researcher may intervene, create consciousness, catalyse social action and change, and in most instances withdraw. This process may underestimate the irrational, multiple, recurring cycles, interlocks and complexities of such phenomena as sexism and racism, and of such conditions as poverty, war and natural disasters.

Theoretical arguments

I will now deal with some of WR researchers' discourses on the theoretical aspects of researching, where available. The first written foray into the topic of feminist research methodology in Sri Lanka was by Hema Goonatilake (1985). One of Goonatilake's initial interests was to outline briefly what feminist research should be in terms of focus and approach. Here, she did not make a distinction between women's research and feminist research; in fact, she sees women's research as feminist research, and as 'research with a difference' (1985: 37). She is one of the first Sri Lankan writers to postulate an emancipatory (Lather 1991; Letherby 2006) research agenda, when she uncompromisingly notes that the aim of research is 'not to maintain social order but to question it and to change it for the better' (ibid.). Goonatilake's seminal article situates women's / feminist research within a Marxist political framework – where research is linked to social change. She proposes that this intends not only to fill the research gaps but also to adopt a 'feminist perspective, to view society through the eyes of women and understand the historical process in the light of their experience as women' (Goonatilake 1985: 37). Goonatilake is, with reference to Smith (1974), promoting a women's standpoint (with regard to empiricist work) here, based on the historically different experience of women as a whole (Chapter 7).

Similarly, for Wanasundera (1995), writing on the same topic, there is a driving political motivation for women's research. There are studies that 'attempt to analyze the position and role of women in society, focussing on women's experience, problems, perceptions, and needs, as well as those that attempt to create a body of knowledge from a female perspective' (Wanasundera 1995: 335). And where there is 'the need to build a knowledge base on the realities of women's lives which could be utilized to bring about attitudinal shifts, policy changes, and action that could remove gender equities' (ibid.), On the issue of research and social transformation, Wanasundera argues that research does not automatically lead to social or attitudinal change; rather, it requires further interventions to be effective. This can be through supportive lobbying, consciousness-raising, policy and programmatic changes (what is argued to be research activism in Chapter 1).

This standpoint assumes that there is some element of commonality in women's experiences that leads to shared needs and interests. Such a worldview is founded on aspirations of unity, and notions of optimism, purity and sisterhood surrounding the political project of feminism during the early stages. Today, consciousness of the diversity of women's identities, needs and standpoints – including those of race (Collins 1990), class (Harstock 2004), lesbianism (Rich 1980) and non-Western feminism (Narayan 2004) etc. – complicate notions of homogeneity, despite understandings of universality and commonality in some experiences.

de Alwis (2004) further problematises this argument on the commonality of politics when she reviews what can be seen as a contradictory relationship between the disciplinary practice of anthropology, and the politics of feminism. Adopting a disciplinary perspective, she argues that certain rules and protocols of anthropology are thought to be analytically prior to political practice, and poses these questions:

> So where does this leave those feminists who wish to pursue the discipline of anthropology? Can we speak from within the domain of feminist politics rather than about it? Is such a disciplinary positioning possible if politics marks the limit of anthropology? How can anthropologists who are also feminists frame research questions about political struggles in which they are actively participating and intervening?
>
> (de Alwis 2004: 123)

In this article, de Alwis provides readings of the Mothers' Front – a women's protest movement of the late 1980s in Sri Lanka (Chapter 5). At one level, she interprets the self-proclaimed non-political role carved out by the Front as calling the political into question and creating new political spaces. She describes how the Front does this by adopting religious distress (through the use of religious rituals) as a form of public protest against the disappearances of family members.[6] This space of religiosity and motherhood that was politically mobilised by these women led to political / ethical dilemmas amongst feminists, as it made them question the meanings of feminisms, differences, women's culture and motherhood. de Alwis (ibid.) herself participates in the debate by speaking from within the domain of feminist politics, and by engaging with this robust activism by non-feminists and the politicisation of so-called women's spaces. She provides a contingent reading of the efficacy of such politics, rather than binary readings of endorsement or rejection.

Jayatilaka (1998) moves the discussion from women / feminism to gender as far as sociological research is concerned. Her paper on research studies of inequality in Sri Lankan society recognises that sociological and anthropological studies have hitherto been blind to the implications of gender inequality in research. She argues that this may have been because gender inequality was generally seen as 'natural' and the norm, while the main concern has been such factors as income, occupations, ethnicity, land ownership, political connections and caste as social facts. Jayatilake (ibid.) contends that Sri Lankan women's access and positioning in education, employment and land as well as their exposure to violence, should be vital factors for stratification studies (alongside other variables). Her interest in gender seems to arise more from the standpoint of the discipline of sociology / anthropology, and her method is based on surveying sociological studies. I will be discussing what can be termed a disciplinary standpoint compiled through savoir in Chapter 7.

Kottegoda (1994), in a brief examination of the gender concept as it is utilised in social and economic studies in Sri Lanka, discusses the common pitfalls of the term in research. To begin with, abstract definitions of gender have primarily assumed an asymmetrical social relationship based on difference, power and silence, and on inequality of access to social resources. She spotlights some common areas of ambiguity in applying gender – such as the unconscious conflation of sex and gender (without problematising the difficulties of separating the two). She further discusses how research focuses on the social relationships between men and women (without calling them gender studies) and, conversely, on women or family-based households, while calling these gender studies. Kottegoda (ibid.) advocates keeping in mind that gender is a relational concept, which includes the examination of men in the distribution of resources / power as well as in other contributory factors such as race, ethnicity and class. She further cautions that in relying too much on women, gender can easily normalise conceptualisations of the characteristics or attributes of gendered behaviour as feminine. She also discusses how Sri Lankan research has not engaged sufficiently in problematising gender – particularly with regard to sexuality, as well as to naturally and socially constructed differences and implications (Chapter 5).

When it comes to the development of specific feminist theoretical frameworks, Schrijvers (1993), who did not favour deductive theorisation in 1995, presents an inductive methodological / theoretical framework from the particular reaches of the Sri Lankan situation. She delineates what she calls a 'transformative research ideal'. This consists of five characteristics of 'dialogical' communication: 1) a dynamic focus on change; 2) the exchange of the researcher and researched positions as subjects and objects; 3) the ideal of egalitarian relations; 4) shared objectives; and 5) the shared power to define the image of reality produced by the research (Schrijvers 1995: 14–15). Based on her experiences of researching with Sri Lankan internal refugees, this methodology strives to establish a collaborative and dialogical effort between the researched and the researcher, to represent the interests of the researched in an egalitarian way. She contends that theory should not only emanate from the specific ground situation, or through an inductive process on the part of the researcher, but that theorisations should originate from the researched. The problems experienced in applying such a methodology included that of the time required for such an intervention, and the possibility of developing 'a methodology that brings to the fore the complexities of change as experienced and influenced by people of different gender, ethnicity, class, culture, and age' (Schrijvers 1993: 59).

This is a key question that preoccupies Schrijvers (1993). Moreover, the importance of capturing / constructing the constant flux and flow of time, the continuous impact of change on individuals, and their own engagement with change, cannot be underestimated. Take the disruptions of war, the mobility of migrant women, and the changing research mandates of international non-governmental organisations (INGOs). These are some of the ontological issues that need accounting for in theorisations (Chapter 4).

Developing such an argument, feminist writer Bandarage (1998) draws a unified theoretical framework for feminism that takes into account the specificities of the local context: including the violence engulfing the country; the dialectics of gender, race / ethnicity and class; and the overwhelming effects of capitalism and westernisation:

> At the theoretical level, the analysis of women and social change in Sri Lanka needs to move beyond the narrow, WID focus on gender, the abstract ahistorical approach of cultural studies, as well as the individualistic human rights approach. Rather, gender issues need to be approached within a broad global political-economic perspective and gender, race / ethnic and class analysis. In other words, the approach to women's liberation in the country has to be placed within overall social transformation or a paradigm shift from domination to partnership at the local and international levels.
>
> (Bandarage 1998: 26)

In her theorisation, Bandarage argues for a movement away from the abstract grand theories of feminisms, to encompass / compose the specificities of local context. I take this to mean the grand causal theories of feminism as articulated by Stanley and Wise (1993), which try to provide reasons for women's oppression and inequalities, as well as grand methodologies of redress such as women's rights frameworks, Women in Development (WID), and Gender and Development (GAD). Bandarage (ibid.) also argues for the necessity of ethical partnerships in the research endeavour. These are seen as requiring solidarity within the various factions of the women's movements.

Furthermore, she advocates the mobilisation of women within an alternative cultural milieu, combining theory with activism, experiential learning, open dialogue, and participatory approaches in her framework. Moreover, 'local languages – Sinhala and Tamil – and local cultural forms such as theatre and music need also be more extensively used in making the feminist discourse and activism more appealing and joyful endeavours' (Bandarage 1998: 27).

Bandarage (ibid.) conceptualises dialogue as the primary means through which differences in ethnicity, religion, and cultural values can be recognised and reconciled as a basis for peace and social reformation. Her theoretical framework is interesting in the way it is rooted in, and strives to unify, the multiple facets of the local context. Furthermore, feminism is approached as 'an ongoing process of growth and empowerment rather than the fait accompli' (Bandarage 1998: 27). Yet, Bandarage's framework (ibid.) becomes problematic when it begins to posit dichotomies and binaries (between academia and struggle, middle-class and 'poorer classes', theory and activism). It fails to take into account the unifications and alliances (although temporary) already taking place within the women's movements. It also does not take into account the possibilities inherent in the paradoxes, complexities and complicities already in existence (for instance, Chapters 1 and 8 discuss collective feminist activism).

Mixed-methods research

While there is a considerable bulk of Feminist empiricist literature, an important development in WR writing has been the mixing of methods. In fact, Goonatilake in 1985 argued for the necessity of quantitative data such as bibliographic data and statistical data, along with qualitative studies, to promote social change for women. She critiqued (though unsubstantiated by reference to specific research) that hitherto many studies were general in nature, and did not account for the complex variations of 'regional, religious and age distinctions, education, employment, income, decision-making, within the household and outside, social relations, political consciousness and participation' (Goonatilake 1985: 36). I would add transgender status and sexual orientation, as well as language and caste differences to this list. Yet, while it is important to account for these differences (Chapter 7), it is imperative not to be bound by them. It is my position that there needs to be a fusion of methods to incorporate both the general and the particular simultaneously. Making meanings requires constructing / highlighting the commonalities and the disparities.

One stated reason for modifying research designs to include quantitative data (from national level surveys as well as from official statistics) and qualitative data (in the form of field investigations and case studies), was the inadequacy of existing data to provide 'insights' (University of Colombo 1979). The methodology of the first Status of Women survey (1979), in particular, reflected mixed methods of data collection (discussions, structured questionnaires, interviews, observations and field living). It contained urban as well as village perspectives, and incorporated eight individual case studies reflecting the views of the writers. The adoption of mixed modes in research such as those by CENWOR (1995a), Jayaweera and Sanmugam (2001), Wickramasinghe and Jayatilaka (2006), has resulted in the ontological construction / representation of a broad panorama as well as of a specific, selective picture. Of course, this may not always ensure a heterogeneous analysis. Nor would it presume to offer 'authentic' representations of reality – if indeed it were possible to do so. However, combining the deductive methods of a research hypothesis with the inductive methods of research questions can augment justificatory arguments for social change. Within the local context, mixed methodology possesses pragmatic value: for consciousness-raising, lobbying, legislative policy and administrative change, and attitudinal and action transformations.

The above identification and construction of methodological types in WR research texts corroborate how meaning was made of research methodology by my interviewees, through different articulations, in the rest of the book. However, such a classification based on type tends to reduce WR work to equal blocs of research, which is not a true picture given the diverse action elements in some feminist empiricist studies, the use of mixed methods, and the theoretical angles spanning all. Given these overlaps and inconsistencies pertaining to methodological types it may be difficult to define each classification in a concrete form. Hence, if meaning is to be made through types, there is a need to account for the overlaps and indefinable features within these classifications.

Other methodological issues

The significance of history

So far, I have discussed the methodological praxis of researchers, not as typologies, but as types of research represented / constructed through my literature review. I now consider two other ontological concerns affecting feminist research – those of positive and negative assumptions pertaining to history and culture.

In 1985, Goonatilake posited an implied comparison between action and historical research by advocating historical research as a means of identifying the basis of women's oppression. She advocated looking at the changing roles and status of women in society during the course of social evolution. Given this classic Marxist / feminist point of view (Maynard 1995; Harstock 2004) that focuses on property relations, changing modes of production and the extent of women's control over the means of production, Goonatilake sees historical research as a methodology of understanding the present structures and ideologies of women's oppression. While the article did not discuss such a proposal beyond bare statements, it was nonetheless an attempt to outline the potential of feminist research. In comparison, Wickramasinghe (2001), similarly to Kelly-Gadol (2008), talks of women's history as a means of restoring women to history and restoring history to women. 'The aim of women's history is to make women a focus of inquiry, a subject of the story, an agent of the narrative. In other words it is to construct women as a historical subject (Wickramasinghe 2001: 33).

While this task of restoration has begun in Sri Lanka, researchers have not always considered how it could be done. Even Wickramasinghe's (ibid.) work on new trends and methodologies in writing history does not explicate the exact ways and means by which researchers could integrate these methodologies into women's history.

Vimaladharma (2003) uses gender theory in historical analysis.[7] He warns feminists doing historical research about the need to engage with several overriding assumptions and standpoints within the local context. First, the need to account for traditionalists who try to construct a golden era, which accorded equal or high position to Sri Lankan women, despite the ambiguity of historical evidence (Kiribamune 1990; Vimaladharma 2003). As a result, issues of discrimination are seen as irrelevant and invalid in the local context. In particular, Vimaladharma (ibid.) refers to assumptions of social and cultural continuity through two millennia of Sri Lankan history. He critiques dismissals of male dominance in preference for instances which are contrary. He also points out how romanticising the past prevents engagement with the gender issues of contemporary times.

Second, he argues for the necessity of engaging with modernists who see patriarchy and male dominance breaking down under colonial rule, resulting in opportunities for women to organise and struggle for emancipation. This thinking, according to Vimaladharma, overlooks the fact that colonial interventions eroded some of the rights to property and status within the family which women enjoyed under indigenous systems. While further research is necessary, I contend that it also ignores some of the oppressive moral impositions of Christianity and the Victorian era, such as legalised marriages, during colonial rule. Vimaladharma proposes that 'the romanticism of the traditionalist and the idealism of the modernist have both to be critically examined using objective analytical criteria' (Vimaladharma 2003: 3). Interestingly, he (ibid.) refers to the concept of patriarchy as being able to provide the relevant analytical criteria to surmount both these drawbacks. While the more theoretically developed strands of patriarchy – discussed as multiple structures (Sangari 2008) or as interplaying with the state, community and household (Agarwal 1988) – would enhance the analysis, a monocausal, singular theoretical perspective may not always be able to address the complicities of these realities. Furthermore, in my view the two oppositional standpoints of traditionalism and modernism both have strategic value in historical research. My epistemological standpoint is such that I see / construct / appropriate the co-existence of commonalities and contrarieties of empowerment and oppression in history, for the political and ethical projects of feminisms.

The cultural factor

In Sri Lanka, a cultural approach (originally founded on literature, the liberal arts and humanities but which now encompasses anthropology as well as the social sciences) has become politically important for feminist research, for a number of reasons. First, the collective national consciousness is fixated on the country's 2500 years of recorded (Buddhist) history and culture to the extent of devaluing Tamil and Muslim histories.[8] Second, the protracted ethnic conflict in the country has heightened and polarised the cultural / ethnic identities of the Tamils, Sinhalese and Muslims. Global developments pertaining to US / UK / India / Al Qaeda and Muslim countries have further exacerbated feelings of insecurity amongst the country's Muslim community. Third, various reactionary forces in the country since Independence (in 1948) have sporadically espoused and distorted culture as a political ideal – if not practice – against the colonial past and against the present currents of glo-balisation. Fourth, culture (paradoxically based on Victorian ideologies of the colonial era, as well as various other religious morals) is manipulated as a powerful force to restrict people's sexualities and gender status. Researchers' emphasis on culture has been for these reasons, as well as to combat the backlash against feminism for being alien to the indigenous cultures (Chapters 1 and 4).

Maunaguru (1995), aligning herself to Althusser (2000), argues the following in regard to Tamil literature:

> The study of literature is an important aspect of feminist studies since literature is part of cultural practice. Social construction of gender takes place through the working of ideology and the ideology of gender is inscribed in everyday discourse and is produced and reproduced in cultural practices.
>
> (Maunaguru 1995: 30)

Gender ideologies (and I would argue, structures, performances and identities) are partially constituted and signified by the dominant cultural myths, perceptions, impulses and practices of each community and the nation at large. Maunaguru (ibid.) argues that because expressive realism is still popular among Tamil literary critics as an approach, they assume that the literary text expresses the truth about the author's experience and world and, by implication, the universal aspects of human nature. However, she sees the text not as a 'transparent media which reflects reality' but rather, as a signifying system that inscribes ideology which is constitutive of reality (Maunaguru 1995: 32). Similarly, in examining / constructing the cultural organisation of sexuality and the meanings assigned to the female body, Tambiah (2004) uses as her base the parliamentary discourse surrounding the changes proposed to the Penal Code in 1995. While the changes would have tightened the laws on sexual offences (including marital rape), and liberalised abortion and homosexuality had they been passed, Tambiah (ibid.) discusses how the entire parliamentary debate was founded on repressive ideologies of gender and the female body; notions of Sri Lankan cultural purity (against the West); the sanctity of the family; and various ethnic and cultural practices. Research on the cultural realm of life signifies / constructs the intangible yet oppressive forces in Sri Lankan society. Nowhere is this done more evocatively than in de Mel's (2007) work on popular culture and the memories and narratives of war-affected women, where she considers the insidious signification and effects of militarisation, war and political violence on all facets of Sri Lankan culture.

The pervasive crosscut of culture is then not only a research topic but also a methodological concern, since it constitutes politicised aspects of ontology or research realities. Given their powers of signification and contact at a sub-liminal level, cultural codes have in general been manipulated against women. However, this does not mean that there are no positive possibilities. Bandarage (1998) advocates an alternative cultural milieu for research activism that is non-violent and based on women's networks (although this has not been clearly defined). The elusive crosscuts of history and culture (acquired and constructed through formal knowledges in this instance) provide critical facets in a feminist methodology – particularly in relation to ontology (see Chapter 4).

***

My literature review of feminist research methodology in Sri Lanka can be summarised as follows (despite the prioritisations involved in summarising). Although attempts to define WR research methodology and compose a historical trajectory of methodological concerns were restricted due to the scarcity of texts, it was nonetheless possible to imply the following types of WR research categories. These were: feminist empiricism, actions research, theoretical work and research using mixed methods. The classifications are based on research types, and are seen as forms of research activism – that aspires to social change through various means. Yet they are not proposed / constructed as exclusive and separate categories but are overlapping issues given postmodernist under-standings. Given the ontological specificities / politics of the local context, history and culture are key factors that need methodological accounting. Both the traditionalist and modernist approaches of historical research are of strategic use for feminism in establishing legitimacy; but an interdisciplinary approach-based culture is one option in responding to the backlash against feminism and the heightened fundamentalist and reactionary forces in the country.

From modernist perspectives then, reviews of local literature (together with global literature reviewing) are a vital method in feminist researching, serving an epistemic function alongside other research methods. Despite being a subjective and selective process, reviewing can collate / construct a back-ground through an indigenous history of ideas, and form a critical assessment of local issues, related to the research topic in question, in terms of formal knowledge making (connaissances). It can delineate and define the field in question, and identify the gaps as well as discursive debates on the topic – while keeping in mind that such definitions and delineations are contingent, local and provisional. Reviewing can serve to partially construct, to contextualise, frame and contribute towards legitimising explicit knowledges – in this instance, on research methodology in Sri Lanka – within knowledge fora. As such it has the capacity to legitimise feminist research in contexts where Women's Studies has not attained academic / institutional acceptability. Aside from being an exercise (that adopts multiple theoretical and epistemological approaches to making meanings), literature reviewing is also a political project that engages with the discursive fields of power and knowledge.

7 Theory
Making and unmaking meaning in theory

Given the somewhat limited feminist theorisations on methodology yielded by my literature review (Chapter 6), the objective of this chapter is to consider women-related (WR) researchers' / writers' unrecorded, understandings (savoir) of feminist theory on methodology (connaissances) – principally through interviews. This research act signifies a somewhat convoluted relationship between savoir and connaissances. I will 'begin' to 'make' theory and 'unmake' theory (connaissances) here primarily from consultations with WR researchers in Sri Lanka. To do so I will pose the following questions. How do WR researchers predominantly perceive of themselves as researchers? What are the key assumptions that they bring to the act of researching? How can these perceptions and assumptions be theorised? I will examine / compose how researchers conceptualise the researcher (and research processes), and reflect on how I myself make and unmake theoretical meaning. To what extent can I extract theoretical meanings from researchers' interviews on research methodology? To what extent can I apply theoretical frameworks from international research methodology to data from interviews? In what ways can I make and unmake meaning in theory?[1]

The pros and cons of applying theorisation

By theorisation, I refer to the process of identifying / applying / deconstructing structures concepts, principles, assumptions, reasonings, hypotheses, and rationales pertaining to the generation / construction of knowledge and meaning-making (Chapter 2). One debate within Sri Lankan Women's Studies discourses centres on the relevance and function of theorisation. On the side of theoretical inconsequence, researchers see applying theory as an imposition on the researched and the research context. This point of view can be traced to the idea of objective reality and political / ethical commitments to its authentic representation (Chapter 6). Theory is rejected in favour of what can be seen as methodological authenticity and accuracy. Schrijvers (1993), who stands vehemently against what she calls a de-personalised (structural) approach to theory, argues that theorisation with the use of models and statistics is highly problematic in representing the voices of the researched:

In the first place, 'structures', 'models', 'systems' and 'statistics' are impersonal and all too often static conceptualizations of social reality, that usually reflect the outsider. They can never capture the complex dialectics shaped by living people, who all exert certain types of influence and power.

(Schrijvers 1993: 59)

She critiques deductive theorisations that are founded on quantitative analysis and a scientific approach to research, and argues that theorisation imposes rigid, alien and stereotypical frameworks that are the conceptualisations of the researcher – who is not part of the researched community.[2] Stanley and Wise (1983, 1993) make a similar point when they argue against typologies as part of theory-making, adding that these can only be caricatures (Chapter 6). Schrijvers (1993) argues further that these frameworks are unable to capture / compose the complex and intricate workings of power amongst the researched.

On the side of theoretical consequence, there is the dominant argument amongst researchers that theory should emanate directly from the experiences of the researcher / researched (Stanley and Wise 1993). Yet this type of grounded theory proposed by Strauss and Corbin (1998), for example, does not occur as a one-directional, inductive process. Invariably, researchers and writers tend to appropriate / recontextualise / utilise key concepts, frameworks and theorisations from global feminisms instinctively and tacitly, according to their reading, conditioning and experiences of women's issues. Consequently, not only theory, but 'research interests and questions arise out of (global) theoretical debates as well as the local debates such as the Mother's Front' (asserted respondent Deepa).

This is because some degree of a priori conditioning on the part of the researcher is unavoidable (Morley 1999). Respondent Dhamani, an academic, considered her work: 'I think I would classify my work as doing ... it is taking some of these theoretical insights and applying them to the Sri Lankan case – nuancing that theory'.

In other words, she promoted adopting global theory and adapting it to the local, according to its ontological landscape. In contrast, African theorists like Oyewumi (1997) have vehemently opposed applying Western theoretical rationales; and some Indian feminists have also rejected the application of Western theorisations (as discussed by John [2004a]) citing arguments of cultural difference and specificity. While Sri Lankan researcher Bandarage (1998) also argues for theorisations based on local specificities, the epistemological act of 'nuancing' theory is still significant when considering theory within the Sri Lankan context. It can be conceptualised in relation to Said's travelling theory:

Like people and schools of criticism, ideas and theories travel – from person to person, from situation to situation, from one period to another. ...

First, there is a point of origin or what seems like one, a set of initial circumstances in which the idea came to birth or entered discourse. Second, there is the distance traversed, a passage through the pressure of various contexts as the idea moves from an earlier point to another new time and place where it will come into a new prominence. Third, – there is a set of conditions – call them conditions of acceptance or, as an inevitable part of acceptance, resistances – which then confront the transplanted theory or idea, making possible its introduction or toleration, however alien it might appear to be. Fourth, the now full (or partially) accommodated (or incorporated) idea is to some extent transformed by its new uses, its new position in a new time and place.

(Said 1983: 226–227)

While 'travelling' and 'nuancing' are methodologically useful concepts for locating and tracing formal theorisations (connaissances), it is equally important to consider whether ideas, implicit understandings, and conceptualisations (savoir) can actually be located in one 'metasource' or individual. Can savoir, or for that matter, connaissances (given that savoir influences connaissances) actually be traced? Moreover, lifelong conscious as well as unconscious knowledges, socialisation processes, and tacit understandings ensure that there are multiple factors influencing both savoir and connaissances (as well as 'indigenous' and Western theorisations, and inductive and deductive research). It therefore becomes important to think in terms of 'multibridity' (Chapter 3) as a vital part of theorisation alongside ideas of travelling and nuancing theory.

In the final count, theory will only have utility value as long as it is considered / constructed as relevant to the particular and the local; whether applied or derived. This may involve recontextualising, applying bits of theory, inducting from ground data and using a middle-order approach (de Groot and Maynard 1993a).

Beginning theory

I decided to focus on theory in this chapter because theory is an aspect of research methodology. At the same time:

methodology is itself theory. It is a theory of methods which informs a range of issues from who to study, how to study, which institutional practices to adopt (such as interpretive practices), how to write and which knowledge to use.

(Skeggs 1997: 17)

As argued in Chapter 6, it is methodology as theory that is not so apparent in Sri Lanka. Methodology has been more an application of methods rather than a theoretical, reflexive or integrated argument for researching.

This was understood / confirmed by my respondents – some of whom did not necessarily want to relate to such abstract methodological terms as epistemology and ontology. As one of my respondents, Vivian, (despite being an academic herself) teasingly but pithily reflected on the implications of my interview schedule:

> But questions can be intimidating in this respect, you suddenly think; you are suddenly made to think of what you don't know. Especially when you indicated that you wanted to talk about the various theories, concepts, methodologies, methods, challenges and problems of researching on women and gender ... although having said it is intimidating, it is also intriguing and interesting. But I also felt a little nervous – because this morning the first thing I thought was – as soon as I opened my eyes – Oh no, Maithree is going to come and talk to me about these very complicated questions ... and I don't know if you noticed but at the beginning I was sweating a little – because of your questions ...
>
> (Vivian)

This was because they had not always defined, recontextualised or theorised these issues according to these particular technical terms and jargon. Not only does this quotation indicate the difficulty of defining / simplifying methodological concepts, but it also exemplifies the intricacy of actually articulating such theoretical issues. These are primarily abstract conceptualisations that this book, on the one hand, tries to transform into practice. On the other, it also tries to translate and relate the concrete practices of research into theoretical conceptualisations. The above quotation signifies the complexities of talking about theory as opposed to writing it; and of doing theory collectively in contrast to doing it individually.

Research methodology seemed to have been apprehended / applied[3] instinctively by many researchers. While this is not to be undervalued, this is the very reason why I partly chose to make and unmake theory on research methodology from the interviews with researchers. Under these circumstances:

> The verbal signs with which people represent their thoughts are thus inert entities to the sociologist until he or she converts them into data by constituting the speakers as relevant subjects, or the remarks as part of a relevant discourse, and providing a theoretical context which these remarks can be deemed to have a bearing on and, when theorized, a place within ...
>
> (Cain and Finch 2004: 520)

I appropriated the following fragments of conversational discourse as 'inert entities' and assembled them as data. However, this did not always allow for the surfacing of theoretical complexities. Theorisations were then also partly reliant on my interpretations of global theorisations, experiences, subjectivity, subconscious, reading interests, tacit understandings, and previous knowledge – as are any theorisations to some degree (de Groot and Maynard 1993a). I posed data as examples / foundations on which I simultaneously constructed modernist / postmodernist theory. Conceptual complexity for this chapter was attempted by theoretically framing local discourses on methodology, by identifying the silences and presences, and by appropriating, recontextualising and contrasting them with global developments in theory. This also involved the epistemological process of analysing, attributing / constructing meanings to specific phenomena, constructing relevance, applying and deconstructing methodologies, and doing so reflexively. I believe that this chapter will legitimise researchers' articulations on and of standpoint within savoir, as far as Sri Lankan Women's Studies is concerned, and will initiate a theoretical debate in terms of connaissances. It will also establish the significance of beginning theorisations through a middle-order approach, as partial or incomplete but defined; provisional until further developed / deconstructed; located in Sri Lanka but also in global theorisations; and politically motivated.

The location / situatedness / standpoints and intersections of knowledge

The realities that the researchers are studying, engaged in and part of are symbiotically linked to how knowledge is conceptualised / produced. In other words, ontology is symbiotic with epistemology and vice versa (Chapters 4 and 5), irrespective of whether they are grand ontologies or localised ones[4] and despite their intersectionality, instability and multiplicity. At this juncture, I consider / construct how knowledge is produced and meanings made within Sri Lanka. Conversely, I also theorise how researchers represent / compose their subjective ontological positionings in their work. I allow Vivian, one of my respondents, to open the theorisation on the location of knowledge (given her own location in a Humanities discipline):

> I'm beginning to believe more and more in the idea of location. Location of – the national, cultural, social, and economic and I think whatever feminist theory or ideology that we use or apply, it is likely to be modified by the location in which we operate, and that location does put certain constraints on us.
>
> (Vivian)

Here Vivian is referring to some of the national currents of strident patriotism that may question the very articulation of feminisms, or to neo-liberal forces that may provoke feminist critiques. She also expanded on the crucial point made by Dhamani earlier about adapting theoretical perspectives to suit the local ontological context. She considers her location within the Sri

Lankan context as sometimes imposing certain constraints on the application of existing (Western) feminist theory.

Consequently, these factors concerning the researcher's location impact on the research process, resulting in knowledge Haraway (1988) terms as being 'situated' (from her multiple locations in the Sciences / Science Studies / Cultural Studies). Skeggs (1997) explicates this point about locatedness / situatedness further:

> I have learnt what it means to be a feminist researcher and position myself accordingly. This positioning process is not without contradiction. Researchers are positioned within institutions, by history, by disciplinary practices, by dominant paradigms, in theoretical fashions, in genre style, by funding arrangements, and so on.
>
> (Skeggs 1997: 18)

The situatedness of knowledge refers to the contextual positionings of the researcher amongst diverse ontological / epistemological factors which may often be paradoxical and intersected. These could be related to external metaphysical realities such as perceptions of time, geography location, and historicism (Engelstad and Gerrard 2005); or they could be internal – the psychologically or culturally or politically specific internal identifications / standpoints of the researcher (Harding 2004).[5] Rich (2003) articulates the array of these possibilities in her essay on a politics of location.

In Sri Lanka, one determining influence on writing and researching is the ontology or epistemology of the historical realities of colonial / neo-colonial experiences and conditions. Yet this alone cannot be taken as the single defining factor of situatedness / locatedness, given other phenomena such as globalisation or the particular subjectivity of the researcher. Given postmodernist questionings of the concept of complete knowledge and the human capacity to fully apprehend knowledge, research generated must be recognised as partial – in the sense of being incomplete and from multiple intersecting standpoints.

To clarify: by standpoints, I mean feminist concerns with subjectivity, identity politics and personal experience (Harding 2004c) that privilege women's ways of knowing (Chapter 2). These are based on the conscious subjectivity and intersections of the researcher; but could well include the writer's unconscious perspectives (Stanley and Wise 1993). Unlike men's experiences which are taken to be the norm, women's knowledges are considered to be 'subjugated knowledges', as conceptualised by Foucault (1980a). Harding (2004a: 1) contends that standpoint theory is about the 'relations between the production of knowledge and practices of power'. These standpoints have become crystallised as epistemological theory that takes into account the multiple facets of identity politics, such as those relating to indigenous women, colour, class, Third Worldism, etc. (Harding 2004c; Hesse-Biber and Yaiser 2004a; Smith 2008). These also include theoretical and ethical issues of differences and intersectionality (Fonow and Cook 1991b, 2005; Mauthner et al. 2002; Hesse-Biber and Yaiser 2004a). The term 'intersectionality' then comes to indicate the multiple fragments of the researchers' identities and shifting standpoints that crosscut or intersect with one another. It can overcome the essentialism of conceptualising a singular standpoint.

The following sections will engage with what has been identified as a women's standpoint, disciplinary / ideological alliances, and the perspectives of mothers, class intersections, counter-nationalist stands, and Asian / South-Asian positions. These classifications are not presented as distinct categories; rather, they constitute the standpoints / intersections / situatedness of Sri Lankan researchers that my respondents offered, and I classified as being significant in processes of meaning-making, during the period of researching. To begin with, I will deal with three differential or oppositional standpoints (Sandoval 2004) against what my respondents consider to be feminisms. They are a women's standpoint, disciplinary / ideological perspectives, and the perspectives of mothers.

A women's standpoint

As argued in Chapter 2 the overarching inference from WR research and writing is that of a global women's paradigm. Amongst the diverse stand-points of researchers within this paradigm is that of a 'women's perspective' besides those of 'feminist' perspectives and gender perspectives (as argued vis-à-vis research categories in Chapter 1). Along with other political, ideological and ethical complicities and complexities involved in researching from such a perspective, the core assumption of a women's standpoint is the collective identity of women as a homogenous group. But women's approaches ema-nating from this standpoint vary from altruism (Chapter 8) to welfare orien-tations; from Women in Development (WID) to democracy; and from rights-based understandings to women's empowerment (Chapter 4). Some of my interviewees considered themselves to be working 'long-term to improve the status of women' as Kiyana put it. Within the local context then, the assumption of researching from a women's standpoint posits women against feminists. Gayathri, a second-generation researcher articulated this opposi-tional standpoint (to feminism):

> Generally I don't like being called a feminist and I have never been a radical feminist. If I work with feminists my work can be described as feminist but I don't like specially to be called feminist because I think I'm into women's rights and the equality of women from a broad perspective of equality of opportunity, non-discrimination and fairness. ...
>
> (Gayathri)

Gayathri subscribed to a 'women's standpoint' because of her broader commitment to liberal values which she sees as going beyond the limitations and compartmentalisations that she associates with the concept of feminism. She did not see feminism as encompassing general issues, or men. Yet the implication of taking a liberal / rights-based women's perspective – with its fundamental silence on the differences between women and men, for example – is not critiqued. Gayathri also implied that she was against the 'radicalism' of feminism. Radicalism may be seen as 'extremist', 'anti-male', 'separatist', 'bra-burning' and 'anti-family' understanding of feminisms. While such researchers do not necessarily reflect the stereotyped, homophobic, and derogatory condemnations of feminisms found in the mainstream media of the country (Chapters 1 and 4), it is possible that an almost defensive stress on anti-feminism may have been a reaction to these evocative, dominant and negative images of feminisms. Another respondent, Zulfika, speculated that because local feminists were perceived as influenced by Western ideologies that were out of sync with local cultures, some WR respondents were hesitant to identify with the term 'feminisms', which led to standpoints that were oppositional to feminisms. A similar scenario, though more developed, is critiqued by John (2004a: 53–54) concerning Indian researchers who also reject such naming, by using stridently postcolonial arguments such as those of an ongoing colonial legacy (Mohanty 1988); by proposing polarising images of 'Indianness' such as Hinduism; and arguing for an inherent superiority of local Indian standpoints.

An oppositional standpoint is felt to give more social credibility and access to a wider women's constituency for the political objectives of research activism. Juxtaposition between women and feminists was also attempted for political and strategic reasons: to facilitate relations with women, and 'not alienate those who did not subscribe to such views – by applying a softly, softly approach' (says another of my respondents, Wasanthi). Given the strategic balancing act which many WR researchers perform (vis-à-vis dress codes and political affiliations as discussed in Chapters 3, 6 and 8), so that the women they are in contact with may not be deterred or alienated, such a standpoint is understandable. However, it is important to note that this anti-feminist (pro-women) standpoint was held in spite of the strict moral standards that some feminists impose on other feminists within the research community (Chapter 8).

The perspective of a mother

A common gender stereotype in the Sri Lankan public consciousness, as in other Asian societies, is that of the mother. Dominant images of mothers range from cultural veneration for the self-sacrifice attributed to and demanded from mothers, to the domineering and oppressive mother-in-law figure. One of my interviewees, Saumi, expressed her views very strongly about focusing on the tie between mothers and children in this perspective: 'I don't think mothers can be separated from children, biologically or in any sense of the word (*when researching*) ... this really could be because of my profession as ... '[6]

In light of her work on the phenomenon of 'female-headed-households' in the country (arising from war and political conflicts), Saumi stressed the almost exclusive importance of the mother for children. Interestingly, such a standpoint was not evident in WR research studies, conveying a certain inconsistency between verbally articulated standpoints and what is practised – and the overall non-adherence to standpoint theorisations in research. However, motherhood featured in a number of interviews. Frequently, the identity of the mother was strongly engrained into women's consciousnesses. Being a mother is often seen as synonymous with being a woman. Single women, lesbian women and transgender persons are not always considered to be valid options for women. A couple of times, I myself have been asked to express opinions 'as a mother' in public forums, despite it being common knowledge that I am childfree. Attribution of such 'maternal thinking', irrespective of whether a woman is a biological mother, has been theorised by Ruddick (1980) as being based on women's potential capacity as mother to bear / nurse children. Clearly, the state of 'childlessness' is not considered to be the norm; in fact, it is not perceived as a natural or normal state. It is rarely assumed to be a considered decision on the part of the couple, but rather seen as an unfortunate deficit in the woman. Kamalini Wijayatilake's research on the diverse experiences of women vis-à-vis cultural practices elaborates on this point: 'a childless couple is considered unfortunate. More so a woman who has not conceived or not given birth to a child, and is considered barren and an ill omen. She is thought of as inauspicious' (Wijayatilake 2001: 147). Furthermore, it is assumed that all women are compelled by a maternal urge, and any exception is 'unnatural'. Moreover, childless / childfree women are conceptualised as being in a state of constant desire to fulfil this lack: 'They're not seen as thanking their lucky stars for not having kids!!' (commented my respondent, Wishva).

It is considered commonplace, and possible for all women, to possess this inherent capacity to express 'a mother's' viewpoint. Consequently, women are expected to perform this gender role, or to express this so-called maternal urge at a social level: for instance, in the presence of children – especially infants. The inherent biological determinism[7] of such thinking is often missed. This was Wishva's perception of a mother's standpoint:

> Okay, because there isn't that much adherence to standpoint theory by researchers, obviously people don't come out and say – okay as a mother I am such and such ... as a mother I feel such and such ... but you know that is what is there – that is the assumption. You can relate that to this whole thing about 'mother and children'. There is this grouping together of women and children for purposes of research ... the inclusion of children into the women's perspective.
>
> (Wishva)

The standpoint of motherhood that is sometimes assumed needs to be worked out theoretically. A 'mother's perspective' continues to efface the perception of women as independent individuals; it also poses constraints to alternative lifestyles and life choices. Therefore such a perspective needs to be theorised as an intersection amongst other intersections – rather than a singular essentialised, biologically determined positioning. The affiliation to motherhood needs to be seen as a personal partiality of some researchers.

Disciplinary and ideological affiliations

Some WR researchers also identified themselves primarily with their disciplinary alliances or related ideological affiliations or theoretical approaches. Others from the sample of respondents interviewed for this study talked of their overall standpoint being a combination of key intersections, self-defining politics, theoretical positionings and disciplinary affiliations. The analytical training of the researcher (whether as a legal analyst, anthropologist, literary critic, educationist, or statistician) was crucial to conceptualisations of these researchers' standpoints: 'I'm a cultural anthropologist and that is part of my identity. I am also interested in gender analysis ... I don't consider myself necessarily as a feminist or Women's Studies person. I consider myself a social scientist' (argued another respondent, Rasika).

Rasika talked about how she perceived her positioning as a feminist or women's studies researcher as a limiting framework – in comparison to a 'professional' standpoint. In this context, feminist, gender or women's perspectives were seen as methods to be applied in research, rather than as methodology. The respondent's identification as a particular kind of academic was the dominant positioning.

Considering the marginal status of Women's Studies in the country compared to other research, and considering the allegations levelled against feminisms (Chapter 6), it is possible that this standpoint of discipline was consciously or even unconsciously adopted so as to provide legitimacy for ensuing research. The rigour of the specific disciplinary practice and the adherence to related methodologies / methods is emphasised. The conscious adoption of an academic or professional identity cannot be ignored, but needs to be theorised as a factor of researcher identification as well as a difference / opposition to a feminist standpoint.

While the rejection of a feminist standpoint to provide legitimacy for research may be politically strategic in the cases of both women's and disciplinary standpoints, the determination of some WR respondents to perceive feminisms as limiting cannot simply be dismissed as a Marxist notion of 'false consciousnesses', or as an appropriation of patriarchal values, or as a lack of feminist knowledge. What is it in a feminist standpoint (that focuses on women) that is seen as 'constraining'? If it is the 'limitation' of focusing only on women, then this has been addressed to some extent by gender studies and work on masculinities in some contexts. Or is it the 'limitation' of 'highlighting women at the expense of men'?

There are occasions, however, when researchers take a disciplinary standpoint from a feminist perspective. For instance, de Alwis (2004a) makes an effort to combine feminist politics with anthropological field research. In a study referred to in Chapter 6, she speaks from within feminist political practice about the Mothers Front in Sri Lanka. This standpoint challenges knowledge produced in the discipline of anthropology, which is generally perceived as a priori, and as not engaging in politics. de Alwis (2004a: 133) performs 'a contingent reading of the political efficacy of the Mothers Front in an attempt to circumvent unproductive binary readings of such movements as either essentializing or empowering, victimized or agentive'. She goes beyond a singular, all-encompassing and essentialising positioning. In her article, she repeatedly combines the discipline / praxis of anthropology with the discipline / praxis of feminism. It is both a methodological approach and a standpoint.

Dhamani, on the other hand, talks of the politics of her theoretical approach.

> Very often my work has been referred to by people as postmodernist, and you know, their term, it is usually complicated and has pejorative meaning, so that something in me, whenever I get this, I want to say, no no I don't think it's postmodernist. But it has some postmodern aspects as well. So I have now kind of got more reconciled to the fact that I'm actually trying to validate postmodernism – not all of it but I think it is still useful to think of in terms of postmodernism … there is a reaction to postmodernism as not political and that all it does is celebrating the fragmentary and therefore not really tied to social reality and processes. … But obviously, we have all been influenced by socialist feminism these are stands that we unconsciously adopt. Though I have not actually read literature that belongs to the socialist feminist movement, there is stuff that I have definitely internalized and used in my work.
>
> (Dhamani)

Dhamani problematised taking on a postmodernist perspective – in a context where researchers have already been influenced by socialist feminism and social democracy (Chapter 8). She provided indications of how the politics of standpoint may involve the attribution of a standpoint, irrespective of the writer's articulated positioning. At the same time, she concedes a degree of unconscious conditioning by uncritical reading. One outcome of this, 'the celebration of the fragmentary' in postmodernist theorising, has enriched standpoint through understandings of the intersections in identity / standpoint.

On the other hand, Kumerini, an interviewee for the book, defines her standpoint as follows:

> In a sense I think I'm basically a social democrat. I think I have now defined my political ideas. So basically not what I am – as far as I know – but what I am not – which is a Marxist – as I tell my friends now – we have all been through the phases of Marxism in our lives. So in that sense my framework is to basically to use feminism as a critique of existing

structures and move towards reform and what it means is basically building my life around international instruments of human rights – including economic, social and cultural rights which is why I call myself a social democrat – I tend to have rights-oriented frameworks.

(Kumerini)

Kumerini saw her feminist politics as stemming from a strong sense of social democracy and from a methodology oriented to women's rights. Her standards lay with the international instruments of the United Nations and the ontological currents of feminist internationalisms (Chapter 4). She categorised Marxism as a defining phase that many researchers go through. In a sense, the epistemological core of standpoint is in differentiation and critique of (in this instance) existing ideological, political and theoretical positions. Kumerini's positioning is defined to some extent by what she is not, rather than what she is: as propounded by de Saussure (2000) in regard to the linguistic sign. This begs the question whether the construction of standpoint necessarily requires an oppositional positioning for its definition (Sandoval 2004) in the long run.

Intersections of class

The following section does not, however, engage with an oppositional standpoint; rather, it is an example of an intersection that complements and nuances some of the standpoints within the WR research community. For example, the consciousness of class, or a formal critique from a Marxist standpoint, lays bare the interactions of power between or amongst specific social classes. A feminist / Marxist standpoint prioritises consciousness of women's oppression with class oppression. Respondent Jayani was very clear that a Marxist standpoint was an adopted perspective, in that it was the class that the researcher identified with as opposed to the class that the researcher came from. 'And here, it is not the class that you were coming from that matters but the class that you are working for that counts – to change society' (Jayani).

The stated consciousness and commitment of the researcher is critical in this understanding since one's standpoint was not seen as intrinsically linked to one's self, in terms of biology, for example (as in the case of a mother's perspective). On a personal level, another interviewee, Vivian, discussed the upper / middle / professional class practice of employing domestic aides to take on family duties during the absence of the mother. She expressed gratitude to the women domestic aides who enabled the privileges that she enjoyed as a researcher and lecturer:

I am always thinking that I am able to do all these things (teaching and researching) because of someone who has taken over my so-called duties as a mother. So that that is one responsibility that I very firmly believe in – and I don't think that I can divorce myself from ... somebody will make the bed, someone will clean the toilets – all those liberties and things that we take for granted around the house will be done.

(Vivian)

The traditional roles and responsibilities of a mother and wife that she has accepted need to be assigned to a paid worker so that she can earn the salary befitting her academic education and skills. Vivian (ibid.) did not seriously question her duties as a mother. A more developed Marxist feminist critique here would call for a further exploration of the issues of unpaid reproductive labour performed by the wife / mother within the family, the financial valuing of manual labour versus intellectual labour, and the implications of the feminisation of work categories related to caring.

A number of research studies that adopt a class perspective (whether as a particular theoretical framework or as an unconscious leaning) see economic empowerment as the main obstacle for many women, particularly at grassroots level. This is particularly the case in research studies that focus on class and labour-related issues. Take the literature on women migrant workers to the Middle East (see de Silva 1981; Dias and Weerakoon 1995; Weerakoon 1998); women workers in the garment industries (see Jayaweera and Sanmugam 2001); and women labourers and casual workers (see Rajapakse 1995; Kottegoda 2004b). The emphasis here falls more on what can be termed as approaches on gender, development and poverty alleviation[8] (Wickramasinghe 2000), as opposed to traditional feminist Marxist / socialist theorisations. Furthermore, as is to be expected within the historical, sociocultural and political positioning of Sri Lanka, the concept of class has compounded meanings. It is associated primarily with poverty and with the urban and rural divide – since a majority of the poor in Sri Lanka are situated in the rural areas. Underdevelopment can be seen as a lack of basic needs and amenities, few opportunities, limited access to credit and training; and these are key features of the poor. Poverty is also linked to other intersections such as gender, ethnicity, language and lack of education (Chapter 1). Thus, instead of seeing development theorisations and socialist theorisations pertaining to women / gender as conflicting, it is important to combine them. While this may be a simplistic analysis, I contend that the adoption of other standpoints sans an economic perspective would undermine the experiences and realities of a majority of women in Sri Lanka. Another of my respondents combined not only the intersections of class and gender, but also her disciplinary training:

Basically I, you see, identify with the oppressed group whether it is caste, class or gender and I have a kind of self-trained discipline in Marxism or Left ideology. Some of the phrases and phraseologies I use unconsciously fall into that frame. But of course class doesn't get framed by gender, so you have to sort of intersect gender – not in isolation can you talk about gender deprivations or class deprivations.

(Thamalini)

Thamalini also highlighted the fact that standpoint and intersections need not necessarily be consciously articulated. One's discourse could reflect these affiliations. The implication here is that neither standpoint nor intersectionality are stable, consistent states of being – whether it be women, motherhood, ethnicity, nationality, regionality or a discipline. Moreover, standpoints and particular intersections can be emphasised during specific historical moments, as will be argued in the next section.

Counter-communal stands

The sporadic ignitions of communal violence in Sri Lanka since Independence in 1948, and the slow burn of war since 1983, have led to periods of heightened communal[9] consciousness amongst all ethnic groups. These identity politics go beyond the benevolent liberal aspirations of ethnocentrism, pluralism or multiculturalism. Within Sri Lanka, they are invariably linked to projects of self-determination, separatism, state and counter-state militarisation, defence and terror. In comparison, nationalisms that arose from colonialism and the modernist project at the turn of the twentieth century, prior to Independence in 1948 from the British, led to the acquisition of certain liberal rights and opportunities for women, politically and economically (Chapter 1).

Today, however, a majority of feminists in Sri Lanka are compelled to engage with / fight against the fundamentalist, ethnocentric ideologies of Sri Lankan Sinhalese, Tamil and Muslim nationalisms. These fundamentalist standpoints espouse racial superiority, bigotry, intolerance, terror, militarisation and the oppression / objectification / radicalisation of women. I use the term 'fundamentalist' to imply essentialism, although Shaheed (2001) objects to the usage of the word fundamentalism because it erases the differences of historical and cultural specificities within countries, communities and regions, and because the term has been given legitimacy in Pakistan. Indian theorist Chhachhi (2005: 222) deconstructs the stability of the concept of communal identity: 'very often identities are constructed on an imagined commonality which is then given objective existence'. She discusses the mobilisation of certain identities as responses to various experiences in life: forced identities and lack of real choice, lead one to 'articulate, underplay or stress this form of identity' (ibid.). Individuals also seek group identities as a subconscious refuge, or to display blatant and strategic power, as in the case of fundamentalist identities (ibid.). At the final count, as Shaheed (2001) says in relation to women living under Muslim laws in Pakistan:

> All forms of what is called "fundamentalism" are ultimately political projects of appropriation of the public, social and personal spaces in which we exist – with the goal of gaining political and economic power. Sometimes such projects aim to maintain power and sometimes to challenge power. The critical element, however, in understanding these forces

that are lumped together under the banner of "Fundamentalism," is to analyze them from the perspective of power.

(Shaheed 2001: 1)

Sri Lankan identity politics have been a predominant sporadic reality since independence (as in many South Asian countries), but more insistently during the last three decades.

> I think there is a whole debate on cultural relativism, issues of identity, and one approach is nationalism. I am interested in looking at Tamil nationalism – being Tamils in different ways. The nationalism that was provided was safe and had some positive movement in its early stages. But what renders it into an oppressive movement?
>
> (Kumerini)

A keen reading of the interview with Kumerini implies an evolution / strands of nationalist standpoints – from aspirations of democratic, libratory politics to oppressive fundamentalisms to counter-communal standpoints, especially in times of crisis. In fact, Haniffa (2008) considers the practices of piety by a da'wa (preaching group) of Muslim women in Sri Lanka as a conscious political stand in response to the heightened ethnicities in the country. These variations convey some of the positionalities possible within identity politics. A feminist counter-nationalist standpoint rejects over-riding ethnocentrisms or fundamentalisms; instead, it promotes an ethnic perspective that is a counter to these dominant strands:

> As I was saying, on the one hand my training, and on the other, my personality – maybe because I come from a particular class I am not so concerned with social and economic issues. But being a Sri Lankan Tamil the identity of a woman becomes very important an issue. At one stage, though I am not particularly plugged into the nation or the ethnic group ... but most of the people that I come across are disturbed identities, you know, people who are have either mixed parentage or people who are visibly against the current of their ethnic groups or at odds with the Sinhalese community ... so identity has become a main focus.
>
> (Kumerini)

Kumerini explains away her lack of a strong racial affiliation as being due to the important intersections of her experiences, personality, and privileged-class background, in contrast to the more dominant viewpoint that fuels Tamil nationalism. She also deconstructs the assumed hegemony, racial purity and consent of communal identities. Similarly, Indian historian Thapar (2007) in her work provides an interesting deconstruction of a Hindu identity as a modern reconstruction of an imagined communal / religious unity in ancient India.

Unlike theorisations of standpoint that privilege difference as a democratic right, a postcolonial distinction or even a postmodern discernment, the dominant ethnic standpoints in Sri Lanka today are instituted and maintained through ideological imposition and militant control. The very act of taking a counter standpoint (to one's ethnicity) as sometimes valued in Western feminist theory can be compromising – given the extremist and sinister outcomes possible for those taking a counter-communal standpoint. As a result, non-dominant standpoints (for instance, Tamil / Muslim / Christian) are relentlessly manipulated or persecuted and intimidated into submission for political gain. This is done through a crisscross of fundamentalist notions and so-called actions of patriotism, allegations of betrayal and treachery, as well as various reprisals.[10] Furthermore, researching, knowledge and meaning-making are located in moments that are heightened by such tensions (Chapter 6). This is more so, right now, as I finalise this book, than ever before – as the bloody battles between the Sri Lankan state and the Liberation Tigers of Tamil Eelam spanning over twenty-five years are deemed to be over – at the cost of massive human consequences on both sides. Given the ongoing brutal repression of the media and other avenues of dissent by the Sri Lankan government, it is not possible to corroborate the conflicting claims of the numbers of people dead and wounded on both sides, and the exact numbers of Tamil civilians currently being interned in so-called welfare camps in the North. As argued by Haavind (2005), the knowledge in this book is situated in time – especially as the current juncture can be regarded as a crucial turning point in Sri Lankan politics when future possibilities seem ambiguous – given the lack of access to independent information.

South Asian / Asian positionings

While Sri Lankan researchers' identification with or alienation from local ethnic, religious, neo-liberal, and counter-Western nationalisms may be at best compounded and oppositional, and at worst perilous, it is another matter when it comes to a regional standpoint. This is especially so when it comes to 'theory coming out of India and South Asia because we know it is rooted in a context that is familiar and common to us' (as asserted by respondent Kamani). Otherwise too, regional associations and affiliations have been made on the basis of presumed commonalities. These comprise suppositions of South Asian nation states as territorial formations within this particular geographical region; shared regional political interactions spanning ancient millennia and the more recent Western colonial enterprises; as well as the dominant and increasingly fundamentalist religions of Hinduism, Islam, Buddhism and Christianity. Local cultures based on common agricultural, family, and religious values; the transitional neo-liberal stage in the development of these countries; highly visual women heads of states during the last three decades (in Sri Lanka, India, Pakistan and Bangladesh); as well as the internal political clashes and militarisation of these frequently authoritarian

nation states and their relations to / impacts on women; are taken to be further foundations for South Asian coalescence. But such positionings are
complicated, as pointed out by Dhamani, one of my interviewees:

> South Asia is my field of research I think it is just because I live here.
> South Asian is also a kind of categorization that is given to me and I've
> reconciled myself to living here and this is my field. And also I suppose
> from the outside because I'm quite often invited as a South Asian Fem-
> inist, right, I guess in a way it is an internalization of some of the ways
> that outsiders look at me, inviting me to various things or how they really
> introduce me at talks particularly in the international scene.
>
> (Dhamani)

For Dhamani, the adoption of a South Asian focus and standpoint was a
naming and categorisation that was imposed on her (the researcher) from
outside, as in the case of some of the other standpoints discussed earlier. Her
knowledge was distinctly perceived as being situated within a South Asian
context. As such, her standpoint seems to have been appropriated as a defence
mechanism in a situation where the option of identities for the researcher
seems limited. There are postcolonial politics at play here. The power to name
has been requisitioned by powerful and established knowledge authorities and
banks, as conceptualised by Said (1978).

Here, it is equally important to consider local and micro-divisions and
divergences of the South Asian region and the multiplicity and distinctions of
its indigenous cultures (for instance, within a country like India). These are
further complicated by geo-politics between over-riding regional colossuses
like India and Pakistan and by inter-regional religious / political fundamentalisms, rivalries and strife in areas such as Pakistan / Afghanistan, Kashmir,
North / East Sri Lanka. Furthermore, not all countries share comparable
colonial experiences, heritages and transformations into independent nations
(take the disparities between India and a country like the Maldives). There
are widely spaced moments in capitalist development / globalisation (for
instance between a country like Bhutan and Sri Lanka), and highly significant
political shifts taking place from monarchies to democracies in countries like
Bhutan and Nepal, while others like Bangladesh, India and Sri Lanka are
victims of the vagaries of 'democratic impulses' that defeat the aspirations of
long-term political stability.

The assumed commonality of geographical regions coming together is
deconstructed by another respondent Kamani in regard to Asian women –
another common group identification:

> I had been more and more preoccupied by the question – what is an
> Asian woman? Actually, if you look at the Time magazine or The Econ-
> omist or whatever, most of the time, by an Asian they mean East Asian.
> Asia has been defined by the Western world – one identity for the whole

of Asia. But it is such a vast region. And how can you compare a country like Japan with one like Afghanistan or even South Asia. If you look at it politically, then some women of some Asian countries have come together on some socio-political issues – but others have not ... There are some regional and sub regional alliances like SAARC, ASIEAN, or Asia Pacific Women's Watch, SANGATH. ... But the whole of identity politics, I see, as relating to a particular stage in capitalism and now globalization ...

(Kamani)

Kamani argued that (as with the South Asian countries) the differences between Asian countries far outweigh the commonalities that have been selectively (and perhaps temporarily) established for political and strategic reasons.

Another key point made by Kamani was her linkage of heightened identities to the global currents of capitalism. She argued that the significance of identity is a reaction to the vast, over-reaching and unifying aspects of globalisation. Of course, if applying a postmodern perspective, then identity politics are indicative of what can be seen as the whole postmodern condition of fragmentation and divergence. Whether it is Asian or South Asian identities / standpoints that were aspired to, they need to be recognised as a strategic means of meaning-making by focusing on commonalities or on differences. Moreover, such a strategy of taking a collective standpoint to expand political camaraderie and unity for the feminist project should only be undertaken with a full knowledge of the complications involved in so doing.

Making and unmaking theory

In this chapter I have made theory on methodology (epistemology) pertaining to some of the sentient interplays of researchers' standpoints, intersections and situatedness within the specific Sri Lankan contexts. I have done this through processes of identifying and applying structures and concepts, making assumptions, providing rationales, reasoning out and coming to conclusions. If we understand standpoint theory as possessing the crucial capacity to express the perspectives of the oppressed (Harding 2004b), then it is possible to identify many other collective standpoints within Sri Lanka. These include politics regarding language use (whether one is primarily proficient in Tamil, Sinhala or English), rural / urban affiliations that are also class indicators, educational status, as well as caste, lesbian and transgender perspectives. Revealing or constructing standpoints and intersections, as well as the situatedness of knowledge, is a form of accountability for the meanings made (Rich 2003), as it 'outs' the researcher in the process of knowledge and meaning-making to the utmost possible degree. The subjectivity of the researcher is politicised and conceptualised, in a collective sense based on assumed commonalities – or understood as oppositional stands based on resistance.

In this chapter I have also unmade theory on methodology pertaining to some of the sentient interplays of researchers' standpoints, intersections and situatedness within the specific Sri Lankan contexts. I have done this through the processes of questioning structures and concepts, deconstructing assumptions, destabilising rationales, unlocking possibilities and allowing for uncertainties. On the whole, in this chapter, feminisms became the core / totalising standpoint against which other standpoints were aligned or measured. Here, the assumed superiority of collective, subjugated knowledge may be questionable, due to its flimsy base of authenticity and its inability to represent itself. The multiple features of standpoint / identification convey that a one-dimensional approach towards identity is problematic: as argued by Maguire et al. (2006). Grillo (2006) points out that intersectionality, in particular, is indicative of the multiplicities and multibridities (Chapter 3) that constitute the researcher's fragmented self as a complex web of interests, identifications and impositions that are related to one another. It blends together the different aspects of a person's identity or standpoint and is a counterbalance to the essentialism of a singular standpoint. However, there will always be contradictions and complicities in identity crosscuts, intersections, overlaps and positionings (Skeggs 1997) given researchers' fluctuating sense of identities at given moments, dependent on the realities experienced. Thus knowledge and standpoints are located in terms of the crosscutting ontologies of communities, ground realities, time, class, biology, ideology, disciplines and regions, both by the researchers themselves and by others. These knowledges are then not only situated in specificity but are also temporal. Here, the question arises as to whether taking a postmodern perspective necessarily nullifies the political objectives of standpoint. In keeping with my overall inclusivist positioning, I maintain my argument that it is the combination of modernist and postmodernist standpoints that can provide a more nuanced political understanding of identity / standpoint as they are more reflective and constructive of both the commonalities and the specificities of the ground situation.

8   Ethics / politics

Feminist ethics / politics in meaning-making

In this final chapter, I will argue that the ethical / political impulses of women-related (WR) research (to be simultaneously understood as savoir and connaissances) are what constitute feminisms in Sri Lanka. How then are ethics / politics conceptualised and how do they operate in local research? I will discuss how key concepts / approaches of feminist politics and ethics such as altruism, liberal democracy and Marxism are engaged with in local research. I will argue that ethics and politics are also forms of strategy / action and methods at the level of feminist activism – despite the shortfalls in impact and achievement. What then are the practical advantages, challenges and limitations of feminist ethics / politics?

This chapter is also my final attempt at reconceptualising the 'categories' of WR research / writing: women, gender and feminisms. Having envisioned women as a global paradigm, and gender as an epistemology, this chapter will argue that 'feminisms' is a form of ethics / politics.

Women's lesser morality versus higher social expectations

Many religious discourses and practices often imply that women's spiritual, moral and mental integrity is lesser than men's (Christ 1992). In Sri Lanka, dominant ontologies pertaining to women's spirituality, morality and character have been rooted in the moral precepts relating to Buddhism, Hinduism, Islam and Christianity. These have led to conflicting and sometimes contrasting moral claims, explanations and practices relating to women. The negative ontological constructions of women in these theological and spiritual norms and religious / cultural practices impose tremendous pressure on women to be good – as has been theorised by feminist psychologists and other writers (Gilligan 1977; Hughes 2002).

This social standard (of a superior morality) that women are conditioned to aspire to can be seen as a partial consequence of the subordinated sexuality of women, and their relegation to care and servicing roles. In Asia, the social control over women is consolidated through intangible myths such as those of the long-suffering woman, the sacrificing mother, the dutiful wife, and the obedient daughter. In Sri Lanka it may be further complicated by the colonial remnants of anglicised Victorian moral codes of character, behaviour and chastity.

Unfortunately, feminists have both internalised and on occasion politicised ideals of moral superiority. There are essentialist portrayals of women as being naturally inclined towards peace and non-violence by Ruddick (1992), or of women as having a special relationship with the environment and Mother Earth (Nesiah 1996). Gilligan (1977), in particular, talks of the different forms of moral reasoning shown by girls and boys – based on care and responsibility on the part of girls, as opposed to justice and rights by boys. Despite the influence of postmodernism and poststructuralism, these arguments take the notion of difference (between men and women) to an extreme of polarised thinking – as universal, homogenous, naturalised and static. This results in higher moral expectations of women as opposed to men; and even higher expectations of feminists as opposed to non-feminists. Women are condemned as morally inferior if they step outside the socially prescribed roles / stereotyped characteristics (for instance, as single mothers, lesbians, older mothers or as being too independent or too severe). Any such perceived indiscretions or deviations from the prescribed moral and ethical norms are staunchly condemned, and sometimes punished. This is achieved not only through structural mechanisms and socio-cultural practices, but also through such means as social ridicule and notions of fear and shame (Wickramasinghe 2002a).

Feminisms as ethics and politics

In Sri Lanka, as elsewhere, feminisms have packed and multiple meanings, and there are negative connotations of colonialism, globalisation, anti-nationalism, elitism and deviancy attributed to the concept (Chapters 1, 3, 4 and 7). As far as positive understandings are concerned, feminisms are based on Marxist / socialist frameworks, liberal democratic ideals, lesbian feminism, Women in Development objectives, patriarchal analysis and empowerment goals, as well as gender mainstreaming. Here I do not attempt to distinguish between these varying theoretical strands (connaissances) and common understandings (savoir) of feminism. I am inclined towards considering them all as forms of 'feminisms' (Warhol and Herndl 1997b; Hesse-Biber et al. 2004), perhaps as part of a continuum (Beasley 1999). This is an inclusivist approach that sees / composes a broad, temporary commonality (though not unity) of objectives in the political / ethical impulses of WR research as being feminist – despite considerable differences.

For the Sri Lankan context, feminist research / writing, defined in political terms, is the following. It is a consciousness, analysis, critique, recommendation or activism:

- Against psychological, ideological, micro / macro / meso and structural forces of power and its transmissions that impact negatively on women.

- For the continuing ethical promotion of alternative choices and commitments towards various degrees of transformation for women (and men) via personal identities, divergent ideologies / discourses, socio-political and cultural policies, structures and practices, micropolitics and personal enactments – locally and internationally.

The term 'feminist' is utilised in WR literature for the following reasons: 1) its capacity to expose the inequalities and power differentials between men and women (and amongst women); 2) its commitment towards progressive structural and individual transformation for women; 3) the ethical means by which researchers aim to achieve these changes. Consequently, the correlations between power, the goal of social change for the better, and ethical methods are the foremost considerations in this conceptualisation of feminist ethics / politics.

Feminist research ethics have traditionally been concerned with the goals, processes and outcomes of research. Birch et al. (2002a) propose a wide-ranging, integrated and holistic approach to ethics, which amalgamates the empirical and the theoretical. They argue that feminists have not always responded ethically to the many issues that arise in researching, and promote the need for continuous ethical thinking. This involves the complex political / ethical issues of, for example, inclusion / exclusion, funding, consent, participation, representation, confidentiality, dissemination, outcomes and follow-up. Furthermore, Doucet and Mauthner (2002) have made a case for an integrated approach, combining these ethical issues of feminist research practice with those of the ethics of epistemology. In contrast, poststructuralist feminists like Ahmed (1998) have raised ontological and epistemological difficulties in engaging with presumptions of universalism and otherness from ethical perspectives.

As far as Sri Lankans are concerned, ethics in politics, governance, social and work institutions, and daily living are continually compromised. The greater part of this book was written when there were ferocious battles raging in the North of the country – with impunity (despite strong concerns for civilian safety). Today, even though the fierce war between the LTTE and the Sri Lankan state is deemed to be over,[1] the current regime continues its brutal repression of democratic actions and perverts the course of democratic institutions; it perpetuates sporadic violence through paramilitary activities (including abductions) with no accountability or larger civic concern. Political opportunism, greed and instability (rather than democracy), has led to frequent legislative elections and political horse-trading. Ethnic and religious fragmentations, and extreme positions of fundamentalisms, are common. Religion, morality and ethics are perverted and politicised for populist reasons. Law and order in day-to-day activities and personal interactions have broken down. The need to inspire ethical thinking and action in the country, a naïve objective perhaps, does not lessen in its urgency. It is relevant not only in feminist research, but in all spheres of activity and at all levels of life. Yet, it is not a goal that is theoretically unproblematic, or without methodological friction.

The ethical problematic of a politics of good

Vivian, an interviewee for the book, expressed this viewpoint:

> As a feminist she says she stands for certain ideals about women, we did not
> expect her to go out and have an affair with another woman's husband.
> She didn't care at all.
>
> (Vivian)

Here, the disparity between political aspirations and personal action is readily condemned. In many ways, feminists are expected to be morally and ethically superior to other women. It is possible that this is because feminists are perceived as openly espousing certain political / ethical ideas pertaining to 'oppression' and 'empowerment', 'iniquity' and 'equality', 'economic subjugation' and the 'upliftment' or 'good' of all women. Furthermore, there is an association between feminisms and sisterhood, collective activism and caring for one another. Any transgression of these stated principles seem to be prone to double censure: due possibly to a somewhat essentialist understanding of the personal as political and vice versa. As with any other political ideology and movement, the political and ethical aspirations of feminisms render it vulnerable to condemnation when there is a perceived contradiction between these aspirations and individual actions. But this can also be seen in the light of the general disapproval and rejection of feminism as Western, and the stereotyping of 'western women and feminisms' as 'morally lax' (Chapters 1 and 4), resulting in higher ethical expectations from local feminists. This conversely assumes that Sri Lankan non-feminists are untainted by such 'moral lapses'. The oppositions and juxtapositions related to feminist images (of the political and the personal, of aspirations and actions, of Western and Sri Lankan, of disapproval and approval, of the immoral and moral) bear significance because of the political need to reach a women's constituency (Chapter 4).

Farida, another respondent, referred to the political / ethical assumptions of WR research as having 'the objective of righting the wrongs and making things better for women' (Farida). The very same impulses within feminisms of doing 'good' for women (whether aspirational or actional) serve to define it. This raises unrealistic expectations of feminisms as ethics / politics. Furthermore, Mauthner (2000) cautions that it would be misleading for feminism or feminist perspectives to be seen as tantamount to ethical ways of working; as this can offer more than it can deliver. Nonetheless, ethics is an underlying concern of feminism – irrespective of what is expected / achieved – and needs to be engaged with pragmatically, as discussed by my respondents.

Edwards and Mauthner (2002) combine the political approaches to theories of ethics and of morality, and concentrate on the values of a feminist ethic of care. In the same vein, Gillies and Alldred (2002: 32) write of 'the need to broaden our conception of ethics to include the political objectives or interventions for research, as well as such questions about the ethics of knowledge relations'.

While these writers are interested in incorporating a political argument into what has been identified by feminists as ethical concerns, my interest is somewhat different. My attention falls on integrating ethics into what has been identified as the political projects of feminisms. This is because politics in research cannot be conceptualised in the abstract, separated from its sister, ethics, or isolated from its parents, epistemology and ontology. Ethics entails a concern about the individual's situation and research impact that goes beyond immediate political interventions. Furthermore, issues of ethics / politics are located / dependent on the research context and researcher subjectivity; from the conceptualisation of the research problem and the identification of politics / ethics, to addressing these issues. Ethics and politics are therefore ontological and epistemological matters.

At this stage, my concern is with what can be identified / conceptualised as a feminist ethics of political intention (Gillies and Alldred 2002) in Sri Lanka. As opposed to ethical aspirations relating to difference or universalism (Ahmed 1998), or exclusions or representation (Walker 2000) theorised in other contexts, my respondents and I identified altruism, liberal democracy and Marxism as constituting the dominant ethical / political motivations for feminist research activism in Sri Lanka. In Diagram 8.1, I portray these as a trio of overlapping impulses. However, I am not suggesting that they are the only political / ethical research impulses of feminisms in the country.

Ethics / politics of altruism

Take the sentiments of altruism as an ethical / political aspiration. In my study, researcher Kiyana made references to her field research, relating to rural women and the conditions of poverty facing them: 'sometimes you feel

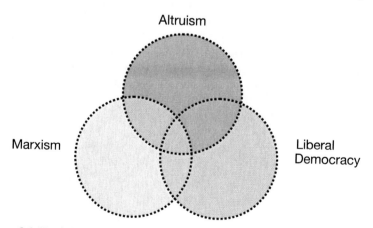

Diagram 8.1 Feminist politics / ethics

you walk into the field with these altruistic views – you know – wanting to do something for these women. To work long-term to improve the status of women' (Kiyana). The researcher identified her own altruistic intentions towards the women concerned. The women's standpoint adopted by her (Chapter 7) required a fusion of research with some form of welfare intervention. The political intent of such an outlook can be read in two ways. It can be read as emanating from the ideologies of compassion and 'dhana' related to the Buddhist and Hindu practices of giving alms and with Christian and Islamic concepts of charity. It can also be read as associated with welfare and development approaches that see women as the passive beneficiaries of development (Buvinic 1983; Moser 1993; Wickramasinghe 2000). The 'benevolence' of such a view is both politically and ethically oppressive and disabling, since it denies the women concerned the full status of both intelligence and agency. The impression of the researched women is as inactive and perhaps even helpless (Chapter 4).

However, this understanding was actively resisted by another of my research informants. 'I don't want to place them (the women concerned) in that marginal position because when you talk to them you find that they are very articulate, very conscious and very alert to the surroundings – both politically and otherwise' (Thamalini). She was very conscious of the fact that the placement of the researched women in a marginal position was an imposition on the researched by the researcher. Marginality in this context was related to the disabling conditions of poverty, war and the tsunami. Such a positioning contradicts and often hides the options, possibilities, agency and action open to the women concerned. Furthermore, altruistic acts of 'giving away money reinforces the power balance between researchers and the respondents which is a big dilemma for all of us working in the field. It is a defensive act that distances them professionally' (Deepa).

Deepa (ibid.) considered the implications of monetary and other donations within the researcher / respondent relationship. It reinforced power gaps and led to a ground culture of expectation from other researchers as well (not to mention the possibility of data corruption). Another criticism of altruism is its capacity to evoke inertia and dependency in recipients. In the case of the tsunami-affected people in Sri Lanka, as time went by, temporary welfare relief and recovery measures led to a culture of demand and dependency. This was especially so in the case of interventions which did not always offer long-term livelihood and other holistic options. What is of importance here (going by the views of Kiyana and Thamalini) is the way in which welfare recipients are constructed in the public consciousness as psychologically defective (Fraser and Gordon 1994)[2] and beyond redemption. One reason for this could be a strong sense of class discomfort / guilt, given the level of abject poverty and suffering encountered by researchers in some situations. There is no doubting the myriad issues faced by women in such a context. Take the example of my experience of a research situation where existing conditions of economic poverty, the burden of multiple roles and domestic violence were compounded by the political forces of civil conflict, and further exacerbated by an environmental disaster like the tsunami (which also led to increased violence against women). I suffered highly complex emotions of compassion, guilt, helplessness and defensiveness when faced with such realities.

The critiques of altruism then pose a different dilemma for researchers. In such an instance, the act of researching seems superfluous when confronted with the depths and dimensions of human suffering. While the women concerned face multiple layers and intersections of oppression, their pressing needs are material and welfare-oriented. Here, there is tremendous pressure on the researcher (implicitly and explicitly) to justify a research intervention that does not guarantee immediate (or any) direct dividends for the researched.

In view of our responsibilities as feminists to researched communities, sentiments of altruism, welfare and charity cannot be dismissed. Interventions can ill afford to ignore the burning material needs of women. On the other hand, research interventions that do not acknowledg women's agency or encourage self-reliance and long-term holistic empowerment (see Sen and Grown 1987; Batliwala 1993; Wickramasinghe 2000) of women[3] are also ethically / politically problematic. Furthermore, when it comes to some empowerment initiatives, there are assumptions made about the availability of women's time / space for organising, their limited access to information, and their powers in the domestic sphere (Banerjee 2008). I will be discussing how researchers try to balance and resolve some of the ethical quandaries relating to the expectations of the researched, through methodological means, later on in this chapter.

Ethics / politics of liberal democracy

Another ethical / political factor that motivates WR research is the goal of democracy. While early democratic values in the country are rooted in the Buddhist philosophy of the sanctity of life, individual rights, equality, meritocracy, convergence and tolerance, modern democracy in Sri Lanka originated in some of the colonial interventions – especially by the British – from the nineteenth century onwards. What are considered political principles first and foremost, are also ethical values that promote standards for how life should be lived:

> If you think that 51% of any given population, (in Sri Lanka) is the population of women, and you see that they suffer more difficulties, more problems as human beings, then ... the research study has to be a vehicle for effective change.
>
> (Gayathri)

Evident from the above quotation by Gayathri is the wider feminist research project of fulfilling the rights of the majority in the population of Sri Lanka – women. Here, it is not only the issue of women's majority representation in the country, but also the issue of women's compounded difficulties, and suffering that comes to the fore. It is possible that the recurring idea of women as 'suffering' – physically and mentally – takes its origins from dominant Buddhist conceptualisations of karma: of life as suffering and women's lives as more unendurable than men's. Consequently, research is perceived as having a moral obligation to promote democratic and effective change – 'to make things better'. This is based on the understanding that critiques, protests and demands for inclusion are adequate responses to women's oppression within a so-called liberal democracy. At the ground level of feminist research activism some of these democratic goals are visible in the anti-war and peace movements, in free-trade zone activism, in campaigns against violence against women, in United Nations initiatives, and in the lobby for women's political representation. Politically, the perspective reflected here and elsewhere in research involves conceptual frameworks pertaining to human rights, women's rights, empowerment, gender equity / equality, and justice. They are also appropriated for ethical purposes.

Kiribamune (1999a), citing Lisewood, argues for women's political participation: 'democratic principles should ensure for everyone competitiveness in the political sphere and that elementary fairness should put women in some proportion to their numbers in the population' (Kiribamune 1999a: 3) In this case, democracy is seen as an ideal which if applied, can ensure women's equitable participation in politics. It assumes that competitiveness is an acceptable value and that it is inevitably fair. Unfortunately, liberal democracy as an abstract ethical aspiration does not necessarily engage with the larger environment of political instability, harassment and violence that does not allow a level playing field for local women's political participation. Associated research on the subject by Kiribamune (1999a) throws light on the structural and psychological deterrents discouraging women's access to politics such as threats of physical violence, public humiliation and character assassination.

One challenge for the feminist democratic impulse, particularly in today's context, is how to relate to the existing conditions of inequity, aggression and political extremism within the country that may stultify research activism. Are feminists to put their agendas on strategic hold until such time as a sense of stability and ease of access to negotiate / lobby with the forces of power prevails? Are they to join together with 'undemocratic' forces on a temporary basis, to maximise possible opportunities to achieve limited democratic objectives? Or are feminists to initiate / continue their resistance against the arrogant usurpation and daily contraventions of legislative, executive and judicial powers in the face of very real dangers of intimidation and physical violence? In which case, are feminists then to make alliances with other civil society groups for the wider political goals of basic human rights?

While these may seem reasonable options, 'the realities' of the situation do not offer such precise alternatives or clear-cut strategies – even within a liberal analysis. Complications include a façade of liberal democracy, created through consecutive mandates by the people in favour of this regime (despite extensive election violations), and highly politicised so-called victories over the LTTE (despite the massive cover-up of casualties and transgressions). The intimidation and harassment of those identified as 'traitors', and the brutal suppression of dissenters are camouflaged by the rhetoric of militarism / militarisation (de Mel 2007) and a pervasive, persuasive 'post-war' ethos of nationalism (Chapter 7). The political harassment and extermination of 'Western elements' (NGOs), those denounced as the traitorous media, and social and women's activists are covered over by a blanket of highly visible small-scale infrastructure projects / exhibitions that give the impression of big development. Diminishing access to the state media (due to rigorous government regulation) and mainstream private media (due to political sycophancy, slavishness and self-censorship) weaken feminist activisms. Given the difficulties of clear-cut condemnation within this ideological space – especially in view of the way in which the war is combined with Sinhala-Buddhist patriotism / authenticity / government support / Sri Lankan-ness as opposed to peace, which is combined with treachery / dissenters / Western-alienness / illegitimacy – feminists are propelled to undertake a number of differential strategies. These include postponement (in terms of the Women's Rights Bill), negotiations within limited spaces and without many dividends (such as political quotas for women), protest on wider issues as part of civil society (against racism and ethnic cleansing), and tentative coalitions for democracy. In other words, feminist objectives may not always be realised in the way that they have been conceptualised. They may require prioritising, strategising, compromise, deferment or collaboration.

Ethics / politics of Marxism

The politics of Marxism have been visible in Sri Lankan women's movements from time to time – from women in the Labour movement of the mid-twentieth century onwards (Muttiah et al. 2006) to more contemporary agitations for better working conditions in the Free Trade Zones (Chapter 1). However, such activities have not been confined to labour rights in the past but have encompassed some of the same issues as the democratic agenda: the repeal of the Prevention of Terrorism Act, the release of the first Tamil woman political prisoner, and a peaceful solution to the ethnic conflict (Samuel 2006a, 2006b).

Usually, the ethics of Marxist action are subsumed within its political objectives. Furthermore, much of Marxist action is in activism rather than research. Respondent Jayani opens the debate by pointing out that the concepts of feminist activism were relative. For instance, it is possible to identify feminisms even when the language of feminisms was not available (Nesiah 1996). Jayani argued that 'virtually anyone could be argued as being feminist'. Citing Marx, she (ibid.) qualified feminism in her understanding as being:

> based on the Marxist theorem that it is not enough to understand society, you had to change it. In applying that feminist consciousness you have to

do something through the women's movements and never give up on the action – which has been there before – even before research started. So it is action research, and continuous action mixed with research.

(Jayani)

For Jayani, there was an ethical obligation to be contingent and emancipatory in feminist research and activism – at the ideological level. On the other hand Thamalini, who works in a women's NGO, emphasised the ethical problem of such emancipatory research in practice:

We used to interact with the women at an ideological level – class is vital. But there are so many structures of oppression that we are not able to handle at the level of a researcher. So we stopped raising consciousness, alongside the research project. Because, what happens after you raise consciousness?

(Thamalini)

Here, Thamalini problematised the classical Marxist concept of consciousness-raising that is seen as leading to emancipatory action. She made the point that consciousness-raising alone is insufficient to deal with the multiple forms of oppression faced by the women concerned. Thamalini's activism was not in organising these communities, but in gender training and lobbying at the different levels and institutions in society. While her organisation's interventions spanned from the individual to the structural, they did not always strengthen the capacity of the researched to direct their own futures, since this requires additional investment and more sustained effort on the part of an NGO. There is an ethical and political dilemma implied in concluding a research intervention in consciousness-raising, when an NGO is not involved in parallel community mobilisation / empowerment. Of course, the question remains as to what extent external forces can be responsible for individual self-determination as well as the degree to which this is possible. This issue resonates with some of the predicaments of the feminist consciousness-raising projects in the West during the 1960s and 1970s (Stanley and Wise 1983a, 1993).

Chapter 7 implies that the respect for differences needs recognition as a key ethical / political value – not only in relation to collective identities, but also individual fragmented subjectivities. The failure to consider commonalities and unities within and across differences (such as coalitions, common interests / political actions undertaken, common standpoints taken) may also lead to essentialism. Consequently, expectations, impositions, obligations, risks, stereotyping, 'othering' and guilt relating to differences are some issues that need to be theorised from ethical / political perspectives.

I have argued so far that the apparent political agenda of feminisms – whether it be altruism, liberal democracy or Marxism – has very strong ethical connotations that are founded on social reform. Researchers have identified / strived to fulfil these abstract political / ethical principles through strategic thinking and tactical interventions. It is precisely this issue of the ethics of political strategising and action that I will be dealing with in the next section.

Thus as far as WR research activism is concerned, the integration of feminist political and ethical aspiration can be conceptualised as in Diagram 8.2.

This diagram is proposed because, in a wider sense, feminisms can be seen as an aspiration of political and ethical principles towards doing good / better – as identified by Edwards and Mauthner citing Kvale (2002: 20). As this may provoke some methodological problems, feminisms can next be seen as strategising in terms of translating political and ethical aspirations into practicable action. In other words, I am referring to the 'utilitarian ethics of consequences' (ibid.). Here of course, questions of possibility and effectiveness need to be addressed. Within the research project, feminisms can be seen as a method of striving to eliminate or to clarify any process-related political and ethical concerns of the researcher. Here again, there are questions as to what extent it is possible to do this: and what purpose the overall objective of epistemologically verifying and reflecting on ethical and political concerns would serve. However, the diagram below does not constitute isolated,

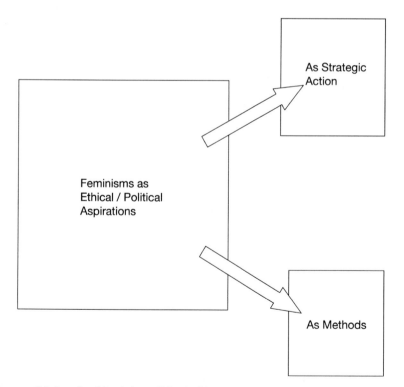

As Strategic Action

Feminisms as Ethical / Political Aspirations

As Methods

Diagram 8.2 Levels of feminist politics / ethics

abstruse activities or models; rather it represents the inter-related features of feminist ethical politics.

Feminist ethics as political strategy and action[4]

> Feminism begins with a reformist, I think it is more of a revolutionary impulse – like to change the world for the better for women specifically, and for everybody else in general – I suppose.
>
> (Vivian)

Respondent Vivian talked about the 'transformative' element of feminist research (Harding 1987b). She looked at this goal in a wider sense, as not only encompassing change for women, or for the individual woman, but also for wider social structures. In order to transform the political and ethical goals of research and writing, Sri Lankan researchers use various types of political strategies / action that can be conceptualised as the operationalisation of feminist political ethics.

Vivian discussed the need for strategy in addressing the issue of feminism as a foreign concept with her characteristic humour:

> I think that feminists and women's activists in Sri Lanka have realised that feminism or any other women's activism is all perceived as a Western import and, therefore as I always say, along with ham, butter, cheese and bacon and sausage which are all seen as Western imports is not good for the local body, does not digest. Feminism too does not digest. So, therefore one has to find a way of introducing the topic of women and women's rights without resorting to a vocabulary perceived as that.
>
> (Vivian)

Here, once again, Vivian referred to some of the ultranationalist and populist sentiments floating around the country against westernisation / globalisation (Chapters 1 and 4), and to how the indigenous is valued almost in physical terms. In the face of resulting antagonism, she argued that it was necessary for feminists in the country to be strategic in raising feminist issues – for pragmatic reasons. This may entail not using the term 'feminist', constructing / representing indigenous histories of women's agitation, and including women in development / poverty frameworks. Such strategic action is deemed necessary so as not to alienate the women's constituency that may, in fact, harbour some of the same anti-Western opinions (Chapter 4).

These political stratagems raise a number of potentially ethical issues. The de-linking of research activism from Western feminisms is ostensibly designed to gain social acceptance and credibility, to slip in a feminist agenda without attracting undue attention from women and their communities. But such a strategy implicates the honesty and integrity of the researcher / activist. While the choice of emphasising one strand of WR activism amongst many (Chapter 4) is a pragmatic option, it is taken as a political measure that creates an oppositional to 'Western feminisms'. Further, such a debate can easily get centred around Sri Lanka's colonial legacy, neo-liberalisation, globalisations, and moral corruption on the one side; and around the demand for purity, the search for and glorification of the indigenous and national sovereignty / integrity, on the other. However, simply debunking fundamentalist and prejudiced worldviews of feminisms as essentialisms merely serves to deepen these chasms and may not serve a political objective. John (2004a), who problematises debates between Indian and Western feminisms offers two lines of enquiry based on the integration of the historical, the cultural and the economic. One is to analyse meanings related to social locations in group identity formation, while the other is to map the ways in which Western theories and thematisations have been restructured and mediated (within the Indian context).

Strategic pragmatism

A more pragmatic approach, that weighs the pros of the political / ethical premise that feminisms are good or appropriate for the women concerned, against that of the cons of strategic action and methods, may be appropriate in field situations. Thus, research impact comes under consideration.

Thamalini questioned the extent to which emancipatory knowledge can lead to individual awareness and actual 'oppositional consciousness', or collective empathy and action. Kiyana referred to an instance where a Muslim survivor of domestic violence actually left her husband, and got a divorce, after consciousness-raising sessions on violence against women. However, the subsequent ostracisation of this woman by her family and community raised different ethical issues – especially in a context where a woman's family and community play vital roles in her life. Gayathri deepened this argument by critiquing the fact that researchers do not follow up at the individual level, where possible. We therefore return to the question: where does the researcher's responsibility for raising consciousness begin and end, given the different levels of oppression and intersections of gender and other inequalities? While Maynard and Purvis (1994a) refer to issues of social responsibility, ongoing support, and boundaries between therapy and research, given the lack of capacity within the Sri Lankan context such follow-up interventions are not always possible. The aim of political action may have been fulfilled, but what of the ethical?

By posing straightforward questions in ways that are founded on oppositions and exclusions, researchers can answer these critical questions relating to the benefits / goodness assumed vis-à-vis the research impact. On the other hand, by posing different questions such as those relating to alternative, partial and provisional outcomes researchers can engage with the same issues of goodness assumed vis-à-vis the research impact at a different level altogether.

This is identified as an ethics of consequences model, and observed to be 'underlain by universalist cost-benefit result pragmatism' (Edwards and Mauthner 2002: 20). I take this to mean that there is a practical rationale in feminist action that weighs up the pros and cons of the political / ethical dimensions of the research intervention. I applied such a rationale to the ethical aspirations of research in the earlier section.

I take the position that neither the ethical aspirations nor actualisations of research take place in a vacuum. Therefore a pragmatic approach is vital if research is to be relevant, useful and inspire change. In fact, I would go on to term this 'strategic pragmatism', due to the strategic nature of such a stance and action. The institution of the Domestic Violence Bill (2005) into legislation in Sri Lanka exemplifies the point. The Women and Media Collective (WMC), a self-identified feminist organisation had, over the years, done a number of studies on violence against women. In the late 1990s, with the help of lawyers, they drafted a Bill on Domestic Violence. This document was used to raise consciousness about, and lobby for legislation against domestic violence at government, legislative, public and women's forums. Due to sustained activism by the WMC, and other women's organisations (such as CENWOR and WERC) and individual activists, the State was prevailed upon to draft its own Domestic Violence Bill. Though there were many theoretical and attitudinal differences between the two Bills (a key issue being the emphasis on children, in the State version), in the end women's groups supported the State version on the pragmatic grounds that any Bill on Domestic Violence sponsored by the State had a number of advantages. It recognised domestic violence as a legislative issue. It raised a degree of public consciousness about the practice. It had the capacity to provide women with some level of protection. Women's groups saw it as 'a strategic battle that had not been finalized but that needed to be fought on many fronts, on many grounds, over a period of time, until we get what we want' (argued my respondent, Wishva).

Such rationalisation exemplifies the position of strategic pragmatism. On the other hand, strategic pragmatism has its own problems. As noted earlier, some of the dominant women's groups and activists are politically and strategically selective in the causes that they espouse: understandably even more so now, given the political context. While feminists have come out strongly on the more pervasive issues such as peace, political participation and domestic violence against women in the past, the more politically tangible developments in the country have not always been taken up. For instance:

> there is a lapse when it comes to collective mobilization on some of the issues we have been working on – example is the violence against women in politics. Remember some years ago, the woman who was stripped when she went canvassing for a mainstream political party. You know, we didn't take a stand on that. Because we have steered clear of party politics.
>
> (Gayathri)

Here Gayathri, a leading women's rights researcher, talked of the problems of bringing women together when it came to a contentious political issue that involved critiquing a political party. Because party politics in the country is perceived as being highly politicised, dirty, corrupt and violent, it has been politically expedient for feminists to steer clear of taking a stand on some of the local political issues. This has been a strategic decision, and a number of feminists justify the stand on the basis that, if they were seen as politically 'neutral' and independent regarding mainstream political divisions, other concerns that are espoused by feminists would acquire legitimacy. This is one instance where strategic pragmatism becomes highly problematic. In one sense, feminist ethics have been compromised for the pragmatic purpose of maintaining feminisms as disengaged from party politics in the country. Yet, given the overall abject lack of integrity within the Sri Lankan political scenario, the very complicated stand of political neutrality (although a myth from a postmodern feminist perspective), is very frequently perceived as a position of opposition. It is my contention that, as feminists, we clearly need to rethink our position in terms of how we engage in or with the mainstream politics in the country. One possible course of action would be to coalesce on an issue basis, within a broad front. Strategic pragmatism is not a positioning that is without problems, but neither is it a positioning without advantages.

Feminist politics / ethics as methods

> We need to think of concrete methods to safeguard ethics.
>
> (Respondent Dhamani)

Hitherto, I dealt with the ethical / political implications of conceptualising and operationalising feminist politics in research / action at a macro level. I now engage with ethics and politics at the micro level: in research methods.

Responsibilities and accountability

Here I do not separate concerns of epistemology from those of research practice. Following Mauthner et al. (2002), I too argue for the ethical responsibility and accountability of a researcher for the feminist politics that she propounds and activates. Accordingly, such responsibility and accountability should be directed towards the entire research process – from the moment of conceptual designing to data analysis, and from writing up to dissemination (Doucet and Mauthner 2002). Yet, given the limitation of space, I confine myself to the following areas: the researcher and her family; the funders of research and research participants; the discipline of Women's Studies and its epistemic community.

My interviewees conveyed that being responsible and accountable for research processes began with the researcher and her family. After all, from a modernist perspective, the researcher needs to be true to herself in researching. This involves her clarity and honesty towards the various choices and decisions she makes; the ontological, ideological, epistemological and theoretical positions that she occupies; and her relationship with those who come in contact with the research process. It also requires candour in regard to research motivations, and responsibilities towards the consequences of research at the societal, institutional, epistemological and personal levels. Yet, such honesty is conceptualised according to postmodernist terms – not as an abstract principle but reliant on pragmatism, provisionality, contingency and conscious subjectivity.

Externally, the researcher is responsible to the people and forces that allow for the opportunity and the freedom to pursue research. This includes the researcher's immediate family, funders, colleagues and support staff. In Chapter 7, I discussed informant Vivian's Marxist interpretation of the two intersections / clash of responsibilities between her children and the contributions of her domestic staff towards the production of her research. While the researcher can acknowledge and give account to the people who provide indirect as well as direct support for the research process, how can the researcher practically recognise or repay such a debt? On the other hand, such obligations may also be located in the ideological valuations imposed on so-called maternal responsibilities (priceless), paid domestic work (undervalued), and academic work (social status and cultural capital).

The personal advantages and benefits of the research for the researcher also need to be made explicit. Researcher Sadia spoke of the ethical considerations of funded research, the need to take into account the monetary aspect of research, and personal economic imperatives that can drive research. Other personal benefits, such as the conferment of educational qualifications and promotions, and the creation of academic or intellectual stature, are considerations that require ethical analysis and explication. Researcher honesty and critical assessment are also necessary regarding funding sources. Some research organisations / researchers currently work in accordance with unofficial internal criteria that arise from global politics. Since the invasion of Iraq by the USA in 2003, for example, they have spurned funding from US state donor organisations. Moreover, there are the implications of the political, economic and ideological challenges faced by researchers and writers due to unfair research practices such as global cutbacks in research funding, the imposition of donor interests, the disparity in payment for local and foreign researchers, and the politics of consultancies.

The self-reflexive exposition and problematisation of these issues would not necessarily 'resolve' the issues concerned. As Mockler (2007) observes, ethical dilemmas are located in a broader context than that of the research enquiry. While self-reflexivity would grant methodological rigour and validity to the research (Chapter 3), it would also accentuate / construct the indeterminate, unsolvable, unstable aspects of meaning-making.

Sensitivity to respondents

Concern about the relationship between researchers and respondents was also raised in my interviews. Take the ethical implications of interviewing women who were affected by war and (sometimes concurrently) the tsunami. The researcher's sensitivity and assurances of confidentiality in engaging with and representing those affected by psychological trauma were key issues. Researchers have to ensure that survivors / victims are not re-victimised through the interview / representation processes. My respondents highlighted the emotional consequences of interviewing the vulnerable such as relieving feelings of pain and suffering, loss and grief, abuse and humiliation, helplessness and despair:

> In writing up cases of violence against women I try to keep to strict human rights methodology and just stick to facts and try to minimise the salacious aspects of that and secondly, I try to give her voice, the voice of the person, than say, my own analysis of it. But you see in her own articulation of it, there is the first-hand experience of violence. You know the moment she reflects on it she sees herself as a victim ...
>
> (Kumerini)

Kumerini (ibid.), a respondent interviewed for my book, raised three issues pertaining to representation. One is that of balancing 'facts' with methodology so as to eliminate the sensationalist and stimulating aspects of violence reportage. While this can be attempted to some extent, the second issue of being 'true' to the voice of the respondent is more complicated, as representation involves selectivity and editing on the part of the researcher. The third issue is one of compassion. Kumerini is highly sensitive to the fact that, in the remembrance and articulation of violence, the respondent is reliving her experiences for the research process. But of course, such retelling may also be 'a cathartic process for the women victims and survivors', as suggested by Wishva, and there may be a deep psychological need to do so.

Sensitivity also includes ensuring that respondents are not exposed to political retaliation by organisations such as the LTTE, JVP or the government of Sri Lanka. There is the importance of 'dealing with women who are politically vulnerable, issues relating to what kind of reprisals can take place – changing names but presenting them in a way that they are not completely alienated from the context' (Dhamani).

Dhamani related an incident where the epistemic value of a particular respondent's narrative of LTTE atrocities was such that exposure in research would have jeopardised the respondent. Changing her name was not an option as she was highly recognisable in the village through her experience of victimisation. Consequently, this woman's account of violence had to be excluded from the research. Several issues come to the fore here – not only that of the grave risk of retaliation for the research respondent, but also those of exclusion in research, authenticity in the representation of the respondent, validity in the representation of the respondent's experience, and the researcher's divided responsibility to the respondent and to the research. The political ethics of research require the prioritising and balancing of the ethical implications of each issue: not only vis-à-vis the research processes but also in regard to the larger reality. Ethical decisions are not only subjective, but they are also contextual in meaning-making.

One more point of interest pertaining to the representation of respondents is how researchers impose their own ideological standpoints and epistemological frameworks upon the respondents (Chapter 6). Take the contentious issue of domestic violence, which some respondents view as the norm and not necessarily to be resisted. Simply writing off such a perspective as false consciousness is problematic as argued by Stanley and Wise (1993). An ethical dilemma arises when conceptualising of the horrendous action of violence set against the needs of the woman in terms of the economic support, family strength and protection required from her husband. Furthermore, Dhamani pointed out 'you may be reading into it a story of tremendous social survival but this may be not what the respondent experiences herself' (Dhamani). Conversely, what the researcher portrays in terms of victimisation may well be perceived by the respondent as a story of survival. The necessity to temper interpretations by allowing or prioritising the respondents' narratives, perhaps by using reflexivity in researcher intervention and inconclusive commentary, are vital in this context.

My own experiences of researching revealed that sensitivity includes toning down or eliminating the overt display of indicators relating to the researcher's identity – in terms of class, race, and language, and including dress and modes of transport. For example, I would not go into drought-stricken, poor villages of Moneragala[5] in the luxurious air-conditioned comfort of an SUV four-wheel drive, dressed in jeans. This would not only flaunt the class, power and privilege of the researcher, but it would also jeopardise rapport with respondents.

Stacey (1991) discusses some of the problematic issues of how researchers, in effect, manipulate respondents for the purpose of collecting / constructing data. Though an element of dishonesty towards respondents cannot be denied here, it is important to question whether, as individuals, we are honest in all our relationships. Are there not particular aspects of identity that we highlight and mask (both consciously and subconsciously) depending on the person / context concerned? Even when there is no necessity to hide one's identity, a softening of identity markers may be required to ensure that the interaction is as equitable as possible, to prevent cultural alienation. It can also be argued given that no interaction is completely honest, it is not possible or necessary to reveal oneself completely to others all of the time. Researchers need, however, to achieve a balance between pragmatism and sensitivity in respondent relationships.

Epistemic community

The researcher's responsibility and accountability within the discipline of Women's Studies and the concept of a feminist epistemic community

(Ramazanoglu and Holland 2002), are other issues that concern Sri Lankan ethical politics. This imagined community, though not homogeneous, implies 'the negotiation of commonalities across differences' (Ramazanoglu and Holland 2002: 139), as well as some degree of empathy and loyalty.

Several ethical issues are important here. One is that of the lack of regard by many researchers for preceding research done by local feminists (Chapter 6). Admittedly there is, on the whole, a paucity of local theorisations. However, researchers do not always convey an awareness of the many empirical studies conducted on such issues as domestic violence or women in the economy; nor do they offer extensive literature surveys. While Sri Lankan feminists of international standing are cited, there is an overall sense that feminist research on certain topics is constantly being reinvented. The lack of comprehensive surveying of local women's studies literature is a highly problematic ethical issue, considering the thirty years of women's research in the country. It is not only an insult to previous research, it also prevents the institution of continuity, engagement and tradition in Sri Lankan Women's Studies. The consequent dearth of lively discussion and debate are detrimental to the robustness of the discipline. While this book is one attempt to lend academic credibility to Sri Lankan Women's Studies, much more needs to be done in terms of writer interactions, literature reviewing and theorising.

Arising from this is the related issue of plagiarism. This may be due to the lack of formal training on ethics and methodology, or simply to academic tardiness. Researchers talked of a number of instances where colleagues have plagiarised their work with impunity. But it was this notion of an epistemic community of feminists, of contributing towards collective knowledge-making, which prevented Dhamani and Gayathri from taking action against plagiarism. I too did not raise the issue when a friend failed, on many occasions, to acknowledge my verbal inputs in her work. Of course, this is to be counterpoised with issues of academic practice, such as the complex issues of intellectual honesty, and the value of intellectual properties, and copyright, which need to be resolved.

Sadia brought up the crucial issue of feminists researching the women's movement: how the collective / collaborative aspects of women's activism got diluted due to lack of acknowledgements and methods of representation. The researcher concerned became the authority on the women's movement. Again, the critical issue of intellectual property rights is foregrounded, along with concerns relating to the ownership and sharing of information, collaborative authorship, and expertise on feminist issues. Several questions need consideration: who should do WR research? Should women activists undertake their own research? How should feminists disseminate data in unwritten form?

One response to these questions and other ethical concerns raised here would be for women's researchers, activists, and research organisations collectively to formulate provisional ethical guidelines on researching. Not as commandments etched in stone, given the unfeasibility of applying a uniform, overarching framework to all situations. But rather, as open-ended, evolving possibilities that would create consciousness and direct researchers on the concerns expressed here (accountability, responsibilities to the epistemic community, sensitivity and representation) as well as other political / ethical issues. Guiding principles for such ethics could be based on 'commitments to contradictions and contextualized moments', 'temporal agreements', 'short-term agendas' and 'bottom lines' as advocated by Manila-based feminists vis-à-vis global feminist critical collaboration (de Vela et al. 2007).

At the epistemological level, this chapter exemplifies how politics / ethics are not only issues of methods and subjectivity, but also ontology, epistemology and theory in operation. My analysis of the politics / ethics in feminist research focused on the difficulties of transforming political and ethical aspirations into research action and methods, given the fracture between modernist theoretical understandings and the intricacies, differences, disunities and instabilities encountered / conceptualised in ground situations. Critiques of altruism need to be reconsidered in the light of respondents' dependency and multiple, intersecting oppressions. Adhering to abstract conceptualisations of liberal democracy has become problematic in heightened situations where the play of violence requires strategising. Marxist impulses reflect on the possibilities and extents of self-empowerment through such action as consciousness-raising. Yet, despite the vast conceptual disparities in the aims of altruism, liberal democracy and Marxism, I have argued for / constructed methodological similarities in their operation. Here, I have discussed the theoretical position of pragmatic strategising as a provisional means of addressing the complexities overwhelming research aspirations, action and impact. Though not without its own problems, strategic pragmatism can prevent a resort to essentialist understandings of aspirations and achievements. The method of reflexivity is also proposed to depict and problematise ethical concerns, even though it does not offer 'resolutions' to ethical dilemmas. Finally, ethical guidelines, again offered provisionally, can direct researchers on some method-related conflicts.

Conclusions

Towards a feminist research methodological matrix – making meanings of meaning-making

A conclusion is a formal ending; a summary of an epistemic construction; an expression of prescriptive findings; a final judgement / deduction based on positivist reasoning or provisional postmodern deconstructions. While conclusions may not be feasible from a postmodernist perspective, there could be intimations of possibilities, contingent and provisional understandings, multiple meanings, and ever-shifting deconstructions. There are expectations of recommendatory solutions that can be perceived as 'hegemonic arrogance' (Morley 1999: 185) from a conclusion. My conclusions are all of the above. Another of the governing conclusions, that of a framework of feminist research methodology, has already been worked into the body of the book. Yet despite the dangers of the certainties of research conclusions (Morley 1999), I firmly believe that researching needs to have a provisional, practical outcome that is useful: at the specific level, or at a wider social level, or at the level of the academic discipline of Women's Studies, or all three. It is on the basis of such an understanding that I have proposed this methodological framework for feminist research methodology. The objective of such an exercise has been to infuse / combine better the abstract methodological concerns of researching, not only with the specificities of a particular research project, but also with larger social concerns. This would not only highlight the political relevance of feminist research but also make the research process more transparent, efficient, useful and methodologically rigorous.

This framework is conceptualised as a methodological matrix emanating from global theorisations, the local ground realities and my theoretical inputs. It has both fixed and stable underpinnings as well as fluid potentials that can be pragmatically engaged with / applied. It is modernist, structuralist, subjective, and constructivist in the way that I categorise commonalities and generalities, and frame and focus, converge and integrate what are considered aspects of feminist research methodology (subjectivity, ontology, epistemology, methods, theory and politics / ethics). It is postmodernist in the way that I construct / engage with differences, fluidities, instabilities, temporalities, intersections and overlaps within; and in the way that it may reflect fragments, contradictions and irrationalities in me.

The matrix is a broad theoretical framework that has the capacity to encompass any research situation. The matrix is concurrently a contingent framework – since its aspects are dependent on the possibilities, certainties, pragmatism and contingencies of each research situation. 'Tracing contingencies means uncovering particular complexes of determinations which contribute to a given outcome' (Andermahr et al. 1997: 47). On eliciting it from / applying it to the Sri Lankan context I was able to account for / compose the particularities, inequalities, subjective, and time / context base of intersections and overlaps of the different aspects of feminist research methodology. For instance, the politics and ethics concerning the representation of women affected by war were also seen / conceptualised as a method, as well as related to the epistemology of researching. Epistemology involving the methodology of gender mainstreaming was perceived / thought of as ontology, since the outcome of such epistemology impacted on women's realities within institutions. This ontology was argued to have resulted in generating further epistemology, in terms of the methods of gender analysis and training. Theories of subjectivities (such as an Asian standpoint) not only reflected on subjectivity but were also epistemology. Theorising / practising subjectivity through reflexivity was also a method. The epistemic project of literature reviewing is also a method of data generation / construction as well as being part of epistemology, ontology and theory. Consequently, aspects of feminist research methodology, while being conceptualised as contingent, had also to be accounted for / unified within a meta-framework on feminist research methodology.

Any project of researching requires a simultaneous process of both theorising and deconstructing in different ways, so as to enrich meaning through multiple dimensions, degrees and densities. While theorising involves analysing to find / construct commonalities, classifications, unifications, rationalities, critiques, definitives, meta-narratives, totalities, and universalisations, it is also open to allegations of superficiality, constructionism and essentialism. Though deconstructing entails looking for / composing differences, specificities, heterogeneity, fragmentations, shifting and multiple meanings, instabilities, contestations and contradictions, it is critiqued for its impracticalities, political nihilisms, futility and crisis in legitimation vis-à-vis ethics (Ahmed 1998: 47). Yet, as shown by my application / construction of the theoretical concept of archaeology to Women's Studies / research activism as well as the concurrent deconstruction of the concept of archaeology in relation to Women's Studies / research activism, both approaches entail some degree of cyclic reasoning, constructionism, differences, commonalities, essentialisms, formulaic assumptions of linkages and binary oppositions that are practised consciously and unconsciously by the researcher (and the reader).

Meanings are multiple and diverse; they are situated historically and culturally, but keep changing collectively and individually (Moi 1999); they are also motivated by subjectivity, contingency and can be differed. Therefore, some of the methodological outcomes of making meanings are generalisations, universalisations, possibilities, simplifications, paradoxes, foundations, paradigms, matrixes, interfaces, categories, continuums, definitions, levels, differences, consensus, overlaps, conflations, specificities, densities, superficialities, dissentions, uniformities, unities, parallels, oppositions, hegemonies, homogeneities, hetero-geneities, ambiguities, simultaneities, assertions, citations, conceptualisations, intersections, diagrams, reconceptualisations, constructions, limitations, dis-coveries, analysis, deconstructions, arguments, namings, descriptions, ascriptive labels, essentialisms, problematisations, complexities, imaginaries, provisionalities and so on. These multiple meanings therefore imply temporality and possibilities for changes, additions and subtractions.

My theoretical input here is to attempt validity and legitimisation for my research through 'a fusion' of the oppositions assumed by the epistemolo-gical threads of modernisms and postmodernisms. Rather than seeing / conceptualising these two approaches as contradictory and in conflict, I saw / conceptualised the two approaches as complementing one another. Thus I have constructed / deconstructed binary oppositions of and conflations within postmodernisms and modernisms. The fusion of these ways of making meanings led to multiple understandings of the research topic rather than a singular understanding.

Dominant theory, epistemology and methodology which demand definitive and critical inputs / perspectives and rejections could be, in the final analysis, a negative and devastating exercise in researching. My work was not neces-sarily founded on the critique of feminist research or research methodology in Sri Lanka. In promoting a more inclusive and accepting approach, I did not intend to establish another binary opposition of inclusivity versus rejection (though it may not be possible to completely avoid such a binary). Rather, my specific outlook was based on the fusion of available methodological approa-ches for strategic purposes, which took into account the underlying conflicting and complementary 'realities' of the ground situation and of individual experiences. It was a pragmatic approach that was concerned with inclusivity of multiple approaches – though not necessarily on an equal footing.

Researching the multiplicities of feminisms can only be complemented by multiple methodologies and multiple constructions / understandings, but within a singular framework. They would have been defeated by a sole theo-risation. However, my theorisation / deconstruction are not proposed as an equal balance of postmodernisms and modernisms; they are not posited as a total or comprehensive theory, epistemology or methodology; or even as the final say on the matter. Rather, this book is an opening word on beginning theory on feminist research methodology.

Table 9.1 **Feminist Research Methodology Matrix.**

The proposed methodological matrix for reflexive feminist researching is summarised / illustrated in the following pages. The first part of each section of the matrix on aspects of research methodology portrays / composes the possibilities of applying / constructing this matrix in general. The second part portrays / composes its application / construction within the Sri Lankan situation. The matrix gives examples of reasons for focusing on the following aspects of research methodology when researching as well as some of the conclusions that can be drawn / composed from doing so. There is space for the reader's inputs as the matrix is conceptualised not as a completed methodological structure but as an evolving, contingent framework.

Aspect of Feminist Research Methodology	Possible Roles in the Research Process	Because	Some Conclusions
Subjectivity	Subjectivity relating to intersections of language / ethnicity / age / class / sexuality / transgender / caste / region / disability / etc. Subjectivity in relation to ontology / epistemology / methods / theory / ethics & politics Subjectivity relating to the theoretical and practical problems of researching Subjectivities relating to feminisms (Sex / Gender / Woman / Women) Subjectivity of experiences Subjectivity of emotions Subjectivity vis-à-vis insecurities, slips and gaps Reader's inputs	All research is subjective The researcher's subjectivity permeates all aspects of research methodology Subjectivity can be seen as an intersection / crosscut of feminist research methodology Accounting for the subjectivity of the researcher enhances objectivity Accounting for subjectivity enhances methodological rigour Reader's inputs	Understanding of subjectivity as part of ontology / epistemology Subjectivity is continuously constituted and resisted; articulated and reversed; positioned and erased Subjectivity can be constructed as singular, stable, all-encompassing and conscious Subjectivity can also be seen as split, fluid, unstable, fragmentary and intersected Ways of expressing / constructing subjectivity include: Reflexivity Standpoint Theorising on experiences Women constitute subjectivity as politically collective experiences and woman as individual experiences Standpoint theory is an epistemology of collective subjectivity Reader's inputs

Table 9.1 (continued)

Aspect of Feminist Research Methodology	Possible Roles in the Research Process	Because	Some Conclusions
Sri Lankan Case	My discipline and work / roles / family / ethnicity and religion / class / politics / language / ontological and epistemological bearings / research context / theoretical and methodological aspects / political and ethical concerns / research methods / analysis and theorisation	The subjectivity of the researcher is generally erased from local research processes Reflexivity very rare To trace / construct / reflect on the interaction between my subjectivity and the research process so as to improve internal validity, enhance methodological credibility – despite expositions of the limitations of research	Reflexivity as a method of accessing / composing / expressing the researcher's subjectivity Subjectivity through reflexivity constructed as selective, conscious and structured Subjectivity through reflexivity constructed as unconscious, unstable and fragmented
Ontology	Feminist understandings of: • Metaphysical realities • Epistemological realities • Theoretical realities • Discursive realities • Creative realities • Imaginary realities • Internal subjective realities • Experiential realties • Subjectivity • Different ontologies of women's oppression	Research focuses on / is part of / contingent on multiple realities Ontology can be seen as an intersection / crosscut of feminist research methodology Research objectives, assumptions and justifications (epistemology) based on ontology	Research processes have to be understood as part of ontology as well as separate from ontology Multiple contesting ontologies can be conceived of / seen as part of / engaging with (and topics of) the research process Multiple contesting ontologies have to be understood not only as separate forces but also as intertwined and overlapping Women constitute ontology (as collective and as individual experiences) Reader's inputs

Table 9.1 (continued)

Aspect of Feminist Research Methodology	Possible Roles in the Research Process	Because	Some Conclusions

	• As Causes
	• As Impacts
	• As Contingent
	• As Over-reaching
	• As Specific
	• Ontologies relating to:
	  • Nature
	  • Social construction
	  • Development
	  • History
	  • Culture
	  • Nations
	  • Institutions
	  • Feminist possibilities
	  • Reader's inputs
		Ontology can direct epistemology (findings / outputs) and vice versa
		Ethics / politics are ontological and subjective concerns
		Contextualising / situating research within research realities enhances relevance and validity	

Sri Lankan Case	Realities relating to researching: • Feminist internationalisms • Feminist localisms • Feminist reformative intents • Feminist personal political interests Gender as an ontology relating to: • Sexual differences • (Heterosexual / transgender / homosexual) • Abstract collective of women • Differentiation as a woman • Gendering of inanimate objects or personification	Ontology can direct epistemology (findings / outputs) and vice versa Ontology can be a tool to address political / methodological attacks on feminist research Conceptualisation / perceptions of reality based on gender	Overlaps and intersections in ontologies related to researching Difficulty in conceptualising / distinguishing between ontology and epistemology given the symbiotic relationship Gender epistemology (knowledge based on gender) directs gender ontology (perceptions of realities) and gender ontology (realities) directs gender epistemology (knowledge based on gender) Savoir directs connaissances and connaissances directs savoir in a cyclic relationship

Table 9.1 (continued)

Aspect of Feminist Research Methodology	Possible Roles in the Research Process	Because	Some Conclusions
	• Gender prototypes for change • Ontological significance of culture • Ontological significance of history		
Epistemology	Feminist understandings of epistemologies related to: • Metaphysics • Theories • Discourse • Creative Arts • Imagination • Subjectivity • Experience Feminist inputs into epistemologies of: • Empiricism • Biological determinism • Rationalism • Culturalism • Marxisms • Postcolonialisms • Poststructuralisms • Psychoanalysis • Western feminisms • Indigenous feminisms • Etc. Feminist epistemologies of: • Gynocriticism	Research objectives, assumptions and justifications (epistemology) based on ontology Ontology can direct epistemology (findings / outputs) and vice versa Epistemology can be seen as an intersection / crosscut of feminist research methodology Ethics / politics may also be epistemological concerns Exploring / constructing / reflecting on epistemology enhances relevance and validity Epistemology can be a tool to address political / methodological attacks on feminist research Reader's inputs	Research processes can be conceived of as engaging with multiple contesting epistemologies Research processes have to be understood as part of epistemology as well as separate from epistemology Difficulty in distinguishing between epistemology and ontology given the symbiotic relationship Feminists have used epistemologies for strategic reasons Some epistemologies seen as essentialist while others are seen as nihilist Women not only a category of research but also a global knowledge paradigm Reader's inputs

Table 9.1 (continued)

Aspect of Feminist Research Methodology	Possible Roles in the Research Process	Because	Some Conclusions
	• Feminising • Gendering • Standpoint Reader's inputs		
Sri Lankan Case	Epistemologies related to feminist researching: • Feminist internationalisms • Feminist localisms • Feminist reformative intents • Feminist personal political interests Gender as an epistemology based on: • Gender theoretical concepts • Gender analysis • Gender political aspirations • Gender methodologies	Epistemologies related to researching drive ontology Research objectives, assumptions and justifications (epistemology) are based on ontology High prevalence of knowledge understandings, assumptions, justifications relating to gender	Difficulty in conceptualising / distinguishing between ontology and epistemology given the symbiotic relationship Gender as an epistemology based on ontology Gender is an epistemology as well as a category of research Gender epistemology (knowledge based on gender) directs gender ontology (perceptions of realities) and gender ontology (realities) directs gender epistemology (knowledge based on gender)
Methods	Methods of data collection / construction Methods of data analysis Methods of writing up Feminist appropriation of / inputs into specific research methods • Reflexivity • Action research • Participatory methods • Interdisciplinary methods • Empirical methods	Research methods are determined by subjectivity, ontology, epistemology, theory and ethics / politics Methods can be seen as an intersection / crosscut of feminist research methodology	Quantitative methods, through generalisations and predefined categories have an impact on policy and political action Qualitative methods embody / compose the particular experiences of individual women and can show nuances and specificities A combination of quantitative and qualitative methods can give multiple dimensions to knowledge

Table 9.1 (continued)

Aspect of Feminist Research Methodology	Possible Roles in the Research Process	Because	Some Conclusions
	Feminist methods such as: • Gender-related needs assessments • Gender frameworks / analysis • Gender monitoring • Gender audits • Gender-related evaluations Reader's inputs	Debate on whether there is a feminist method Assumptions pertaining to a clash of paradigms Feminist knowledge seen / constructed as multi / trans / interdisciplinary Reader's inputs	Mixed methods can provide validity through triangulation Interdisciplinary / multidisciplinary / transdisciplinary methods provide holistic understandings Knowledge partial, contingent and situated despite the methods used Literature reviewing is important as a feminist method because it can provide legitimacy to Women's Studies in academia Reader's inputs
Sri Lankan Case	Focus on literature reviewing as a research method of data collection / construction Literature reviewing as an epistemic project of: • Linear evolution and consistency • Gaps, interruptions, multiple strands and directions	Research tends to ignore literature reviewing as a method Citations may ignore local research and concentrate on the global	Literature reviewing is a method Literature reviewing is ontology as it provides background Literature reviewing gives an epistemic evolution of the topic Literature reviewing is subjective and selective and therefore indicates the gaps, interruptions, multiple strands and directions in knowledge Literature reviewing is theory as it can theorise / deconstruct the research subject Literature reviewing is epistemology as it could generate knowledge theories Literature reviewing can provide legitimacy to Women's Studies in academia Lack of a literature review may pose ethical / political issues

Table 9.1 (continued)

Aspect of Feminist Research Methodology	Possible Roles in the Research Process	Because	Some Conclusions
Theory	Inductive theory (grounded) Deductive theory (application) Middle-order theory (moving between induction and deduction) Travelling theory Interdisciplinary theories Standpoint theories Feminist theories from various disciplines Feminist theories of: • Equality • Difference • Empowerment • Patriarchy • Gender Reader's inputs	Theory can 'interpret' data and help to 'construct' 'knowledge' and 'meaning' Possibility of theory to address the diversity of feminisms? For positivists, theory needs to be objective and verifiable for the production of scientific knowledge For non-positivists, theory can be subjective and falsifiable For poststructuralists, theory has lost its prestige and authority Theory can have formal frameworks / axioms / propositions, configurations Theory can be an essential guide to practice and politics Theory can 'interpret' data and help to 'construct' Deconstruction can de-stabilise theory theory / meaning Theory needs adaptation to different research contexts Reader's inputs	Concurrent theorisations from modernist / postmodernist paradigms to make multiple meanings simultaneously as a response to the diversity of feminisms 'Oppositional' paradigms seen to / constructed to co-exist as a response to the diversity of feminisms Theories that do not account for both commonalities and differences can be essentialist Elements of essentialism in all theory Women not only a category of research but also a knowledge paradigm Grand theories are suspect Theory is contingent and unstable, and situated Reader's inputs

Table 9.1 (continued)

Aspect of Feminist Research Methodology	Possible Roles in the Research Process	Because	Some Conclusions
Sri Lankan Case	Theorisations on: • Women's standpoints • Mother's viewpoints • Disciplinary and ideological perspectives • Class perceptions • Counter-communal stands • Asian / South Asian positionings Debate on the pros and cons of theorisation Beginning theory Nuancing theory	The situatedness, standpoints and intersections of the researcher influence knowledge generated Or The subjectivity of the researcher engages with / impacts on the research process Knowledge situated in time / location / theory, etc. The lack of theorisation in general may require the researcher to 'begin' theorisation from ground data Western theorisations may need adaptation to non-Western contexts	Standpoints cannot be conceptualised as separate categories but as intersecting / overlapping Tensions between collective standpoints and individual positionings Need to simultaneously build on commonality in standpoints while accounting for individual differences Understanding of the instability of the self in the face of changing times / circumstances Risks involved in expressing a standpoint under certain political circumstances Theory on standpoints is epistemology (theory on knowledge) and ontology (understanding of reality) Possibility of theorising and deconstructing at the same time Provisional and new understandings that are context- and subjectivity-based
Politics / Ethics	Ethics and politics related to the following: • Research objectives • Research topic • Data collection methods • Data analysis methods • Ontological assumptions • Epistemological standpoints • Research funding	Power plays in the research process Politics / ethics seen as symbiotic Need to anticipate problems relating to ethics / politics	Some ethical / political concerns of epistemology, ontology, theory and subjectivity can only be reflected on and problematised Politics / ethics constitute ontology (based on understandings of reality) and epistemology (theories of knowledge)

Table 9.1 (continued)

Aspect of Feminist Research Methodology	Possible Roles in the Research Process	Because	Some Conclusions
	• Colleagues / collaborators / support staff • Family & others • Benefits for the researcher • The researched • Theoretical / analytical perspectives • Previous research • Discipline & research community • General public • Language • Cultural concerns • Historical concerns • Insider / outsider issues • Outputs of research • Outcomes of research Reader's inputs	Ethics / politics can be seen as intersections / crosscuts of feminist research methodology Ethics / politics need to be considered at every step in the research process if research outcomes are to complement research objectives, be relevant and just Ethics / politics issues in researching can be general, personal and relative Ethics / politics need to be considered as concerns of epistemology as well as research practice Reader's inputs	Codes of Ethics & Procedural Guidelines to minimise damage in empirical research Pragmatic strategising to achieve something – as opposed to nothing Action research to benefit the participants Participatory research to democratise / equalise power balances Interpretive sufficiency to promote depth and breadth of understanding Performativity to show multiple readings of the text Multimodal & cross-cultural representation to ensure diversity and multiple interests Standpoint theory to expose the location of collective interests Reflexivity to reveal dilemmas in research and strengthen validity Reader's inputs

Table 9.1 (continued)

Aspect of Feminist Research Methodology	Possible Roles in the Research Process	Because	Some Conclusions
Sri Lankan Case	Ethics / politics of aspirations *Altruism *Liberal democracy *Marxism Ethics / politics as strategy and action Ethics / politics relating to data collection / construction methods Ethics as a politics of good?	Politics / ethics seen as symbiotic Disjunction between research objectives and outcomes Ethics seen as related to methods Power plays in the research process Influences of religions	Some politics / ethics are not values that are purely inspirational, but can be operationalised at the levels of strategy / methods Need for a degree of strategic pragmatism in translating ethical / political aspirations into action Feminisms redefined as the ethics / politics of researching (not only a category of research) Some ethical / political concerns of epistemology, ontology, theory and subjectivity can only be reflected on and problematised

Notes

Introduction

1 Modernism refers to dominant understandings of the world mainly centred on assumptions of rationality, positivism, realism and empiricism (and is distinguished from the European artistic movement at the turn of the nineteenth century).
2 Postmodernisms refer to understandings of 'realities' from perspectives that are anti-foundational, pragmatic, pluralistic, contingent, local and provisional.
3 I have capitalised Women's Studies when referring to the discipline while women's studies refer to research studies.
4 The term 'epistemology' is used in relation to theorisations on knowledge production.
5 This relates to theorisations of knowledge production and meaning-making through research.
6 The term 'women's research activism' is used to emphasise the point that research is a form of political activism irrespective of its ideological leanings.
7 It takes into account the subjective, ontological, epistemological, theoretical, ethical, political and technical aspects of research processes.
8 Ontology refers to understandings of the nature / perception of realities.
9 Literature on methodology with stated feminist ideological leanings.
10 This refers to literature on women as a subject.
11 Discourse incorporates speech, writing, knowledge practices; it is a way of representing knowledge about a particular topic at a given time.
12 The perspective of reality based on conscious awareness, subjective intentionality and objects.
13 This refers to researchers who are retained to conduct consultancies (including gender policies and evaluations) for non-governmental organisations (NGOs) and international non-governmental organisations (INGOs).

1 The local context: Archaeology of women's research activism

1 This refers to the ways in which certain discourses as well as theoretical, academic and knowledge conventions conform or prioritise certain structures and methodologies in writing such as profiles, histories, genealogy or archaeology.
2 This argument has also been framed in terms of ontology leading to epistemology and epistemology leading to ontology (Chapters 4 and 5).
3 Sri Lanka.
4 Sinhalese.
5 This is discussed at length in Chapters 4, 7 and 8.
6 These include the Girls' Friendly Society and the Ceylon Women's Union (1904), the *Lanka Mahila Samithi* (1929), and the Women's Franchise Union (1927). The latter attracted many women (from prominent political families to wives of labour

and nationalist leaders of the 1920s). The Women's Political Union of the 1920s, and later the All Ceylon Women's Conference, continued to champion women's rights, equal pay and women's access to all professions.

7 This is the right to equal opportunities in fields such as employment, education and politics.

8 These are areas of life which are of specific concern to women such as domestic violence, abortion and sexual harassment.

9 Different gender needs of men and women as well as the different interests in how gender impacts on any issue.

10 This is the particular standpoint of a collective identity or perspective.

11 *The Second Sex* was originally published in 1949 in French.

12 This is based on conversations with Kumari Jayawardena, Eva Ranaweera and Bernadeen de Silva.

13 Feminists like Nawal El-Saadhavi, Noeline Hayzer, Kamla Bhasin and Elizabeth Reid visited the country.

14 Some of these women were involved in UNIYW celebrations.

15 This was founded on equal rights, development, legislative changes and justice.

16 Women's Liberation.

17 Community-based organisations.

18 These were funded by agencies such as the United Nations and its related bodies, the US, Norwegian, Dutch, Canadian and Swedish bi-lateral organisations.

19 This includes the Institute of Social Studies (The Hague) and Institute for Development Studies (University of Sussex) as well as UK and US universities.

20 The commonalities in women's activism are evident from the attendees at many Asian / South-Asian feminist conferences.

21 Canadian International Development Agency.

22 This is evident from CENWOR national conventions as well as university research symposia.

23 Research activism is distinguished from action research (Chapter 6) which leads to the empowerment / integration of the researched into the research process.

24 Spivak (1993) uses the term in postcolonial discourse to mean those outside hegemonic power structures.

25 John (2004a) discusses the feminist debate in India on the issue of indigenous versus Western theorisations.

26 I use this to mean an overarching system of male dominance.

27 However, WR academics published their work via NGOs.

28 Technical research from the NGOs also does not see the light of publication.

29 Take the BA course on Women in Agriculture (University of Peradeniya); MA in Women's Studies (University of Colombo); BA Multi-disciplinary Gender Stream (University of Colombo).

30 These have been by the Women and Media Collective and the Women's Education and Research Centre.

31 These are the Universities of Peradeniya, Colombo, and Kelaniya.

32 This is a norm of thinking that the destinies of people are solely guided by their biological make-up (Chapters 2, 5, 7 and 8).

33 Interviewees made references to studies on women's work and family strategies, subcontracting, the impact of macro-economic reforms and poverty, undertaken jointly with research centres from other countries.

2 A paradigm: Women – a paradigm in global knowledge production

1 The axiom that social realities are constructed, but they vary across different times and locations, and are changeable through individual and collective political action.

2 'Multibridity' is used to indicate the multiple influences defining a person's life: being simultaneously informed of the indigenous, as well as the global – though not necessarily uniformly.
3 Given that ontology (being or existences in / of realities) involves the consciousness of or knowing such realities, ontology cannot be divorced from epistemology.
4 The last two categories were discussed to some extent in the earlier section.
5 Culturalism is used to denote rationales for knowledges based on ethnic practices, religious beliefs and cultural traditions.
6 In Chapter 3 I will argue that reflexivity is both a standpoint and a method. As such, my discussion here is limited.
7 These were initiatives in development that specifically targeted women and aimed to integrate them into development primarily as beneficiaries under welfare, but also as participants under equity, efficiency and anti-poverty approaches, and lately as decision-makers.

3 Subjectivity: Reflecting on the self as / in making meaning

1 The positivist paradigm in knowledge-making values empiricism, scientific methods such as observation, and aims of objectivity as the basis for knowing.
2 The word 'post-eras' is used to refer to contemporary ontological / epistemological uncertainties and pluralisms due to the knowledge, theoretical and political movements of psychoanalysis, postmodernisms and postcolonialisms that destabilise dominant understandings of the world based on positivism.
3 Some arguments emanating from cultural studies that the goals of feminism have been achieved or that feminism is no longer relevant in some contexts or that its politics have been negated through the influence of poststructuralism.
4 Manual data analysis involved less exertion of my limbs than using a software program requiring extensive work at the computer would have done.
5 Social Constructionism refers to the idea of the constructed rather than essential nature of realities whereas Social Constructivism hinges on the understanding of 'objective reality' as being contingent and rhetorical.
6 There are many postmodernist characteristics in modernist ways of making meaning. Cross-disciplinary examples include efforts at 'representing reality' within the Modernist cultural movement by twentieth-century writers like Virginia Woolf, Dorothy Richardson, James Joyce and T. S. Eliot.
7 Structuralism was originally conceptualised as the subjective attribution of relations to objects found in reality so as to form a synthesis or unity; but later theorised to encompass subjects themselves in these structures.
8 This refers to regional and international linkages, alliances and influences between feminists of varying hues generated by the UN as well as other informal networks.
9 Recently, Samuel (unpublished) has worked on grey literature that emanated from women's activism amongst Sinhala-speaking groups.
10 It deals with the theories of interpretation not only of texts but also of the nature of reality and human understanding.
11 First-generation researchers have been researching from before 1975 (not applicable to this sample). Second-generation researchers have been researching since the 1970s. Third-generation researchers have been researching since the late 1990s.

4 An ontology: Research realities in meaning-making

1 Meta-cognitive knowledge pertains to one's knowledge about how one's cognition operates.
2 Ontological politics refer to the political dynamics of the 'realities' within the research context and process.

3 This was in relation to a proposed Bill on Women's Rights, which had a provision guaranteeing women's rights to the body, and which was interpreted as the right to abortion. Currently, abortion is illegal in Sri Lanka.

4 I cite two examples – Radhika Coomaraswamy (UN Special Rappateur on Violence Against Women 1994–2004) and Savithri Goonesekere (Expert Committee to the UN Convention on the Elimination of all forms of Discrimination Against Women 1999–2001).

5 These include Development Alternatives with Women for a New Era (DAWN), Women Living Under Muslim Law (WLUML), Association of African Women for Research and Development (AAWORD), and Kartini Asia Network.

6 I will be engaging more comprehensively with what I construct as general ontology of gender and gender epistemology in Chapter 5.

7 These include the Framework for Gender Livelihood Analysis in Disasters or the Harvard Gender Roles Framework of Analysis, and the Gender Analysis Matrix.

8 Examples include gender diagnosis or gender-related planning.

9 Take the example of the Domestic Violence Bill of 2005.

10 Liberation Tigers of Tamil Elam.

11 Sri Lanka Freedom Party (SLFP).

12 I identify the combination of personal politics of researching and research ethics as construing research feminisms in Sri Lanka (Chapter 8) and researcher standpoints and intersections (Chapter 7).

5 An epistemology: Making meanings of being / doing gender

1 An early version of this chapter was published under Wickramasinghe, M. (2006) 'An epistemology of gender – an aspect of being as a way of seeing', in *Women's Studies International Forum*, 29 (6), 606–611.

2 A line of thinking that sees the destinies of human beings as biologically decided, and not as individually and socially determined.

3 Selective and subjective thinking that constructs relationships between things, on the basis of unification and order.

4 This refers to the denial of selfhood of others in order to secure the self of the centred subject.

5 The acquisition of gender identities is conceptualised as socialisation.

6 This is a city in the north of the island. The northern area of Sri Lanka is home to a majority of Tamil people.

7 The Sinhalese claim their racial roots to the Aryans.

8 This is the concept of practice being illuminated by a priori theory, and simultaneously, theory being illuminated by practice.

6 A method: Literature reviewing as making meaning

1 This signifies a discursive project of identifying / constructing a body of previous textual knowledge, or connaissances, on a research topic.

2 A genealogy would necessarily focus on the gaps and discontinuities between ideas (or ideologies) and practices so as to destabilise / deconstruct their seemingly pre-given, stable, linear, monolithic and totalising aspects.

3 A typology implies not only a category but also the evolution of the category.

4 As noted in Chapter 1, action research refers to research that empowers and integrates the researched into the research process.

5 Sporadic waves of warfare due to Sri Lanka's ethnic conflict in the North and East of the country have periodically displaced Muslim, Tamil and Sinhala populations.

6 This is in the context of both the JVP / government conflict as well as the LTTE / government conflict in the late 1980s.

7 As stated earlier, my literature review does not include research done by men. However, I am making an exception in the case of Vimaladharma because of the capacity of his work to exemplify some of my thinking on research methodology in Sri Lanka.

8 It also ignores the colonial interventions of the Portuguese, Dutch and British since the sixteenth century or treats them as historical aberrations.

7 Theory: Making and unmaking meaning in theory

1 Such a reflexive exercise of constructing and deconstructing theory is not confined to this chapter alone; it is a process that intermittently runs through the entire book.

2 In contrast, she proposes a transformative methodological framework based on experiences of working amongst Sri Lankan IDPs (see Chapter 6).

3 Further research is required in this area to consider the exact ways in which researchers unconsciously utilise research methodology.

4 In Chapter 2 I argue for varying types of ontologies; from grand ontologies of postmodernism or modernism; to more localised ones of feminist internationalism or personal politics.

5 Chapter 2 deals with ontological and epistemological conceptualisations.

6 Saumi works in a profession related to children.

7 The line of thinking that the physiological differences between men and women is the sole determinant of their different social roles, characteristics and relations (Chapters 3 and 7).

8 This involves Women in Development (WID) and Gender and Development (GAD) approaches.

9 The word 'communal' has been used since colonial times to describe violence amongst ethnic groups in Sri Lanka. Today there is a shift towards the use of the word 'ethnic' possibly due to an understanding of identity politics as opposed to community strife.

10 There include reprisals by the state and paramilitary groups, the LTTE, fundamentalist political parties like the JVP and Jathika Hela Urumaya (JHU), the media as well as society at large.

8 Ethics / politics: Feminist ethics / politics in meaning-making

1 The limited access to the North, the suppression of independent information and dissenting opinions make a clear assessment of the political situation somewhat difficult.

2 In fact, Fraser and Gordon provide a genealogy of the term 'dependency' in US welfare interventions, highlighting the political and economic implications, and the psychological stigma – especially for single black mothers.

3 Admittedly, empowerment is a contested term. I use it here to indicate women's control over gender divisions, resources, sexuality, body and fertility, education and training, information and knowledge, mobility, governance and decision-making as well as the spirit and psyche.

4 Action here refers to political action.

5 Moneragala is one of the poorest districts in Sri Lanka.

Bibliography

Abeysekera, M. (2005) 'Gender relief and rehabilitation', *The Island*, 8 March 2005.

Abeysekera, S. (1995) 'Women and the media, Sri Lanka – the decade from Nairobi to Beijing', in CENWOR (ed.) *Facets of Change – Women in Sri Lanka 1986 – 1995*, Colombo: Centre for Women's Research.

——(2000) 'Women and the media in Sri Lanka: the post Beijing Phase', in CENWOR (ed.) *Post-Beijing Reflections: Women in Sri Lanka 1995 – 2000*, Colombo: Centre for Women's Research.

——(2005) 'Communities beyond the pale: sex workers' rights and human rights in Sri Lanka', in G. Misra and R. Chandiraman (eds) *Sexuality, Gender and Rights – Exploring Theory and Practice in South and Southeast Asia*, New Delhi / Thousand Oaks / London: Sage Publications.

Adkins, L. (1995) *Gendered Work*, Buckingham: Open University Press.

——(2004) 'Reflexivity: freedom or habit of gender?', in L. Adkins and B. Skeggs (eds) *Feminism after Bourdieu*, Oxford / Massachusetts: Blackwell Publishing.

Agarwal, B. (1988) 'Patriarchy and the "modernizing" state: an introduction', in B. Agarwal (ed.) *Structures of Patriarchy, State, Community and Household in Modernizing Asia*, New Delhi: Kali for Women.

Ahmed, S. (1998) *Differences that Matter – Feminist Theory and Postmodernism*, Cambridge: Cambridge University Press.

Alcoff, L. (1988) 'Cultural feminism versus poststructuralism: the identity crisis in feminist theory', *Signs Journal of Women in Culture and Society*, 13 (3), 405–436.

——(2008) 'The problem of speaking for others', in A. M. Jaggar (ed.) *Just Methods*, Boulder / London: Paradigm Publishers.

Alcoff, L. and Potter, E. (1993) *Feminist Epistemologies*, New York and London: Routledge.

Althusser, L. (1977) *Lenin and Philosophy and Other Essays*, London: New Left Books.

——(2000) 'Ideology and ideological state apparatuses', in J. Rivkin and M. Ryan (eds) *Literary Theory: An Anthology*, Oxford: Blackwell Publishers.

Amarasuriya, N. R. (1995) 'Women in science and technology', in CENWOR (ed.) *Facets of Change – Women in Sri Lanka 1986 – 1995*, Colombo: Centre for Women's Research.

Andermahr, S., Lovell, T. and Wolkowitz, C. (1997) *A Concise Glossary of Feminist Theory*, London: Arnold.

Ariyabandu, M. M. and Wickramasinghe, M. (2003) *Gender Dimensions in Disaster Management – A Guide for South Asia*, Colombo: Intermediate Technology Development Group South Asia.

Auerbach, N. (1978) *Communities of Women: Ideas in Fiction*, Massachusetts: Harvard University Press.

Ball, S. (1990) 'Self doubt and soft data: social and technical trajectories in ethnographic fieldwork', *International Journal of Qualitative Studies in Education*, 3 (2), 157–171.

Bandarage, A. (1988) 'Women and capitalist development in Sri Lanka', *Bulletin of Concerned Asian Scholars*, 20 (2), 57–81.

——(1998) *Women and Social Change in Sri Lanka: Towards a Theoretical Framework*, Colombo: Centre for Women's Research.

Bandaranaike, S. (1975) 'Man and woman as part of one unity', *Ceylon Daily News*, 26 June 1975.

Banerjee, N. K. (2008) 'The enabling process of Empowerment', in M. E. John (ed.) *Women's Studies in India*, New Delhi: Penguin Book in India.

Barrett, M. (1988) *Women's Oppression Today: Problems in Marxist Feminist Analysis*, London: Verso.

Barron, L. (2006) 'Literature review', in V. Jupp (ed.) *The Sage Dictionary of Social Research Methods*, London / Thousand Oaks / New Delhi: Sage Publications.

Bartky, S. (1978) 'Towards a phenomenology of feminist consciousness', in M. Vetterling-Braggin (ed.) *Feminism and Philosophy*, Totowa: Littlefield Adams.

Basu, A. (2003) 'Globalisation of the local / localisation of the global: mapping transnational women's movements', in C. R. McCann and S. Kim (eds) *Feminist Theory Reader – Local and Global Perspectives*, New York / London: Routledge.

Batliwala, S. (1993) *Women's Empowerment in South Asia: Concepts and Practice*, New Delhi: Asian South-Pacific Bureau of Adult Education / Food and Agriculture Organisation.

Batliwala, S. and Dhanraj, D. (2007) 'Gender myths that instrumentalise women: a view from the Indian front line', in Cornwall, A., Harisson, E. and Whitehead, A. (eds) *Feminisms in Development – Contradictions, Contestations and Challenges*, London / New York: Zed Books.

Beasley, C. (1999) *What is Feminism? An Introduction to Feminist Theory*, London: Sage Publications.

Bernstein, B. (1990) *The Structuring of Pedagogic Discourse – Class Codes and Control* (Vol. 14), London: Routledge.

Bhabha, H. K. (1994) *The Location of Culture*, London / New York: Routledge.

Bhavnani, K. (1993) 'Tracing the contours – feminist research and feminist objectivity', *Women's Studies International Forum*, 16 (2), 95–104.

Birch, M. and Miller, T. (2002) 'Encouraging participation: ethics and responsibilities', in M. Mauthner, M. Birch, J. Jessop and T. Miller (eds) *Ethics in Qualitative Research*, Thousand Oaks: Sage.

Birch, M., Miller, T., Mauthner, M. and Jessop, J. (2002a) 'Introduction', in M. Mauthner, M. Birch, J. Jessop and T. Miller (eds) *Ethics in Qualitative Research*, Thousand Oaks: Sage.

——(eds) (2002b) *Ethics in Qualitative Research*, Thousand Oaks: Sage.

Boserup, E. (1970) *Women's Role in Economic Development*, London: Allen and Unwin.

Bourdieu, P. and Wacquant, L. (1992) *An Invitation to Reflexive Sociology*, Chicago, IL: University of Chicago.

Braidotti, R. (1994) *Nomadic Subjects: Embodiment and Sexual Difference in Contemporary Feminist Theory*, New York: Columbia University Press.

Brah, A. (1993) 'Questions of difference and international feminism', in S. Jackson (ed.) *Women's Studies – Essential Readings*, New York: New York University Press.

——(2003) 'Diaspora, border and transnational identities', in R. Lewis and S. Mills (eds) *Feminist Postcolonial Theory – A Reader*, New York: Routledge.

Bryman, A. (2004) *Social Research Methods*, Oxford: Oxford University Press.

Burrell, G. and Morgan, G. (1979) *Sociological Paradigms and Organisational Analysis*, Aldershot: Gower Publishing.

Butler, J. (1993) *Bodies that Matter – on the Discursive Limits of 'Sex'*, New York / London: Routledge.

——(1999) *Gender Trouble – Feminism and the Subversion of Identity*, New York: Routledge.

Buvinic, M. (1983) 'Women's issues in third world poverty: A policy analysis', in M. Buvinic, M. A. Lycette and W. P. McGreevy (eds) *Women and Poverty in the Third World*, Baltimore, MD / London: John Hopkins University Press.

Cain, M. and Finch, J. (2004) 'Towards a rehabilitation of data', in C. Seale (ed.) *Social Research Methods – A Reader*, London / New York: Routledge.

Cat's Eye (2000a) 'Hate speech and homophobia in Sri Lanka', in M. de Alwis (ed.) *Cat's Eye – A Feminist Gaze on Current Issues*, Colombo: Cat's Eye Publications.

——(2000b) 'National liberation and women's liberation', in M. de Alwis (ed.) *Cat's Eye – A Feminist Gaze on Current Issues*, Colombo: Cat's Eye Publications.

——(2000c) 'A tribute to Doreen Wickremasinghe', in M. de Alwis (ed.) *Cat's Eye – A Feminist Gaze on Current Issues*, Colombo: Cat's Eye Publications.

Caws, P. (1995) 'Structuralism', in J. Kim and E. Sosa (eds) *A Companion to Metaphysics*, Malden, MA / Oxford / Victoria: Blackwell Publishing.

CENWOR (ed.) (1985) *UN Decade for Women – Progress and Achievements of Women in Sri Lanka*, Colombo: Centre for Women's Research.

——(1995a) *Facets of Change – Women in Sri Lanka 1986 – 1995*, Colombo: Centre for Women's Research.

——(1995b) *Facing Odds – Women in the Labour Market*, Colombo: Centre for Women's Research.

——(1998) *Women in the Economy – Trends and Policy Issues*, Colombo: Centre for Women's Research.

——(2000) *Post Beijing Reflections: Women in Sri Lanka, 1995 – 2000*, Colombo: Centre for Women's Research.

——(2001) *Sri Lanka Shadow Report on the UN Convention on the Elimination of All Forms of Discrimination against Women*, Colombo: Centre for Women's Research.

Chakravarti, U. (2008) 'Archiving the nation-state in feminist practice – a South Asian perspective', occasional paper no 51, New Delhi: Centre for Women's Development Studies.

Charmaz, K. (2002) 'Qualitative interviewing and grounded theory analysis', in J. F. Gubrium and J. A. Holstein (eds) *Handbook of Interview Research*, Thousand Oaks, CA: Sage.

Chaudhuri, M. (2004) 'Introduction', in M. Chaudhuri (ed.) *Feminism in India*, London / New York: Zed Books.

Chhachhi, A. (2005) 'Forced identities – the state, communalism, fundamentalism, and women in India', in Khullar, M. (ed.) *Writing the Women's Movement – A Reader*, New Delhi: Asian Centre for Women's Studies / Zubaan.

Chodorow, N. (1978) *The Reproduction of Mothering*, Berkeley, CA: University of California Press.

Christ, C. P. (1992) 'Feminists – sojourners in the field of religious studies', in C. Kramarae and D. Spender (eds) *The Knowledge Explosion – Generations of Feminist Scholarship,* New York / London: Teachers College Press, Columbia University.

Cixous, H. (1976) 'The laugh of the medusa', *Signs*, 1 (4), 36–55.

Coffrey, A., Beverley, H. and Atkinson, P. (1996) 'Qualitative data analysis: technologies and representations', *Sociological Research Online*, 1 (1). Available from: www.socresonline.org.uk/socresonline/1/14.html (accessed 7 November 2006).

Cohen, L. and Manion, L. (1997) *Research Methods in Education*, London: Routledge.

Cole, E. B. and Coultrap-McQuin, S. (eds) (1992) *Explorations in Feminist Ethics – Theory and Practice*, Bloomington / Indianapolis, IN: Indiana University Press.

Collins, P. H. (1990) *Black Feminist Thought: Knowledge, Consciousness and the Politics of Empowerment*, New York / London: Routledge.

——(1991) 'Learning from the outsider within – the sociological significance of black feminist thought', in M. M. Fonow and J. A. Cook (eds) *Beyond Methodology – Feminist Scholarship as Lived Research*, Bloomington, IN: Indiana University Press.

——(2004) 'Comment on Hekman's "truth and method: feminist standpoint theory revisited": where's the power?', in S. Harding (ed.) *The Feminist Standpoint Theory Reader – Intellectual and Political Controversies*, New York / London: Routledge.

Coomaraswamy, R. (2004) 'Engendering the constitution-making process', in R. Coomaraswamy and D. Fonseka (eds) *Peace Work – Women, Armed Conflict and Negotiations*, Colombo: International Centre for Ethnic Studies.

Cornwall, A., Harrison, E. and Whitehead, A. (2007) *Feminisms in Development – Contradictions, Contestations and Challenges*, London / New York: Zed Books.

de Alwis, M. (1994a) 'The articulation of gender in cinematic address: Sinhala cinema in 1992', in S. Thiruchandran (ed.) *Images*, Colombo: Women's Education and Research Centre.

——(1994b) 'Towards a feminist historiography – reading gender in the text of the nation', in R. Coomaraswamy and N. Wickramasinghe (eds) *Introduction to Social Theory*, Colombo: International Centre for Ethnic Studies / Knoark Publishers.

——(ed.) (2000) *Cat's Eye – A Feminist Gaze on Current Issues*, Colombo: Cat's Eye Publications.

——(2001) 'Ambivalent maternalisms: cursing as public protest in Sri Lanka', in S. Meintjes, A. Pillay and M. Turshen (eds) *The Aftermath: Women in Post-conflict Transformation*, London: Zed Books.

——(2004a) 'Feminism', in D. Nugent and J. Vincent (eds) *A Companion to the Anthropology of Politics*, Cornwall: Blackwell Publishing.

——(2004b) 'The costs of belonging: international civic society and feminism', in A. J. Canagaratna (ed.) *Ethnicity, Pluralism and Human Rights – Neelan Tiruchelvam Commemoration Conference Papers*, Colombo: International Centre for Ethnic Studies.

de Alwis, M. and Jayawardena, K. (2001) *Casting Pearls – The Women's Franchise Movement in Sri Lanka*, Colombo: Social Scientists Association.

de Beauvoir, S. (1972) *The Second Sex*, New York: Vintage.

Debold, E., Tolman, D. and Brown, L. M. (1996) 'Embodying knowledge, knowing desire: authority and split subjectivity in girls' development', in N. Goldberg, J. Tarule, B. Clinchy and M. Belenky (eds) *Knowledge, Difference and Power*, New York: Basic Books.

Deem, R. and Brehony, K. J. (1994) 'Why didn't you use a survey so you could generalise your findings? Methodological issues in a multiple site case study of school governing bodies after the 1988 Educational Reform Act', in D. Halpin and B. Troyna (eds) *Researching Educational Policy – Ethical and Methodological Issues*, London: The Falmer Press.

de Groot, J. and Maynard, M. (1993a) 'Facing the 1990s: problems and possibilities for women's studies', in J. De Groot and M. Maynard (eds) *Women's Studies in the 1990s – Doing Things Differently?* New York: St Martin's Press.

——(eds) (1993b) *Women's Studies in the 1990s – Doing Things Differently?* New York: St Martin's Press.

de Lauretis, T. (1989) 'The essence of the triangle, or taking the risk of essentialism seriously: feminist theory in Italy, the US and Britain', *Differences: A Journal of Feminist Cultural Studies*, 1 (2), 3–37.

Delphy, C. (1981) 'For a materialist feminism', *Feminist Issue*, 1 (2), 69–76.

——(1981) 'Women in stratification studies', in H. Roberts (ed.) *Doing Feminist Research*, London / Boston / Melbourne / Henley: Routledge and Kegan Paul.

de Man, P. (1999) 'Semiology and rhetoric', in J. Wolfreys (ed.) *Literary Theories – A Reader and Guide*, New York: New York University Press.

de Mel, N. (1994) 'Women as gendered subject and other discourses in contemporary Sri Lankan fiction in English', in S. Thiruchandran (ed.) *Images*, Colombo: Women's Education and Research Centre.

——(1996) 'Static signifiers – metaphors of woman in contemporary Sri Lankan war poetry', in K. Jayawardena and M. de Alwis (eds) *Embodied Violence – Communalising Women's Sexuality in South Asia*, New Delhi / London / New Jersey: Zed Books / Kali for Women.

——(2001) *Women and the Nation's Narrative – Gender and Nationalism in 20th Century Sri Lanka*, Colombo: Social Scientists' Association.

——(2007) *Militarizing Sri Lanka – Popular Culture, Memory and Narrative in the Armed Conflict*, Los Angeles / London / New Delhi / Singapore: Sage Publications.

de Mel, N. and Muttetuwegama, R. (1997) 'Sisters in arms: The eksath kantha peramuna', *Pravada*, 4 (10 & 11), 22–26.

de Mel, N. and Samarakkody, M. (2002) *Writing an Inheritance – Women's Writing in Sri Lanka 1860 – 1948*, Colombo: Women's Education and Research Centre.

Department of Census and Statistics (Sri Lanka) (1995) *Women and Men in Sri Lanka*, Colombo: Department of Census and Statistics / Ministry of Finance, Planning, Ethnic Affairs and National Integration.

——(1997) *Changing Role of Women in Sri Lanka*, Colombo: Department of Census and Statistics / Ministry of Finance and Planning.

Derrida, J. (1976) *Of Grammatology*, Baltimore / London: John Hopkins University Press.

——(1998) 'Archive fever: a Freudian impression', Chicago, IL: University of Chicago Press.

——(1999) 'Letter to a Japanese friend', in J. Wolfreys (ed.) *Literary Theories – A Reader and Guide*, New York: New York University Press.

de Saussure, F. (2000) 'Course in general linguistics', in J. Rivkin and M. Ryan (eds) *Literary Theory: An Anthology*, Oxford: Blackwell Publishers.

de Silva, N. (1981) 'Sri Lankan housemaids in the Middle East', *Logos*, 20 (4 December), 33–38.

de Silva, W. (1995) 'Political participation of women in Sri Lanka', in CENWOR (ed.) *Facets of Change – Women in Sri Lanka 1986 – 1995*, Colombo: Centre for Women's Research.

de Vela, T. C., Trice, J. N. and Ofreneo, M. A. (2007) *Positioning in Global Feminist Critical Collaboration – Self-reflexive Talk among Manila-based Feminists*, Monograph Series 2 (1), Manila, Isis International-Manila.

de Zoysa, D. A. (1995) *The Great Sandy River – Class and Gender Transformations among Pioneer Settlers in Sri Lanka's Frontier*, Amsterdam: Centre for Asian Studies / Netherlands Foundation for the Advancement of Tropical Research.

Dias, M. (1979) 'Socio-cultural factors affecting the status of women', in University of Colombo (ed.) *Status of Women*, Colombo: University of Colombo.

——(1983) *Migration to the Middle East – Sri Lanka Case Study*, Colombo: United Nations Educational, Scientific and Cultural Organisation.

——(1985) 'Participation of women in community action', in CENWOR (ed.) *The UN Decade for Women: Progress and Achievements of Women in Sri Lanka*, Colombo: Centre for Women's Research.

Dias, M. and Weerakoon, N. (1995) 'Migrant women domestic workers from Sri Lanka – trends and issues', in CENWOR (ed.) *Facets of Change – Women in Sri Lanka 1986 – 1995*, Colombo: Centre for Women's Research.

Dillon, J. and Maguire, M. (eds) (1997) *Becoming A Teacher – Issues in Secondary Teaching*, Buckingham: Open University Press.

Doucet, A. and Mauthner, N. (2002) 'Knowing responsibly: linking ethics, research practice and epistemology', in M. Mauthner, M. Birch, J. Jessop and T. Miller (eds) *Ethics in Qualitative Research*, Thousand Oaks: Sage.

Dube, L. (2002) 'The meaning and content of marriage in matrilineal Muslim society', in L. Sarkar, K. Sharma and L. Kasturi (eds) *Between Tradition, Counter Tradition and Heresy*, New Delhi: Rainbow Publishers.

du Bois, B. (1983) 'Passionate scholarship – notes on values, knowing and method in feminist social science', in G. Bowles and R. D. Klein (eds) *Theories of Women's Studies*, London / New York: Routledge and Kegan Paul.

Dunne, M., Pryor, J. and Yates, P. (2005) *Becoming a Researcher – A Research Companion for the Social Sciences*, Maidenhead: Open University Press.

Dworkin, A. (1981) *Pornography: Men Possessing Women*, London: Women's Press.

Eagleton, T. (1983) *Literary Theory: An Introduction*, Blackwell: Oxford.

Economic Review (1976a) 'A role for women in the rural economy', *Economic Review*, 2 (6), 22.

——(1976b) 'Women and development', *Economic Review*, 2 (6), 2–22.

Edwards, R. and Mauthner, M. (2002) 'Ethics and feminist research – theory and practice', in M. Mauthner, M. Birch, J. Jessop and T. Miller (eds) *Ethics in Qualitative Research*, Thousand Oaks, CA: Sage.

Emmanuel, S. (2006) *Dealing with the Women's Militancy – An Analysis of Feminist Discourses from Sri Lanka*, Colombo: Social Policy Analysis and Research Centre / University of Colombo.

Employers' Federation of Ceylon (2003) *Guidelines for Sexual Harassment*, Colombo: Employers' Federation of Ceylon.

Engelstad, E. and Gerrard, S. (eds) (2005) *Challenging Situatedness*, Eburon Delft: Eburon Academic Publishers.

Felski, R. (1997) 'The doxa of difference', *Signs Journal of Women in Culture and Society*, 23 (1), 1–21.

Feminist Study Circle (undated) *Feminism is Relevant – Part I – History, Politics and Economics*, Colombo: Feminist Study Circle.

Fernando, V. and de Mel, J. H. (1991) *Non-Governmental Organisations (NGOs) in Sri Lanka – An Introduction*, Colombo: NGO Water Supply and Sanitation Decade Service.

Finch, J. (1984) '"It's great to have someone to talk to" The ethics and politics of interviewing women', in C. Bell and H. Roberts (eds) *Social Researching – Politics, Problems, Practice*, London: Routledge and Kegan Paul.

Fine, M. (1994) 'Dis-stance and other stances: negotiations of power inside feminist research', in A. Gitlin (ed.) *Power and Method – Political Activism and Educational Research*, New York: Routledge.

Firestone, S. (1979) *The Dialectic of Sex: The Case for Feminist Revolution*, London: The Women's Press.

Flax, J. (1987) 'Postmodernism and gender relations in feminist theory', *Signs Journal of Women in Culture and Society*, 12 (4), 621–643.

Flick, U. (2006) 'Triangulation', in V. Jupp (ed.) *The Sage Dictionary of Social Science Methods*, London / Thousand Oaks / New Delhi: Sage Publications.

Fonow, M. M. and Cook, J. A. (1991a) 'Back to the future: A look at the second wave of feminist epistemology and methodology', in M. M. Fonow and J. A. Cook (eds) *Beyond Methodology: Feminist Scholarship as Lived Research*, Bloomington / Indianapolis, IN: Indiana University Press.

——(eds) (1991b) *Beyond Methodology – Feminist Scholarship as Lived Research*, Bloomington: Indiana University Press.

——(2005) 'Feminist methodology: new applications in the academy and public policy', *Signs Journal of Women in Culture and Society*, 30 (4), 2211–2236.

Fontana, A. (2002) 'Postmodern trends in interviewing', in J. F. Gubrium and J. A. Holstein (eds) *Handbook of Interview Research*, Thousand Oaks: Sage.

Foucault, M. (1972) *The Archaeology of Knowledge and the Discourse on Language*, A. M. Sheridan Smith (trans.), New York: Pantheon Books.

——(1980a) *The History of Sexuality* (Vol. 1), R. Hurley (trans.), New York: Vintage.

——(1980b) 'Two Interviews', in C. Gordon (ed.) *Michel Foucault Power/Knowledge – Selected Interviews and Other Writings 1972–1977*, Essex: Pearson Education.

——(1991) 'Nietzsche, Genealogy, History', in P. Rabinow (ed.) *The Foucault Reader*, London / New York / Victoria / Ontario / Auckland: Penguin Books.

——(1998) *Aesthetics, Method, and Epistemology*, in J. D. Faubion (ed.), R. Hurley and others (trans.), New York: New Press.

Franklin, S. and Stacey, J. (1988) 'Dyketactics for difficult times: A review of the "homosexuality, which homosexuality?" conference', *Feminist Review*, 29 (May 1988), 136–150.

Fraser, N. and Gordon, L. (1994) 'A genealogy of dependency: tracing a keyword in the US welfare state', *Signs Journal of Women in Culture and Society*, 19 (2), 309–336.

Fraser, N. and Nicholson, L. J. (1990) 'Social criticism without philosophy: an encounter between feminism and postmodernism', in L. J. Nicholson (ed.) *Feminism / Postmodernism*, New York / London: Routledge.

Friedan, B. (1963) *The Feminine Mystique*, New York: W. M. Norton.

Frye, M. (1990) 'The possibility of feminist theory', in D. L. Rhode (ed.) *Theoretical Perspectives on Sexual Difference*, New Haven, CT / London: Yale University Press.

Ghai, A. (2008) 'A disabled feminism?', in M. E. John (ed.) *Women's Studies in India*, New Delhi: Penguin Books.

Gillies, V. and Alldred, P. (2002) 'The ethics of intention – research as a political tool', in M. Mauthner, M. Birch, J. Jessop and T. Miller (eds) *Ethics of Qualitative Research*, Thousand Oaks, CA: Sage.

Gilligan, C. (1977) 'In a different voice: women's conceptions of self and morality', *Harvard Educational Review*, 47 (4), 481–517.

Gilman, C. P. (1979) *Herland*, New York: Pantheon.

Gluck, S. B. and Patai, D. (eds) (1991) *Women's Words, Women's Words, Women's Words, the Feminist Practice of Oral History*, New York: Routledge.

Gomez, M. and Gomez, S. (2001) *Preferring Women – Gender and Politics in Sri Lanka*, Colombo: Canadian International Development Agency.

Gomez, S. and Gomez, M. (1999) *From Rights and Shame to Remedies and Change – Gender Violence in Sri Lanka*, Colombo: Canadian International Development Agency.

Goonatilake, H. (1985) 'Research and information on women', in CENWOR (ed.) *UN Decade for Women: Progress and Achievements of Women in Sri Lanka*, Colombo: Centre for Women's Research.

——(1986) 'The emergence of a new educated proletariat: The case of young female workers in the Free Trade Zones', Paper presented at the 42nd Annual Sessions of the Sri Lanka Association for the Advancement of Science (SLAAS), Colombo: Sri Lanka Association for the Advancement of Science, December 1986.

Goonesekere, S. (1995) 'Realising gender equity through law: Sri Lanka's experience of the post-Nairobi Decade', in CENWOR (ed.) *Facets of Change – Women in Sri Lanka 1986 – 1995*, Colombo: Centre for Women's Research.

——(2000) 'The Beijing commitments and the Sri Lankan legal system', in CENWOR (ed.) *Post-Beijing Reflections in Sri Lanka*, Colombo: Centre for Women's Research.

Gordon, C. (ed.) (1980) *Michel Foucault Power/Knowledge – Selected Interviews and Other Writings 1972–1977*, Essex: Pearson Education.

Greer, G. (1971) *The Female Eunuch*, London: Paladin.

Griffiths, M. (1998) *Educational Research for Social Justice*, Buckingham / Philadelphia, PA: Open University Press.

Grillo, T. (2006) 'Anti-essentialism and intersectionality: tools to dismantle the master's house', in E. Hackett and S. Haslanger (eds) *Theorising Feminisms – A Reader*, New York / Oxford: Oxford University Press.

Gross, E. (1987) 'Conclusion: what is feminist theory?', in C. Pateman and E. Gross (eds) *Feminist Challenges – Social and Political Theory*, Boston, MA: North Eastern University Press.

Gunawardena, C. (ed.) (2005) *Not Adding Up: Looking Beyond the Numbers – Gender Equity in Higher Education in Sri Lanka*, Colombo: Open University of Sri Lanka.

Haavind, H. (2005) 'How my texts are situated in time and may change the future', in E. Engelstad and S. Gerrard (eds) *Challenging Situatedness*, Eburon Delft: Eburon Academic Publishers.

Hackett, E. and Haslanger, S. (eds) (2006) *Theorising Feminisms – A Reader*, New York / Oxford: Oxford University Press.

Halpin, D. and Troyna, B. (eds) (1994) *Researching Educational Policy – Ethical and Methodological Issues*, London: The Falmer Press.

Hammersley, M. (2006) 'Induction', in V. Jupp (ed.) *The Sage Dictionary of Social Research Methods*, London / Thousand Oaks, CA / New Delhi: Sage Publications.

Haniffa, F. (2008) 'Piety as politics amongst Muslim women in contemporary Sri Lanka', *Modern Asian Studies*, 42 (2/3), 347–375.

Haraway, D. (1988) 'Situated knowledges: the science question in feminism and the privilege of the partial perspective', *Feminist Studies*, 14 (3), 573–599.

——(1990) 'A manifesto for Cyborgs: science, technology and socialist feminism in the 1980s', in L. J. Nicholson (ed.) *Feminism / Postmodernism*, New York / London: Routledge.

Harding, S. (1987a) 'Introduction: is there a feminist method?', *Feminism and Methodology*, Bloomington: Indiana University Press, 1–14.

——(ed.) (1987b) *Feminism and Methodology*, Bloomington, IN: Indiana University Press.

——(1989) 'Feminist justificatory strategies', in A. Gary and M. Pearsall (eds) *Women, Knowledge and Reality*, Boston, MA: Unwin Hyman.

——(1990) 'Feminism, science and anti-enlightenment critiques', in J. L. Nicholson (ed.) *Feminism / Postmodernism*, London: Routledge.

——(2004a) 'Introduction: standpoint theory as a site of political, philosophic, and scientific debate', in S. Harding (ed.) *The Feminist Standpoint Theory Reader – Intellectual and Political Controversies*, New York / London: Routledge.

——(2004b) 'Rethinking standpoint epistemology: what is strong objectivity?', in S. Harding (ed.) *The Feminist Standpoint Theory – Intellectual and Political Controversies*, New York / London: Routledge.

——(2004c) *The Feminist Standpoint Theory Reader – Intellectual and Political Controversies*, New York / London: Routledge.

Harding, S. and Norberg, K. (2005) 'New feminist approaches to social science methodologies', *Signs Journal of Women in Culture and Society*, 30 (4), 2009–2015.

Harre, R. (2006) 'Phenomenology', in V. Jupp (ed.) *The Sage Dictionary of Social Research Methods*, London / Thousand Oaks, CA / New Delhi: Sage Publications.

Harstock, N. (2004) 'The feminist standpoint: developing the ground for a specifically feminist historical materialism', in S. Harding (ed.) *The Feminist Standpoint Theory Reader – Intellectual and Political Controversies*, New York / London: Routledge.

Hart, C. (1998) *Doing a Literature Review – Releasing the Social Science Imagination*, London / Thousand Oaks / New Delhi: Sage Publications.

Hepburn, A. (2006) 'Constructionism', in V. Jupp (ed.) *The Sage Dictionary of Social Research Methods*, London / Thousand Oaks / New Delhi: Sage Publications.

Hesse-Biber, S. N., Leavy, P. and Yaiser, M. L. (2004) 'Feminist approaches to research as a process – reconceptualising epistemology, methodology, and method', in S. N. Hesse-Biber and M. L. Yaiser (eds) *Feminist Perspectives on Social Research*, Oxford / New York: Oxford University Press.

Hesse-Biber, S. N. and Yaiser, M. L. (2004a) 'Difference matters: studying across race, class, gender, and sexuality', in S. N. Hesse-Biber and M. L. Yaiser (eds) *Feminist Perspectives on Social Research*, New York / Oxford: Oxford University Press.

——(eds) (2004b) *Feminist Perspectives on Social Research*, Oxford / New York: Oxford University Press.

Hesse-Biber, S. N. and Leavy, P. L. (eds) (2007) *Feminist Research Practice*, Thousand Oaks, CA / London / New Delhi: Sage Publications.

Hey, V. (2006) 'The politics of performative resignification: translating Judith Butler's theoretical discourse and its potential for a theory of education', *British Journal of Sociology of Education*, 27 (4), 439–457.

Holland, J. and Ramazanoglu, C. (1994) 'Coming to conclusions – power and interpretation in researching young women's sexuality', in M. Maynard and J. Purvis (eds) *Researching Women's Lives from a Feminist Perspective*, London: Taylor and Francis.

Holstein, J. A. and Gubrium, J. F. (1995) *The Active Interview*, London: Sage.

Hubbard, R. (1990) 'The political nature of "human nature"' in D. L. Rhode (ed.) *Theoretical Perspectives on Sexual Difference*, New Haven, CT / London: Yale University Press.

Hughes, C. (2002) *Key Concepts in Feminist Theory and Research*, London: Sage Publications.

International Labour Organisation (ed.) (2000) *Structural Adjustment, Gender and Employment – The Sri Lankan Experience*, Geneva: International Labour Office.

International Labour Organisation and Employers' Federation of Ceylon (2005) *Guidelines for Company Policy on Gender Equity / Equality*, Colombo: International Labour Organisation.

Irigaray, L. (1974) *Speculum of the Other Woman*, trans. G. C. Gill, Ithaca, NY: Cornell University Press.

Islam, N. (2008) 'Research as an act of betrayal: researching race in an Asian community in Los Angeles', in A. M. Jaggar (ed.) *Just Methods – An Interdisciplinary Feminist Reader*, Boulder, CO / London: Paradigm Publishers.

Jackson, C. and Pearson, R. (1998) *Feminist Visions of Development – Gender Analysis and Policy*, London / New York: Routledge.

Jacobs, J. M. (2003) 'Earth honoring: western desires and indigenous knowledges', in R. Lewis and S. Mills (eds) *Feminist Postcolonial Theory – A Reader*, New York: Routledge.

Jagger, A. M. (1989) 'Love and knowledge – emotion in feminist epistemology', in A. Garry and M. Pearsall (eds) *Women, Knowledge and Reality – Explorations in Feminist Philosophy*, Boston: Unwin Hyman.

——(2004) 'Feminist politics and epistemology: the standpoint of women', in S. Harding (ed.) *The Feminist Standpoint Theory Reader – Intellectual and Political Controversies*, New York / London: Routledge.

——(2008) (ed.) *Just Methods – An Interdisciplinary Feminist Reader*, Boulder, CO / London: Paradigm Publishers.

Jain, J. (2005) '"Ladki Ki Jaat?" Theorising the women question', in Final Report: Project Developing Indian Perspectives on Feminist Theory and Methodology Department of Women and Child Development / Women's Studies Centre University of New Delhi.

Jarviluoma, H., Moisala, P. and Vilkko, A. (2003) *Gender and Qualitative Methods*, London / Thousand Oaks, CA / New Delhi: Sage Publications.

Jayaratne, T. E. (1983) 'The value of quantitative methodology for feminist research', in G. Bowles and R. D. Klein (eds) *Theories of Women's Studies*, London / New York: Routledge and Kegan Paul.

Jayaratne, T. E. and Stewart, A. J. (1991) in M. M. Fonow and J. A. Cook (eds) *Beyond Methodology – Feminist Scholarship as Lived Research*, Bloomington, IN: Indiana University Press.

Jayasinghe, V. (1981) 'Employment of female domestic aides in the UAE', *Economic Review*, 7 (1), 7–9.

Jayatilaka, S. R. D. S. (1998) *Study of Inequality in Sri Lankan Society – The Gender Blindness in Sociological and Anthropological Studies*, CENWOR Sixth National Convention on Women's Studies, Colombo: Centre for Women's Research, March 1998.

Jayawardena, K. (1975) 'The participation of women in the social reform, political and labour movements of Sri Lanka', *Logos*, 13 (2), 17–25.

——(1985) 'Some aspects of feminist consciousness in the decade 1975 – 1985', in CENWOR (ed.) *The UN Decade for Women: Progress and Achievements of Women in Sri Lanka*, Colombo: Centre for Women's Research.

——(1986) *Feminism and Nationalism in the Third World*, London: Zed Books.

——(1993) *Dr. Mary Rutnam – A Canadian Pioneer for Women's Rights in Sri Lanka*, Colombo: Social Scientists' Association.

——(1994) 'Religious and cultural identity and the construction of Sinhala Buddhist womanhood', *Nivedini*, 2 (1), 111–139.

——(1995a) 'The women's movement in Sri Lanka 1985 – 95 – a glance back over ten years', in CENWOR (ed.) *Facets of Change – Women in Sri Lanka 1986–1995*, Colombo: Centre for Women's Research.

——(1995b) *The White Woman's Other Burden – Western Women and South Asia During British Rule*, New York: Routledge.

Jayawardena, K. and de Alwis, M. (eds) (1996) *Embodied Violence – Communalising Women's Sexuality in South Asia*, New Delhi / London / New Jersey: Zed Books and Kali for Women.

——(2002) 'The contingent politics of the women's movement in Sri Lanka after independence', in S. Jayaweera (ed.) *Women in Post-Independence Sri Lanka*, Colombo: Vijitha Yapa Publications.

Jayawardena, K. and Jayaweera, S. (1985) 'The integration of women in development planning', in N. Hayzer (ed.) *Missing Women: Development Planning in Asia and the Pacific*, Kuala Lumpur: Asia and Pacific Development Centre.

Jayaweera, S. (1979) 'Women in the economy', in University of Colombo (ed.) *Status of Women*, Colombo: University of Colombo.

——(1985a) 'Integration of women in development planning', in CENWOR (ed.) *The UN Decade for Women: Progress and Achievements of Women in Sri Lanka*, Colombo: Centre for Women's Research.

——(1985b) 'Women and education', in CENWOR (ed.) *The UN Decade for Women: Progress and Achievements of Women in Sri Lanka*, Colombo: Centre for Women's Research.

——(1995) 'Introduction', in CENWOR (ed.) *Facets of Change – Women in Sri Lanka (1986–1995)*, Colombo: Centre for Women's Research.

——(2000) 'Gender dimensions of change: a micro-level analysis', in International Labour Organisation (ed.) *Structural Adjustment, Gender and Employment*, Geneva: International Labour Organisation.

——(2002a) 'Women in education and employment', in S. Jayaweera (ed.) *Women in Post-Independence Sri Lanka*, Colombo: Centre for Women's Research.

——(ed.) (2002b) *Women in Post-Independence Sri Lanka*, Colombo: Vijitha Yapa Publications.

——(2005) *The Impact of the Tsunami on Households and Vulnerable Groups in Two Districts in Sri Lanka*, Colombo: Centre for Women's Research.

Jayaweera, S. and Sanmugam, T. (2001) *Women in Garment and Textile Industries in Sri Lanka – Gender Roles and Relations*, Colombo: Centre for Women's Research.

John, M. E. (2004a) 'Feminisms in India and the West – recasting a relationship', in M. Chaudhuri (ed.) *Feminism in India*, New Delhi: Kali for Women / Women Unlimited.

——(2004b) 'Gender and development in India – 1970s–1990s', in M. Chaudhuri (ed.) *Feminism in India*, New Delhi: Kali for Women / Women Unlimited.

John, M. E. (2008) 'Introduction', in M. E. John (ed.) *Women's Studies in India*, New Delhi: Penguin Books.

Jupp, V. (ed.) (2006) *The Sage Dictionary of Social Research Methods*, London / Thousand Oaks / New Delhi: Sage Publications.

Kabeer, N. (2003) *Gender Mainstreaming in Poverty Eradication and the Millennium Development Goals – A Handbook for Policy-makers and Stakeholders*, London: Commonwealth Secretariat / International Development Research Centre / Canadian International Development Agency.

Kandiyoti, D. (1988) 'Bargaining with Patriarchy', *Gender and Society*, 2 (3), 274–290.

Karl, M. (1995) *Women and Empowerment – Participation and Decision-Making*, London: Zed Books.

Kelly-Gadol, J. (2008) 'The social relation of the sexes: methodological implications of women's history', in A. M. Jagger (ed.) *Just Methods: An Interdisciplinary Feminist Reader*, Boulder / London: Paradigm Publishers.

Khanduja, S. (2005) 'Curricular and pedagogical strategies in women's studies: the Indian context', in P. Juyal and the Faculty of Isabella Thorburn College, *Women's Studies in India: Some Contemporary Counters*, Seoul: Ewha Women's University Press.

Kiribamune, S. (1990) 'Women in pre-modern Sri Lanka', in S. Kiribamune and V. Samarasinghe (eds) *Women at the Crossroads – A Sri Lankan Perspective*, New Delhi: Vikas Publishing House Private Limited.

——(1999a) 'Climbing the greasy pole: opportunities and challenges in women's access to electoral politics in Sri Lanka', in S. Kiribamune (ed.) *Women and Politics in Sri Lanka – A Comparative Perspective*, Kandy: International Centre for Ethnic Studies.

——(ed.) (1999b) *Women and Politics in Sri Lanka – A Comparative Perspective*, Kandy: International Centre for Ethnic Studies.

Kiribamune, S. and Samarasinghe, V. (eds) (1990) *Women at the Crossroads – A Sri Lankan Perspective*, New Delhi: Vikas Publishing House Private Limited.

Klein, R. D. (1983) 'How to do what we want to do – thoughts about feminist research methodology', in G. Bowles and R. D. Klein (eds) *Theories of Women's Studies*, London: Routledge and Kegan Paul.

Knox, R. (1966) *An Historical Relation of Ceylon*, Colombo: Tisara Prakasakayo.

Kottegoda, S. (1994) *Examining Gender: Is it Relevant?* CENWOR Fourth National Convention on Women's Studies, Colombo: Centre for Women's Research, March 1994.

——(1999) *Women in Poverty in Sri Lanka – Trends and Characteristics*, Documentation of Discussions at the Strengthening of Vocational Training Project (SVTP) Colombo: Poverty Impact Unit, Centre for Poverty Analysis, July 1999.

——(2003) 'Interventions in poverty alleviation: women recovering from poverty or women recovering the family from poverty?', in Centre for Poverty Analysis (ed.) *Poverty Issues in Sri Lanka, Poverty in Sri Lanka*, Colombo: Centre for Poverty Analysis / Sri Lanka Association for the Advancement of Science.

——(2004a) *Poverty, Migration and Family: the Politics of Gender in Sri Lanka*, CENWOR Ninth National Convention on Women's Studies, Colombo: Centre for Women's Research, March 2004.

——(2004b) *Negotiating Household Politics – Women's Strategies in Urban Sri Lanka*, Colombo: Social Scientists' Association.

Kramarae, C. and Spender, D. (eds) (1992) *The Knowledge Explosion – Generations of Feminist Scholarship*, New York / London: Teachers' College Press, Columbia University.

Kramarae, C. and Treichler, P. (1985) *A Feminist Dictionary*, Boston, MA / London / Henley: Pandora Press.

Krishnaraj, M. (2006) 'Is gender easy to study? Some reflections', *Economic and Political Weekly*, 21 October 2006.

Kuhn, T. (1970) *The Structure of Scientific Revolutions*, Chicago: University of Chicago Press.

Lal, J. (1996) 'Situating locations: The politics of self, identity, and "other", in living and writing the text', in Diane Wolf (ed.) *Feminist Dilemmas in Fieldwork*, Boulder, CO: Westview Press.

Lather, P. (1986) 'Research as praxis', *Harvard Educational Review*, 56 (3), 257–277.
——(1991) *Getting Smart – Feminist Research and Pedagogy with/in the Postmodern*, London / New York: Routledge.
Law, J. (2004) *After Method – Mess in Social Science Research*, London and New York: Routledge – Taylor and Francis Group.
Leach, F. (2003) *Practicing Gender Analysis in Education*, Oxford: Oxfam.
Leavy, P. L. (2007) 'The feminist practice of content analysis', in S. N. Hess-Biber and P. L. Leavy (eds) *Feminist Research Practice*, London / Thousand Oaks, CA / New Delhi: Sage Publications.
Letherby, G. (2003) *Feminist Research in Theory and Practice*, Buckingham / Philadelphia, PA: Open University Press.
——(2006) 'Emancipatory research', in V. Jupp (ed.) *The Sage Dictionary of Social Research Methods*, London / Thousand Oaks, CA / New Delhi: Sage Publications.
Lewis, R. and Mills, S. (eds) (2003) *Feminist Postcolonial Theory – A Reader*, New York: Routledge.
Licuanan, P. B. (2006) *Staying the Course: Linking the MDGs, Beijing and CEDAW*, Colombo: Centre for Women's Research.
Loganathan, B. (2001) *Gendering Humanitarianism: An Annotated Bibliography on Gender and Capacity Building in Armed Conflict*, Colombo: International Centre for Ethnic Studies.
Lund, R. (1989) *Women and Rural Development in the Mahaweli Area – A Feminist Appraisal*, paper presented at the CENWOR First National Convention on Women's Studies, Colombo: Centre for Women's Research, March 1989.
Lyons, T. (1999) 'Gender and development: African Women and Western feminisms, and the dilemmas of doing feminist field work in Africa', Outskirts online journal, Vol. 4. Available from: www.chloe.uwa.edu.au/outskirts/archive/volume4/lyons (accessed 6 March 2009).
MacKinnon, C. (1982) 'Feminism, Marxism, method and the state: an agenda for theory', *Signs*, 7 (3), 515–544.
MacLure, M. (2003) *Discourse in Educational Research*, Buckingham: Open University Press.
Maguire, M. (2005) '"Not footprints behind but footprints forward": working class women who teach', *Gender and Education*, 17 (1), 1–18.
Maguire, M. and Ball, S. (1994) 'Researching politics and the politics of research: recent qualitative studies in the UK', *Qualitative Studies in Education*, 7 (3), 269–285.
Maguire, M., Wooldridge, T. and Pratt, A. S. (2006) *The Urban Primary School*, Maidenhead: Open University Press.
Manchanda, R. (2001) (ed.) *Beyond Victimhood and Agency*, New Delhi: Sage Publications.
Mani, L. (1992) 'Multiple mediations: feminist scholarship in the age of multinational reception', in H. Crowley and S. Himmelweit (eds) *Knowing Women – Feminism and Knowledge*, Cambridge: Polity Press / Open University.
March, C., Smyth, I. and Mukhopadhyay (1999) *A Guide to Gender Analysis Frameworks*, Oxford: Oxfam.
Martin, J. R. (1994) 'Methodological essentialism, false difference, and other dangerous traps', *Signs Journal of Women in Culture and Society*, 19 (3), 630–657.
Mason, J. (2002) *Qualitative Researching*, Thousand Oaks, CA: Sage Publications.
Maunaguru, S. (1995) 'Women in contemporary Sri Lankan Tamil fiction', *Nivedini*, 3 (2), 30–44.

Mauthner, M. (2000) 'Snippets and silences: ethics and reflexivity in narratives of sistering', *International Journal of Social Research Methodology*, 3 (4), 287–306.

Mauthner, M., Birch, M., Jessop, J. and Miller, T. (eds) (2002) *Ethics in Qualitative Research*, London: Sage.

Mauthner, N. and Doucet, A. (1998) 'Reflections on a voice-centered relational method – analysing maternal and domestic voices', in J. Ribbens and R. Edwards (eds) *Feminist Dilemmas in Qualitative Research – Public Knowledge and Private Lives*, London: Sage.

Maynard, M. (1993) 'Feminism and the possibilities of a postmodern research practice', *British Journal of Sociology of Education*, 14 (3), 327–331.

——(1995) 'Beyond the "Big Three": the development of feminist theory in the 1990s', *Women's History Review*, 4 (3), 259–281.

——(2004) 'Methods, practice and epistemology: The debate about feminism and research', in C. Seale (ed.) *Social Research Methods – A Reader*, London / New York: Routledge Taylor and Francis Group.

Maynard, M. and Purvis, J. (1994a) *Researching Women's Lives from a Feminist Perspective*, London: Taylor and Francis.

——(1994b) 'Doing feminist research', in M. Maynard and J. Purvis (eds) *Researching Women's Lives from a Feminist Perspective*, London: Taylor and Francis.

Mazundar, V. (2008) 'The making of a founding text', in M. E. John (ed.) *Women's Studies in India*, New Delhi: Penguin Books.

Meerachakravorthy (1998) 'Gender concept – another dimension of understanding', *Nivedini – Journal of Gender Studies*, 6 (1/2), 22–29.

Meintjes, S., Pillay, A. and Turshen, M. (2001) (eds) *The Aftermath: Women in Post-conflict Transformation*, London: Zed Books.

Mendis, S. K. (ed.) (2002) *Gender Resource Book for Teachers*, Colombo: Centre for Women's Research.

Mies, M. (1983) 'Towards a methodology for feminist research', in G. Bowles and R. D. Klein (eds) *Theories for Women's Studies*, London: Routledge and Kegan Paul.

——(1991) 'Women's research or feminist research? The debate surrounding feminist science and methodology', in M. M. Fonow and J. A. Cook (eds) *Beyond Methodology – Feminist Scholarship as Lived Research*, Bloomington, IN: Indiana University Press.

Miller, T. and Bell, L. (2002) 'Consenting to what? Issues of gate-keeping and "informed" consent', in M. Mauthner, M. Birch, J. Jessop and T. Miller (eds) *Ethics in Qualitative Research*, Thousand Oaks, CA: Sage.

Miller, C. and Razavi, S. (1998a) 'Introduction', in C. Miller and S. Razavi (eds) *Missionaries and Mandarins: Feminist Engagement with Development Institutions*, London: Intermediate Technology Publications / United Nations Research Institute for Social Development.

——(eds) (1998b) *Missionaries and Mandarins: Feminist Engagement with Development Institutions*, London: Intermediate Technology Publications / United Nations Research Institute for Social Development.

Miller, J. (2000) *Violence against Sex Workers in Sri Lanka – Causes, Consequences and Remedies*, Colombo: International Centre for Ethnic Studies.

Millett, K. (1971) *Sexual Politics*, London: Sphere Books.

Ministry of Health and Women's Affairs (1993) *Status of Women (Sri Lanka)*, Colombo: Ministry of Health and Women's Affairs.

Ministry of Women's Affairs (2003) *Handbook on Gender Disaggregated Data – Sri Lanka*, Colombo: Ministry of Women's Affairs.

Mockler, N. (2007) 'Ethics in practitioner research: dilemmas from the field', in A. Cambell and S. Groundwater-Smith (eds) *An Ethical Approach to Practitioner Research*, London / New York: Routledge Taylor and Francis Group.

Mohanty, C. T. (1988) 'Under western eyes: feminist scholarship and colonial discourses', *Feminist Review*, 30, 65–88.

——(2003) 'Feminist encounters: locating the politics of experience', in C. R. McCann and S. Kim (eds) *Feminist Theory Reader – Local and Global Perspectives*, New York / London: Routledge.

Mohanty, M. (2008) 'On the concept of empowerment', in M. E. John (ed.) *Women's Studies in India*, New Delhi: Penguin Book in India.

Moi, T. (1999) *What is a Woman? And Other Essays*, Oxford: Oxford University Press.

Morley, L. (1996) 'Interrogating patriarchy – the challenges of feminist research', in L. Morley and V. Walsh (eds) *Breaking Boundaries: Women in Higher Education*, London / Washington, DC: Taylor & Francis.

——(1999) *Organising Feminisms – The Micropolitics of the Academy*, New York: St Martin's Press.

Morley, L. and Walsh, V. (1996) *Breaking Boundaries: Women in Higher Education*, London: Taylor and Francis.

Moser, C. (1993) *Gender Planning and Development – Theory, Practice and Training*, London / New York: Routledge.

Ms. (2005a) 'Gender dimensions of disasters', *The Sunday Leader*, 2 January 2005.

——(2005b) 'Paying attention to gender issues in the face of the Tsunami', *The Sunday Leader*, 30 January 2005.

Muttiah, W., Thiruchandran, S. and Wanasinghe, S. (eds) (2006) *Socialist Women of Sri Lanka*, Colombo: A Young Socialist Publication.

Naples, N. A. (2003) *Feminism and Method – Ethnography, Discourse Analysis and Activist Research*, New York / London: Routledge.

Narayan, U. (2004) 'The project of a feminist epistemology: perspectives from a non-western feminist', in S. Harding (ed.) *The Feminist Standpoint Theory Reader*, New York / London: Routledge.

Nesiah, V. (1996) *Debates in the Feminist Movement*, Colombo: Social Scientists' Association.

Nicholson, L. J. (ed.) (1990) *Feminism / Postmodernism*, New York / London: Routledge.

Nzegwu, N. (2002) 'Questions of agency: development, donors and women of the South', *Jenda: A Journal of Culture and African Women Studies*, 2 (1). Available from: www.jendajournal.com/vol2.1/nzegwu.html (accessed 15 February 2009).

Oakley, A. (1972) *Sex, Gender and Society*, London: Temple Smith.

——(1981) 'Interviewing women: a contradiction in terms', in H. Roberts (ed.) *Doing Feminist Research*, London / Boston / Melbourne / Henley: Routledge and Kegan Paul.

——(2000) *Experiments in Knowing Gender and Method in the Social Sciences*, Cambridge: Polity Press / Blackwell Publishers.

——(2002) 'Research evidence, knowledge management and educational practice: lessons for all?' Paper for High-level Forum on Knowledge Management in Education and Learning, Oxford, March 2002.

——(2005) *The Anne Oakley Reader – Gender, Women and Social Science*, Bristol: The Policy Press.

Olesen, V. L. (2000) 'Feminisms and qualitative research at and into the millennium', in N. K. Denzin and Y. S. Lincoln (eds) *Handbook of Qualitative Research*, Thousand Oaks: Sage.

Oluwelwe, S. (2000) 'Africa', in A. M. Jaggar and I. M. Young (eds) *A Companion to Feminist Philosophy*, Malden / Oxford / Victoria: Blackwell Publishing.

Otani, H. and Widner, R. L. (2005) 'Metacognition: new issues and approaches: guest editor's introduction', *Journal of General Psychology*. Available from: www.findarticles.com/p/articles/mi_m2405 (accessed 20 February 2006).

Overholt, C., Anderson, M., Cloud, K. and Austin, J. E. (1984) *Gender Roles in Development – A Case Book*, Bloomfield, IN: Kumarian Press.

Oyewumi, O. (1997) *The Interaction of Women – Making an African Sense of Western Gender Discourses*, Minnesota: University of Minnesota Press.

Palriwala, R. (2002) 'Rhetorics of motherhood: politics, policy and family ideologies in India', in L. Sarkar, K. Sharma and L. Kasturi (eds) *Between Tradition, Counter Tradition and Heresy*, New Delhi: Rainbow Publishers.

Pateman, C. and Gross, E. (eds) (1987) *Feminist Challenges – Social and Political Theory*, Boston: North Eastern University Press.

Peiris, K. (1995) 'Mobilisation of community action by women', in CENWOR (ed.) *Facets of Change – Women in Sri Lanka 1986 – 1995*, Colombo: Centre for Women's Research.

Platt, J. (1981) 'On interviewing one's peers', *British Journal of Sociology*, 32 (1), 75–91.

Potter, J. and Weatherell, M. (1987) *Discourse and Social Psychology*, London: Sage.

Raj, M. K. (1988) 'Women's studies: A case for a new paradigm', *Economics and Political Weekly*, 28 (8), 892–894.

Rajapakse, D. A. (1995) 'Inter-locking class and gender: Mahawali women's (subjective) class experiences at times of drought', in CENWOR (ed.) *Facing Odds – Women in the Labour Market*, Colombo: Centre for Women's Research.

Rajasingham-Senanayake, D. (2001) 'An ambivalent empowerment: The tragedy of Tamil women in armed conflict', in R. Manchanda (ed.) *Beyond Victimhood and Agency*, New Delhi: Sage Publications.

Ramazanoglu, C. and Holland, J. (1999) 'Tripping over experience: some problems in feminist epistemology', *Discourse: Studies in the Cultural Politics of Education*, 20 (3), 381–392.

——(2002) *Feminist Methodology Challenges and Choices*, London / Thousand Oaks, CA / New Delhi: Sage Publications.

Ranasinghe, C. P. (1957) *The Buddha's Explanation of the Universe*, Colombo: Lanka Buddha Mandalaya Fund.

Ranaweera, E. (1992) 'Shame / Women / Gajaman Nona', CENWOR Third National Convention on Women's Studies, Colombo: Centre for Women's Research, March 1992.

Rao, A. (1991) *Women's Studies International – Nairobi and Beyond*, New York: The Feminist Press at the City University of New York.

Reay, D. (1995) 'The fallacy of easy access', *Women's Studies International Forum*, 18 (2), 205–213.

——(1996) 'Insider perspectives or stealing the words out of women's mouths: Interpretation in the research process', *Feminist Review*, 53, 57–73.

——(1998) 'Rethinking social class – qualitative perspectives on class and gender', *Sociology*, 32, 259–275.

Rege, S. (2008) 'Writing caste, writing gender: Dalit women's testimonies', in M. E. John (ed.) *Women's Studies in India*, New Delhi: Penguin Books.

Reinharz, S. (1983) 'Experiential analysis: a contribution to feminist research', in G. Bowles and R. D. Klein (eds) *Theories of Women's Studies*, London: Routledge.

——(1992) *Feminist Methods in Social Research*, New York / Oxford: Oxford University Press.

Reinharz, S. and Chase, S. E. (2002) 'Interviewing women', in J. F. Gubrium and J. A. Holstein (eds) *Handbook of Interview Research*, Thousand Oaks: Sage.

Reuben, E. (1978) 'In defiance of the evidence: notes on feminist scholarship', *Women's Studies International Quarterly*, 1 (3), 215–218.

Rhedding-Jones, J. (1997) 'The writing on the wall: doing a feminist post-structural doctorate', *Gender and Education*, 9 (2), 193–206.

Rhode, D. L. (ed.) (1990) *Theoretical Perspectives on Sexual Difference*, New Haven / London: Yale University Press.

Ribbens, J. (1989) 'Interviewing – an unnatural situation?', *Women's Studies International Forum*, 12 (6), 579–592.

Ribbens, J. and Edwards, R. (eds) (1998) *Feminist Dilemmas in Qualitative Research – Public Knowledge and Private Lives*, London: Sage.

Rich, A. (1980) 'Compulsory heterosexuality and lesbian experience', *Signs Journal of Women in Culture and Society*, 5 (4), 631–660.

——(2003) 'Notes towards a politics of location', in C. R. McCann and S. Kim (eds) *Feminist Theory Reader – Local and Global Perspectives*, New York / London: Routledge.

Richardson, L. (2000) 'Writing as a method of inquiry', in N. K. Denzin and Y. S. Lincoln (eds) *Handbook of Qualitative Research*, Thousand Oaks: Sage.

Riddell, S. (1989) 'Exploiting the exploited? The ethics of feminist educational research', in R. Burgess (ed.) *The Ethics of Educational Research*, London: Falmer Press.

Roberts, H. (ed.) (1981) *Doing Feminist Research*, London / Boston, MA / Melbourne / Henley: Routledge and Kegan Paul.

Rosaldo, M. and Lamphere, L. (eds) (1974) *Women, Culture and Society*, Stanford: Stanford University Press.

Rowbotham, S. (1973) *Hidden from History*, London: Pluto.

Rubin, G. S. (2006) 'Thinking sex: notes for a radical theory of the politics of sexuality', in E. Hackett, and S. Haslanger (eds) *Theorising Feminisms – A Reader*, New York / Oxford: Oxford University Press.

Ruddick, S. (1980) 'Maternal thinking', *Feminist Studies*, 6 (2), 342–367.

——(1992) 'From maternal thinking to peace politics', in E. B. Cole and S. Coultrap-McQuin (eds) *Explorations in Feminist Ethics – Theory and Practice*, Bloomington / Indianapolis: Indiana University Press.

——(2006) 'Notes towards a maternal peace politics', in E. Hackett and S. Haslanger (eds) *Theorising Feminisms – A Reader*, New York / Oxford: Oxford University Press.

Rupesinghe, K. (1981) *A Preliminary Analysis of Female Labour in Garment Industries in Sri Lanka*, Colombo: Social Scientists' Association Seminar on Women Workers in Export-oriented Industries and Tourism.

Ruwanpura, K. N. (2006) *Matrilineal Communities, Patriarchal Realities – A Feminist Nirvana Uncovered*, New Delhi: Social Scientists' Association / Zubaan.

Said, E. W. (1978) *Orientalism*, London: Routledge Kegan Paul.

——(1983) *The World, the Text and the Critic*, Cambridge: Harvard University Press.

Samuel, K. (1999) *Women's Rights Watch – Year Report 1999*, Colombo: Women and Media Collective.

——(2001) 'Gender difference in conflict resolution', in I. Skjelsbaek and D. Smith (eds) *Gender Peace and Conflict*, New Delhi / Oslo: International Peace Institute / Sage Publishers.

——(2006a) *A Hidden History – Women's Activism for Peace in Sri Lanka 1982 – 2002*, Colombo: Social Scientists' Association.

——(2006b) *Feminist Trends in the Women's Action Committee 1982–1990*, Colombo: Thesis submitted for a Masters in Women's Studies, University of Colombo.

Sandoval, C. (2004) 'US third world feminism: the theory and method of differential oppositional consciousness in the postmodern world', in S. Harding (ed.) *The Feminist Standpoint Theory Reader*, New York: Routledge.

Sangari, K. (2008) 'Politics of diversity: religious communities and multiple patriarchies', in M. E. John (ed.) *Women's Studies in India*, New Delhi: Penguin Books.

Sangari, K. and S. Vaid (1989) 'Recasting women - an introduction', in K. Sangari and S. Vaid (eds) *Recasting Women: Essays in Colonial History*, New Delhi: Kali for Women.

Saran, R. (1985) 'Use of archives and interviews in research on educational policy', in R. Burgess (ed.) *Strategies of Educational Research – Qualitative Methods*, London: Falmer Press.

Schalkwyak, J., Thomas, H. and Woroniuk, B. (1996) *Mainstreaming: A Strategy for Achieving Equality between Men and Women – A Think Piece*, Stockholm: Swedish International Development Agency / Department of Policy and Legal Services.

Scheurich, J. J. and McKenzie, K. B. (2005) 'Foucault's methodologies – archaeology and genealogy', in N. K. Denzin and Y. S. Lincoln (eds) *The Sage Handbook of Qualitative Research*, Thousand Oaks, CA / London / New Delhi: Sage Publications.

Schrijvers, J. (1993) 'Question of gender in development planning-women's experience in a new settlement of the Mahaweli Project', *Asia Pacific Journal of Rural Development*, 3 (1), 44–63.

——(1995) 'Dilemmas of a transformative research ideal – refugees and resettlement in Sri Lanka', *Nivedini*, 3 (2), 7–29.

——(1996) 'Researching in the eastern province', *Voice of Women*, 4 (4), 19–20.

——(1998) 'Internal refugees in Sri Lanka: the interplay of ethnicity and gender', *Nivedini – Journal of Gender Studies*, 6 (1/2), 30–63.

Scott, J. (2006) 'Textual analysis', in V. Jupp (ed.) *The Sage Dictionary of Social Research Methods*, London / Thousand Oaks, CA / New Delhi: Sage Publications.

Scott, J. W. (1991) 'Gender: A useful category of historical analysis', in A. Rao (ed.) *Women's Studies International – Nairobi and Beyond*, New York: The Feminist Press at the City University of New York.

——(2000) 'Fictitious unities – gender, east and west', Paper presented at the 4th European Feminist Research Conference, Bologna, Italy, September 29, 2000.

——(2003) 'Deconstructing equality versus difference: or, the uses of poststructuralist theory for feminism', in C. R. McCann and S. Kim (eds) *Feminist Theory Reader – Local and Global Perspectives*, New York / London: Routledge.

Scott, S. (1984) 'The personable and the powerful: gender and status in sociological research', in C. Bell and H. Roberts (eds) *Social Researching – Politics, Problems, Practice*, London: Routledge and Kegan Paul.

Seale, C. (1999) *The Quality of Qualitative Research*, London / Thousand Oaks, CA / New Delhi: Sage Publications.

Sen, G. and Grown, C. (1987) *Development, Crisis and Alternative Visions – Third World Women's Perspectives*, New York: Monthly Review Press.

Shaheed, F. (1997) 'The state of research on women in Pakistan', Keynote paper presented at First National Conference on New Directions in Research for Women, Aga Khan University, Karachi (30–31 May) AKU-Karachi, 11–21.

——(2001) 'An interview with Farida Shaheed', *Association for Women's Rights in Development.* Available from: www.awid.org/eng/Issues-and-Analysis/Library/An-Interview-with-Farida-Shaheed (accessed 31 January 2009).

Shiva, V. (2008) 'Democratizing biology: reinventing biology from a feminist, ecological, and third world perspective', in A. M. Jaggar (ed.) *Just Methods – An Interdisciplinary Feminist Reader,* Boulder / London: Paradigm Publishers.

Showalter, E. (1979) 'Towards a feminist poetics', in M. Jacobus (ed.) *Women Writing and Writing about Women,* London: Croom Helm.

Skeggs, B. (1994) 'Situating the production of feminist ethnography', in M. Maynard and J. Purvis (eds) *Researching Women's Lives from a Feminist Perspective,* London: Taylor and Francis.

——(1997) *Formations of Class and Gender – Becoming Respectable,* London / Thousand Oaks, CA / New Delhi: Sage Publications.

Skjelsbaek, I. and Smith, D. (2001) (eds) *Gender Peace and Conflict,* New Delhi / Oslo: International Peace Institute / Sage Publishers.

SLWNGOF (1999) *Sri Lanka Shadow Report on the UN Convention on the Elimination of All Forms of Discrimination Against Women,* Colombo: Sri Lanka Women's NGO Forum.

Smith, B. (2005) 'Beyond concepts: ontology as reality representation', in A. Varzi and L. Vieu (eds) *Proceedings of FOIS 200 – International Conference on Formal Ontology and Information Systems,* Turin, 4–6 November 2004. Available from: www.ontology.buffalo.edu/bfo/BeyondConcepts.pdf (accessed 15 February 2009).

Smith, D. (1974) 'Women's perspective as a radical critique of sociology', *Sociological Inquiry,* 44, 1–3.

——(2004) 'Women's perspective as a radical critique of sociology', in S. Harding (ed.) *The Feminist Standpoint Theory Reader,* New York / London: Routledge.

Smith, L. T. (2008) *Decolonizing Methodologies – Research and Indigenous Peoples,* London / New York: Zed Books / Dunedin: University of Otago Press.

Soysa, P. (1985) 'Health and nutritional status of women', in CENWOR (ed.) *The UN Decade for Women: Progress and Achievements of Women in Sri Lanka,* Colombo: Centre for Women's Research.

Spivak, G. C. (1976) 'Translator's preface', in J. Derrida (ed.) *Of Grammatology,* Baltimore, MD / London: John Hopkins University Press.

——(1990) 'The problem of cultural self-representation', in Sarah Harasym (ed.) *The Postcolonial Critics: Interviews, Strategies, Dialogues,* New York and London: Routledge.

——(1993) 'Can the subaltern speak?', in P. Williams and L. Chrisman (eds) *Colonial Discourse and Postcolonial Theory – A Reader,* Cambridge: Harvester Wheatsheaf.

Stacey, J. (1991) 'Can there be a feminist ethnography?', in S. B. Gluck and D. Patai (eds) *Women's Words, Women's Words, Women's Words, the Feminist Practice of Oral History,* New York: Routledge.

Stake, R. E. (2005) 'Case studies', in N. K. Denzin and Y. S. Lincoln (eds) *Sage Handbook of Qualitative Research,* Thousand Oaks, CA / London / New Delhi: Sage.

Stanley, L. (1990a) 'Feminist praxis and the academic mode of production – an editorial introduction', in L. Stanley (ed.) *Feminist Praxis,* London / New York: Routledge.

——(ed.) (1990b) *Feminist Praxis,* London / New York: Routledge.

Stanley, L. and Wise, S. (1983a) 'Back into the personal or our attempt to construct feminist research', in G. Bowles and R. D. Klein (eds) *Theories of Women's Studies,* London / New York: Routledge and Kegan Paul.

——(1983b) *Breaking Out – Feminist Consciousness and Feminist Research*, London: Routledge and Kegan Paul.

——(1993) *Breaking Out Again – Feminist Ontology and Epistemology*, London / New York: Routledge.

Strauss, A. and Corbin, J. (1998) *Basics of Qualitative Research-Techniques and Procedures for Developing Grounded Theory*, Thousand Oaks, CA / London / New Delhi: Sage Publications.

Tambiah, Y. (2004) '(Im)moral citizens: Sexuality and the Penal Code in Sri Lanka – ethnicity, pluralism and human rights', in A. J. Canagaratna (ed.) *Neelan Tiruchelvam Commemoration Conference Papers*, Colombo: International Centre for Ethnic Studies.

Thapar, R. (2007) *Imagined Religious Communities? Ancient History and the Modern Search for a Hindu Identity*, New Delhi: Critical Quest.

Thiruchandran, S. (ed.) (1994) *Images*, Colombo: Women's Education and Research Centre.

——(1997) 'A construction of gender in the social formation of Jaffna: some thematic observations', *Nivedini*, 5 (2), 50–80.

——(2001) *Feminine Speech Transmissions*, New Delhi: Vikas Publishing House (Pvt.) Ltd.

Thorne, B. (2008) '"You still taking notes?" Fieldwork and problems of informed consent', in A. M. Jaggar (ed.) *Just Methods*, Boulder, CO / London: Paradigm Publishers.

Ulluwishewa, R. (1991) 'Development planning and gender inequality: A case study of Mahaweli development project in Sri Lanka', *Geojournal*, 23 (2), 107–112.

United Nations Development Fund for Women (UNIFEM) South Asia Regional Office / CENWOR (2004) *CEDAW Indicators for South Asia: An Initiative*, Colombo: Centre for Women's Research

University of Colombo (ed.) (1979) *Status of Women – Sri Lanka*, Colombo: University of Colombo.

Vidyaratne, S. (2004) *Monetary Valuation of Unpaid Work and Disaggregation of GDP by Sex*, Colombo: Centre for Women's Research.

Vimaladharma, K. P. (2003) *Women in the Kandyan Kingdom*, Kandy: Varuni Publishers.

Visweswaran, K. (1994) *Fictions of Feminist Ethnography*, Minneapolis, MI / London: University of Minnesota Press.

Walby, S. (1990) *Theorizing Patriarchy*, Oxford: Basil Blackwell.

Walker, M. U. (2000) 'Moral epistemology', in A. M. Jaggar and I. M. Young (eds) *A Companion to Feminist Philosophy*, Malden, MD / Oxford / Victoria: Blackwell Publishing.

Wanasundera, L. (1986) *Women of Sri Lanka – An Annotated Bibliography*, Colombo: Centre for Women's Research.

——(1990) *Women of Sri Lanka – An Annotated Bibliography Supplement 1*, Colombo: Centre for Women's Research.

——(1995) 'Research and information', in CENWOR (ed.) *Facets of Change – Women in Sri Lanka (1986–1995)*, Colombo: Centre for Women's Research.

——(1997) *Women of Sri Lanka – An Annotated Bibliography Supplement 2*, Colombo: Centre for Women's Research.

——(1998) *Women Affected by Armed Conflict – A Bibliographic Summary*, Colombo: Centre for Women's Research.

——(2001) *Women of Sri Lanka – An Annotated Bibliography Supplement 3*, Colombo: Centre for Women's Research.

——(2002) *Women of Sri Lanka – An Annotated Bibliography Supplement 4*, Colombo: Centre for Women's Research.

——(2005) *Women of Sri Lanka – An Annotated Bibliography Supplement 5*, Colombo: Centre for Women's Research.

Warhol, R. R. and Herndl, D. P. (1997a) 'About feminisms', in R. R. Warhol and D. P. Herndl (eds) *Feminisms – An Anthology of Literary Theory and Criticism*, New Brunswick, NJ: Rutgers University Press.

——(eds) (1997b) *Feminisms – An Anthology of Literary Theory and Criticism*, New Brunswick, NJ: Rutgers University Press.

Waring, M. (2008) 'Counting for something? Recognizing women's contribution to the global economy through alternative accounting systems', in A. M. Jagger (ed.) *Just Methods: An Interdisciplinary Feminist Reader*, Boulder, CO / London: Paradigm Publishers.

Warren, C. (2002) 'Qualitative interviewing', in J. F. Gubrium and J. A. Holstein (eds) *Handbook of Interview Research – Context and Method*, Thousand Oaks: Sage.

Watson, B. and Maguire, M. (1997) '*Multicultural* matters', in J. Dillon and M. Maguire (eds) *Becoming a Teacher–Issues in Secondary Teaching*, Buckingham: Open University Press.

Wee, V. and Shaheed, F. (2008) *Empowering Themselves: A Framework that Interrogates and Transform*, The Research Programme Consortium on Women's Empowerment in Muslim Contexts (Gender, Poverty and Democratisation from the Inside Out), Pakistan, Southeast Asia Research Centre / City University of Hong Kong.

Weedon, C. (1987) *Feminist Practice and Poststructuralist Theory*, Oxford: Basil Blackwell.

——(2003) 'Subjects', in M. Eagleton (ed.) *A Concise Companion to Feminist Theory*, Oxford: Blackwell Publishing.

Weerakoon, N. (1998) 'International female labour migration', in CENWOR (ed.) *Women in the Economy – Trends and Policy Issues*, Colombo: Centre for Women's Research.

Weston, K. (2004) 'Fieldwork in lesbian and gay communities', in S. N. Hesse-Biber and M. L. Yaiser (eds) *Feminist Perspectives on Social Research*, Oxford / New York: Oxford University Press.

Whitbeck, C. (1989) 'A different reality: feminist ontology', in M. Pearsall and A. Garry (eds) *Women, Knowledge and Reality*, Boston, MA: Unwin Hyman.

Wickramasinghe, M. (1997) 'The concept of patriarchy: an essential tool for the feminist project', *Options*, 12 (4th Quarter), 13–17.

——(2000) *From Theory to Action – Women, Gender and Development*, Colombo: Friedrich Ebert Stiftung.

——(2002a) 'Fundamentals of feminist critical theory', *Journal of Faculty of Humanities University of Kelaniya*, III (2000/2001), 282–300.

——(2002b) 'Gender identity and gender relations', in S. K. Mendis (ed.) *Gender Resource Book for Teachers*, Colombo: Centre for Women's Research.

——(2006) 'An epistemology of gender – an aspect of being as a way of seeing', *Women's Studies International Forum*, 29 (6), 606–611.

——(2007) 'Imported or indigenous knowledges feminist ontological / epistemological politics', in N. de Mel and S. Thiruchandran (eds) *At the Cutting Edge – Essays in Honour of Kumari Jayawardena*, New Delhi: Women Unlimited.

——(2009) 'Women – a new paradigm in knowledge production', in K. Kumarasinghe (ed.) *Volume to Felicitate 50 Years of the University of Kelaniya*, Kelaniya: University of Kelaniya.

——(2009) 'The possibilities and challenges of postcolonial situatedness, standpoints and intersectionality', in S. Thiruchandran and D. Karunanayake (eds) *Continuities/Departures: Essays on Postcolonial Sri Lankan Women's (Creative) Writing in English*, Colombo: Women's Education and Research Centre.

Wickramasinghe, M. and Jayatilaka, W. (2006) *Beyond Glass Ceilings and Brick Walls – Gender at the Workplace*, Colombo: International Labour Organisation.

Wickramasinghe, N. (2001) *History Writing: New Trends and Methodologies*, Colombo: International Centre for Ethnic Studies.

Wijayatilake, K. (2001) *Unravelling Herstories – A Three Generational Study*, Colombo: Centre for Women's Research.

——(2002) *All Her Worldly Goods – Women's Property and Inheritance Rights*, Colombo: Centre for Women's Research.

Wijayatilake, K. and Zackeriya, F. (2001) *Sexual Harassment at Work – Plantation Sector*, Colombo: International Labour Organisation.

Wijewardene, S. (2007) 'But no one has explained to me who I am now … : "Trans" self-perceptions in Sri Lanka', in S. E. Wieringa, E. Blackwood and A. Bhaiya (eds) *Women's Sexualities and Masculinities in a Globalising Asia*, New York: Palgrave.

Wilkinson, S. (2004) 'Focus groups: a feminist method', in S. N. Hesse-Biber and M. L. Yaiser (eds) *Feminist Perspectives on Social Research*, New York / Oxford: Oxford University Press.

Williams, P. and Chrisman, L. (eds) (1993) *Colonial Discourse and Postcolonial Theory – a Reader*, Cambridge: Harvester Wheatsheaf.

Wittig, M. (1981) 'One is not born a woman', *Feminist Issues*, 1 (2), 47–54.

——(1992) *The Straight Mind and Other Essays*, Hempstead: Harvester Wheatsheaf.

Women's Education and Research Centre (1998) *Code of Ethics for Gender Representation in the Electronic Media*, Colombo: Women's Education and Research Centre.

Women's Franchise Union of Ceylon (1928) *Women and the Vote*, Colombo: Bastian and Company.

Yin, R. K. (2003) *Case Study Research Design and Methods*, London: Sage.

Young, K. (1988) 'The social relations of gender', in P. Mohammed and C. Shepherd (ed.) *Gender in Caribbean Development*, Jamaica: Women and Development Studies Group.

Zackeriya, F. and Shanmugaratnam, N. (2001) *Stepping Out: Women Surviving amidst Displacement and Deprivation*, Colombo: Muslim Women's Action and Research Front.

Zinsser, J. P. (1990) 'The United Nations Decade for Women: a quiet revolution', *The History Teacher*, 24 (1), 19–29.

Index

Abeysekara, Manel, 17, 97
Abeysekara, Sunila, 19, 20, 24
accountability, 161–62
action research, 48, 116–18
Adkins, L., 56
Afghanistan, 144
Africa, 37, 42, 46 *see also* South Africa;
   Yorubaland; Zimbabwe
Agarwal, B., 46
Ahmed, S., 149
Alcoff, L., 41
Alldred, P., 150–51
Al Qaeda, 125
Althusser, L., 32, 56, 125
altruism, 151–53
Andermahr, S., 45, 168
archaeology, 4, 13–30
Aruni (respondent), 25
Asia, 37, 147; Asian positionings,
   143–45; Asian viewpoint, 18; *see also*
   East Asia; South Asia; South East
   Asia
Auerbach, N., 38
Australia, 38

Balasuriya, Tissa, 19, 20
Ball, S., 80
Banadaranaike, Sirimavo, 17–18
Bandarage, A., 85, 90, 121–22, 126, 129
Bangladesh, 143, 144
Batliwala, S., 46–47
Bebel, August, 19
Bhaba, H.K., 59
Bhutan, 144
Birch, M., 48, 149
Blyton, Enid, 3
Boserup, E., 18, 44
Bosnia, 38
Bourdieu, P., 56

British, 16 *see also* UK
Buddhism/Buddhists, 16, 18, 27, 59, 71,
   101, 125, 143, 147, 152, 153, 154
Butler, J., 35, 62, 96, 101

Cain, M., 69, 131
Canada, 38
Canadian International Development
   Agency (CIDA), 23
Castro, Fidel, 19
Centre for Society and Religion (CSR),
   19, 20
Centre for Women's Research
   (CENWOR), 79, 123, 160
Ceylon Labour Union, 16
Chhachhi, A., 141
Christianity, 15–16, 124, 143, 147, 152
CIDA (Canadian International
   Development Agency), 23
Cixous, H., 35
class: author's positioning, 59–60;
   intersections of, 139–41
Code of Ethics on Gender
   Representation for the Electronic
   Media, 107
Collins, P.H., 60
Colombo, 85, 108, 109; University of,
   18–19, 79
Communist Party (CP), 16, 17
confidentiality, 66–67
connaissances, 13, 14, 15, 17, 24–27,
   30, 32–33, 73, 76, 93, 108, 110, 128,
   130
Cook, Judith, 113
Coomaraswamy, R., 106–7
Corbin, J., 129
Costa, Della, 19
counter-communal stands, 141–43
CP (Communist Party), 16, 17

CSR (Centre for Society and Religion), 19, 20
cultural approach, 125–26

Dassanayake, Mala, 20
data analysis, 5, 44–45, 69–70
de Alwis, 65, 75, 86, 88, 96, 119–20, 137–38
de Beauvoir, S. 18, 93
Deepa (respondent), 152
de Groot, J., 45, 70
Delphy, Christine, 33, 44
de Man, P., 67
de Mel, N., 15, 99–100, 102, 104, 105, 110, 126
democracy *see* liberal democracy
democratic agenda *see* liberal/ democratic agenda
Derrida, J., 63, 67, 110
de Saussure, F., 139
de Silva, Bernadeen, 18, 20
Dhamani (repondent), 29, 79, 80, 129, 132, 138, 144, 161, 163, 164, 165
disciplinary and ideological affiliations, 137–39; author's positioning, 58, 60
District Integrated Rural Development Schemes, 85
Domestic Violence Bill (2005), 160
Doucet, A., 149, 161
Dunne, M., 8, 51

East Asia, 46 *see also* Asia
Economic Review, 18
Edwards, R., 150, 157
Eksath Kantha Peramuna (EKP; United Women's Front), 16
Emmanuel, S., 90
empiricist approach, 114–15
empowerment, 46–47
English language, 7, 15, 20, 22–23, 60–61, 67
epistemic community, 21–22, 32, 164–65
epistemology: author's positioning, 62–64; feminist, 39–43, 79, 86, 88–92; gender as, 5, 52, 93–109, 168; in methodological matrix summary, 173–74; and ontology, 73–74, 90–92, 95–99, 108–9, 132, 168; and women as paradigm, 31, 33, 39–43, 48
equality, 17–18, 46, 106
essentialism, 42–43
ethics *see* politics/ethics
Europe, 37, 95; Eastern, 38
Enlightenment, 40, 65, 95

Far East, 38
Farida (respondent), 21, 150
feminist internationalisms, 76, 78–81, 91
feminist localisms, 77, 84–87, 91
feminist personal political interests, 77, 87–90, 91
feminist structural reformative intents, 77, 81–83, 91
Finch, J., 69, 131
Fonow, Mary Margaret, 113
Foucault, M., 4, 13–14, 32, 41, 62, 95, 110, 133
Free Trade Zones (FTZs), 84, 155
Friedan, B., 18
FTZs (Free Trade Zones), 84, 155

GAD (Gender and Development) movement, 17–18, 38, 81, 121
Gauri (respondent), 100
Gayathri (respondent), 134–35, 153, 159, 160–61, 165
gender: analysis, 102–5; concept of, 25, 47, 93–95, 120; cultural factors, 125; as epistemology, 5, 52, 93–109; and historical analysis, 124; methodologies, 107–8; ontology, 81–83, 95–99, 108–9; political aspirations, 105–7; social construction of, 113–14; and subjectivity, 35; theoretical concepts, 99–102; and understanding of development, 38
Gender and Development (GAD) movement, 17–18, 38, 81, 121
gender mainstreaming, 81–83 107–8, 168
Gender Project: 'Gender in Commonwealth Higher Education', 64
Gillies, V., 150–51
Gilligan, C., 35, 48, 148
Gilman, C.P., 38
global knowledge production, women as paradigm in, 31–49
Goonatilake, Hema, 15, 18, 29, 113, 115, 116–17, 118, 122, 123–24
Goonewardene, Vivienne, 17
Greer, G., 18
Grillo, T., 146
Gross, E., 46
Guide for a Code on Sexual Harassment, 107
Guidelines on Company Policy for Gender Equity/Equality, 107
Gynocriticism, 41

Haavind, H., 143
Haniffa, F., 142
Haraway, D., 115, 133
Harding, S., 8, 58, 73, 98–99, 115, 133
Hart, C., 111
Hinduism, 135, 143, 147, 152
history: historical trajectory, 113–14;
    significance of, 123–24; *see also*
    archaeology
Holland, J., 32, 56

identity, 100–101, 141–42
ideological and disciplinary affiliations,
    137–39
IMF (International Monetary Fund), 20
India, 15, 19, 38, 40, 46, 65, 125, 135,
    142, 143, 144, 159
Institute of Education, University of
    London, 64
internationalisms, feminist, 76, 78–81,
    91
International Monetary Fund (IMF),
    20
intersectionality, 6, 134, 146;
    intersections of class, 139–41
interviews, 68–69, 163
intuition, 3
Iraq, 162
Ireland, 38
Irigaray, L., 34
Islam, 143, 147, 152 *see also* Muslims
Israel, 38

Jaffna, 101
Jalani (respondent), 82
Janatha Vimukthi Peramuna (JVP), 85,
    163
Jarviluoma, H., 93
Jayani (respondent), 87, 139, 155–56
Jayatilaka, W., 106, 120, 123
Jayawardena, K., 16, 18, 20, 65, 101
Jayaweera, Swarna, 17, 18, 103, 104,
    123
John, M.E., 40, 135, 159
Joint Gender Committee, 86
JVP (Janatha Vimukthi Peramuna), 85,
    163

Kamani (respondent), 29, 143, 144–45
Kandiyoti, D., 46
Kant, Immanuel, 95
Kantha Handa (Voice of Women), 20
Kanthava Samajaya Vimukthiya
    (Women, Society, Liberation), 19

Kantha Vimukthiya (Women's
    Liberation), 19–20
Kashmir, 144
Kelly-Gadol, J., 124
Khanduja, S., 48
Kiribamune, S., 154
Kiyana (respondent), 25, 134, 151–52,
    159
Knox, Robert, 15
Kolontai, Alexandra, 19
Kottegoda, S., 120
Krishnaraj, M., 13, 47
Kuhn, Thomas, 32, 33
Kumerini (respondent), 138–39, 142,
    163
Kvale, 157

Labour Movement, 20
Labour Party, 16
Lamphere, L., 18
Lanka Sama Samaja Pakshaya (LSSP),
    16, 17
Lather, P., 32
Law, J., 74
Lenin, Vladimir, 19
lesbians, 24, 36
Letherby, G., 8, 110–11
liberal democracy, ethics/politics of,
    153–55
liberal/democratic agenda, 17
Liberation Tigers of Tamil Eelam
    (LTTE), 85, 86, 143, 149, 155,
    163
Lisewood, 154
literature reviewing, 6, 44, 52, 67, 110–
    27
local context, 13–30, 64
localisms, feminist, 77, 84–87, 91
location of knowledge, 132–33
Logos, 20
London University: Institute of
    Education, 64
LSSP (Lanka Sama Samaja Pakshaya),
    16, 17
LTTE (Liberation Tigers of Tamil
    Eelam), 85, 86, 143, 149, 155, 163
Lyons, T., 41

Maguire, M., 80, 146
Mahaweli Development Scheme, 84,
    85
Maldives, 144
Mao Tse-tung, 19
Marga Institute, 19

Marx, Karl, 32
Marxism, 19–20, 32, 40, 47, 65, 66, 75, 87, 88, 113, 117, 118, 123, 138, 139, 140, 147, 166; ethics/politics of, 155–56
Mason, J., 79, 94–95, 111
Maunaguru, S., 125
Mauthner, M., 150, 157, 161
Mauthner, N., 149, 161
Maynard, M., 45, 70, 94, 159
methods: author's positioning, 67–72; feminist, 43–45, 161–66; literature review, 6, 44, 52, 67, 110–27; in methodology matrix summary, 174–75; politics/ethics, 161–66
Mexico: first UN Conference on Women (1975), 17
Middle East, 38, 46, 84
Mies, Maria, 19, 57, 116
Millet, K., 18
Ministry of Plan Implementation, 18
Ministry of Women's Affairs, 18
mixed-methods research, 122–23
Mockler, N., 162
modernism, 1, 6, 34, 62, 63, 109, 126, 146, 167, 169
Mohanty, C.T., 65
Moneragala, 164
moral inferiority, 147, 148
moral superiority, 147–48, 150
Morley, L., 56–57, 69, 113
Moser, C., 25
mother, perspective of, 135–37
Mother's Front, 85, 86, 119, 129, 138
Muslims, 20, 47, 68, 125, 141, 142, 159 *see also* Islam
Muttetuwegama, Manori, 18
Muzundar, 19

Naples, N.A., 62
Narayan, U., 40, 65, 116
National Committee, 17
Nepal, 144
New Zealand, 38, 40
nuancing, 6, 129, 130

Oakley, A., 44, 71, 93
Oluwelwe, S., 42
ontological politics, 76–92
ontology: author's positioning, 61–62, 64; and epistemology, 73–74, 90–92, 95–99, 108–9, 132, 168; feminist, 36–39; gender, 95–99, 107, 108–9, 168; in methodological matrix summary,

171–72; research realities, 5, 52, 64, 73–92; and women as paradigm, 33, 34, 35, 36–39
Oyewumi, O., 34, 129

Pakistan, 38, 141, 143, 144
paradigm, women as, 4, 31–49
patriarchy, 46, 99–100, 124
Penal Code Amendment (1995), 24, 125–26
politics/ethics, 6, 47–48, 52, 66–67, 105–7, 147–66, 177–78; *see also* ontological politics
Positivism, 40
postmodernism, 1, 6, 34, 39, 62, 63, 65, 78, 109, 133, 138, 145, 146, 167, 169
pragmatism, strategic, 159–61
Prevention of Terrorism Act, 155
Purvis, J., 159

Queer theory, 36, 101

Rajapakse, D.A., 103
Ramazanoglu, C., 32, 56
Ranweera, Eva, 18
Rasika (respondent), 98, 101, 107, 137
reflexivity, 4–5, 44, 48, 55, 56–58, 71–72
Reinzharz, S., 116
respondents, sensitivity to, 163–64
responsibilities, researcher's, 161–62
Ribbens, J., 44
Ricardo, 32
Rich, A., 133
Rosaldo, M., 18
Rowbotham, Sheila, 18, 19
Ruddick, Sara, 38–39, 136, 148

Sadia (respondent), 22, 23–24, 89, 162, 165
Said, E.W., 129–30, 144
Sakunthala (respondent), 27
Samarakkody, M., 15
Samuel, K., 19–20, 86
Sangari, K., 46
Sanmugam, T., 103, 123
SAP (Structural Adjustment Programme), 20, 84
Saumi (respondent), 135–36
savoir, 13, 14, 15, 17, 20, 24, 26, 27–30, 32, 33, 73, 95, 108, 110, 128, 130
Schrijvers, J., 103, 117, 118, 120–21, 128–29
Scott, J.W., 96
sensitivity to respondents, 163–64

sexuality, 24, 36, 89–90, 125–26
Shaheed, F., 47, 141–42
Shiva, Vandana, 39
Sinhala/Sinhalese, 7, 16, 19, 20, 23, 59, 60, 61, 67, 68, 101, 104–5, 122, 125, 141
situatedness of knowledge, 6, 133
Skeggs, B., 130, 133
SLFP (Sri Lanka Freedom Party), 17
SLWNGOF (Sr Lanka Women's Non-Governmental Organisations Forum), 79
Smith, D., 41, 118
Smith, L.T., 40
South Africa, 38
South America, 37, 38
South Asia, 38, 46, 104; positionings, 143–45; *see also* Asia
South East Asia, 46 *see also* Asia
Spivak, G.C., 42–43
Sri Lanka Freedom Party (SLFP), 17
Sri Lanka Women's Non-Governmental Organisations Forum (SLWNGOF), 79
Stacey, J., 69, 164
Stake, R.E., 67
standpoints, 6, 41–42, 78, 133–45, 146
Stanley, L., 32, 42, 78, 94, 114, 121, 129, 164
Status of Women Survey, 18–19, 122–23
strategic pragmatism, 159–61
Strauss, A., 129
Structural Adjustment Programme (SAP), 20, 84
structural reformative intents, feminist, 77, 81–83, 91
subjectivity, 4–5, 33, 34–36, 41, 51–52, 55–72, 145, 168, 170–71
Surya Mal Movement, 16

Tambiah, Y., 24, 125–26
Tamil, 7, 16, 20, 23, 60, 61, 67, 68, 101, 122, 125, 141, 143
textual analysis, 67
Thailand, 15
Thamalini (respondent), 140–41, 152, 156, 159
Thapar, R., 142
theory, 6, 27, 45–47, 52, 64–66, 70–71, 86–87, 99–102, 110–11, 118–22, 128–46, 168, 176–77
Thiruchandran, S., 88, 101
transgender, 101–2
travelling theory, 129–30
Trotsky, Leon, 19

UK, 37, 125 *see also* British
UN *see* United Nations
UNCEDAW (United Nations Convention on the Elimination of all forms of Discrimination Against Women), 17, 18, 79, 80
United National Party (UNP), 20
United Nations (UN), 17, 18, 19, 30, 37, 46, 79, 80–81, 139, 154; Conference on Women (Mexico 1975), 17; Convention on the Elimination of all forms of Discrimination Against Women (UNCEDAW), 17, 18, 79, 80; Decade of Women (1975–85), 1, 19; Declaration on Human Rights (1948), 17; International Year of Women (UNIYW; 1975), 1, 15, 17, 18, 20, 62, 113
United Women's Front (Eksath Kantha Peramuna; EKP), 16
UNIYW (United Nations International Year of Women, 1975), 1, 15, 17, 18, 20, 62, 113
UNP (United National Party), 20
USA, 37, 38, 125, 162

Vimaladharma, K.P., 124
Vivian (respondent), 75, 87, 131, 132–33, 139–40, 150, 158, 162

Wadhani (respondent), 102
Wanasundera, L., 22–23, 84, 113–14, 115, 116, 118–19
Waring, M., 44
Wasanthi (respondent), 26, 135
Wee, V., 47
Weedon, C., 36
WERC (Women's Education and Research Centre), 160
Western ideas/the West, 7, 18, 37, 38, 41, 42, 46, 47, 56, 65, 73, 75–76, 89, 158, 159
Whitbeck, C., 74
Wickramasinghe, M., 106, 123, 124
WID (Women in Development), 38, 46, 121, 134
Wijayatilake, K., 88, 100, 105–6, 136
Wijewardene, S., 24, 97, 101–2
Wilkinson, S., 44
Wise, S., 32, 42, 78, 94, 114, 121, 129, 164
Wishva (respondent), 82, 136, 160, 163

Wittig, M., 36, 94
Women and Media Collective (WMC), 160
Women for Peace, 85
Women in Development (WID), 38, 46, 121, 134
Women's Bureau of Sri Lanka, 18
Women's Education and Research Centre (WERC), 160

Women's Franchise Union of Ceylon, 16
women's standpoint, 134–35
World Bank, 20, 28, 89

Yorubaland, 34

Zackeriya, F., 105–6
Zimbabwe, 41
Zulfica (respondent), 25–26, 135